THE CIVILIZATION OF THE AMERICAN INDIAN

The Ten
Grandmothers

By ALICE MARRIOTT

NORMAN
UNIVERSITY OF OKLAHOMA PRESS

For Casey *and* Dad

About the Kiowas

IN SOME PARTS OF THIS COUNTRY, notably the Southeast and the Southwest, it is possible to reconstruct the past cultures of living Indian tribes from material objects which they or their forbears have left behind. This is not true in the Great Plains region. The area was probably sparsely settled, and then only marginally, when the whites brought horses to the tribes of the Southwest and the Mississippi Valley. The spread of peoples into the Plains is, by comparison with the occupation of other areas, recent.

In writing of a plains tribe, therefore, one deals less with tangibles than in other sections of the country. One begins with living memories, works back to their recollections of other memories, and is then turned loose in the uncharted sea of legend. All legends, it is true, no matter how vague they first seem, have some relation to the everyday life of the people who produced them, but not all legends make that relationship immediately apparent.

In telling of the Kiowas then, it was necessary for me to recognize certain limitations. Their legends, and a few scattered documents left by early white explorers, placed them as far north as the Yellowstone in the late seventeenth century. Within the memories of remembered grandparents, they had journeyed once as far south as British Honduras. Within living memory, they have been settled in western Oklahoma, the Oklahoma and Texas panhandles, and southern Kansas. The need for tipi poles carried them occasionally into the mountains of southern Colorado; trade took them to Taos, the easternmost pueblo. Most of the time, however, they lived in or near the Wichita Mountains, and their knowledge of other tribes was greatest in that vicinity.

By all of their enemies the Kiowas were respected, indeed feared, for their fighting ability. Their relations with the Crows, Blackfeet, and Shoshonis were good, and they were on terms of armed neutrality with the Cheyennes and the Arapahoes. They carried on intermittent warfare with the Utes and the Navajos to the northwest of their usual haunts. They were on terms of open enmity with the Osages and the Pawnees to the northeast, but they early made peace with the Comanches, with whom they shared a general hunting and camping range.

There is a Kiowa legend that, in the days when the Kiowas lived in the north, they were a large tribe. A quarrel arose between two band chiefs, and the tribe separated, one group remaining in the north; the other, the group that still call themselves the Kiowas, traveling south. Old Kiowas think the other band may have been the Crows, although they recognize the difference between their own language and customs and those of the northern tribe. Some Kiowas recognize a resemblance between their language and that of Taos. The name Kiowa-Tanoan linguistic stock is in use by linguists.

It is difficult to relate the tribe to another any more closely. Their material culture is certainly that of the Southern Plains: the Kiowas lived a nomadic life, subsisting on the buffalo herds which they followed, and varying their diet with other meats and with wild plant foods. Their whole concept of possession was based on impermanent residence. They have no recollection of an agricultural tradition, and agriculture is only sparsely reflected in their legends. In their manufactures, their social organization based on the band, their war concept, and their use of the Sun Dance, they were like their neighbors, the Southern Cheyennes and Arapahoes, and less like the Comanches.

Like most other plains tribes, they developed a series of tribal palladia. Among the Kiowas these were ten medicine bundles, known as the Ten Grandmothers. Around them centered a series of legends about twin culture heroes, called the Half Boys. The contents of the bundles are now unknown, although the bundles themselves still exist. Because of their sacredness, even the guardians of the bundles were forbidden to open them. Once a year the ten guardians carried the bundles into a ceremonial tipi where, alone, a priest, who had inherited the right, ceremonially opened them, inspected the contents, cleansed them by prayer and ceremonial smoking, and closed them again. When the last man who had this right died, in the 1890's, the bundles had been opened for the last time. Since then the Ten Grandmothers have been as sacred and as valued as ever—offerings and prayers are still made to them—but they have not been opened.

Physically, the Kiowas are dark-skinned and are inclined to be short, stocky, and thick-chested. Their heads are brachycephalic. There has been enough inter-marriage with whites and with members of other tribes to allow variant types to creep in, however, so that at the present time it is difficult to generalize about physical types.

About the Kiowas

Socially, the Kiowas have not had a good character from early travelers, explorers, and missionaries. Even Mooney regretfully classified them below Sioux and Cheyennes in a listing of moral characteristics. That may still be true; or there may have been a decided change in character in a generation and a half; or I may not have known enough Sioux and Cheyennes to be a fair judge. My own experience has been, nevertheless, that the Kiowas are friendly, generous, courteous, and hospitable on the whole, and that if there are some exceptions, those same exceptions would exist in any other group of human beings.

The clothing of the Kiowas was relatively simple: moccasins, breechclout, and shirt, all of deerskin, for men; boot-moccasins and dresses of the same material for women. Children's clothing, which was first put on them when they were three or four years old, was adult clothing scaled down to size. Both sexes and all ages wore winter robes of buffalo or deerskin, dressed with the hair on. Men often, and women occasionally, wore summer robes, dressed without hair. Since metal was obtainable at an early date, the Kiowas learned to use it to make hair-plates, belts, earrings, finger-rings, bracelets, necklaces, and horse trappings. By 1852 a wealth of metal ornament had become a distinguishing feature of the costume of the tribe, and Marcy identified them at a distance by "the flashing of their silver ornaments in the sun."

The Kiowas lived in tipis made of buffalo hides. The tipi was built on a four-pole foundation, to which twenty poles were added to fill out the circle. It faced east except when it was pitched in the Sun Dance circle, when it faced the center of the enclosure. The tipi front was fastened with small, painted sticks, and there was a rawhide door hung over the opening. In warm weather the sides were rolled up for two or three feet above the ground. Tipis are still set up in summer camps and are the ritual shelters for peyote meetings. Domed brush arbors were, and still are, built as summer shelters.

One of the most engrossing and important parts of the Kiowas' lives was the societies. Men's societies had little formal age-grading. There was a feeling that a man would be more at home with men of his own age and interests, and so matters adjusted themselves. Little boys were Rabbits, youths were Herders, and after maturity a man joined whichever one of the six dancing societies he liked. He could stay all his life in one group or could go on to others, as the spirit moved him or invitations to join other societies were offered. The societies took turns policing the buffalo drives, the one to act being indicated by the Sun Dance priest. There was also a dancing society for women known as Calf Old Women, which operated on the same basis as the men's societies. Members were old women, membership was by invitation only, and their sole purpose in meeting, as far as is known, was to feast. No known survivors were encountered.

Slightly different from the dancing societies mentioned was the group of "religious societies." These were the Crazy Dogs (great warriors' society); the Buffalo Doctors (for the treatment of wounds, hence all flowing of blood, hence today tuberculosis and other respiratory diseases); the Owl Doctors (for prophecy and the finding of lost articles); the Eagle Shields (who excelled in sleight-of-hand and shamanistic trick work, but commonly used their power for good); and the Sun Dance Shields (whose duty was to guard the Taime or Sun Dance image and its keeper). Associated with the religious societies was a group of old women known as the Bear Women, whose meetings and purposes were deeply secret and who seem to have inspired terror in most persons. No admitted survivors of this society and no one who admitted to a knowledge of its activities could be found. Membership in the religious societies was by invitation only, and acceptance of the invitation was mandatory.

The Kiowa year count, a painted mnemonic record, begins with 1832–33, when the Kiowas captured money from white traders. From that year on, each summer and each winter is named for a specific event, and from the summer of 1833 to that of 1888 the Sun Dance sites are known and identifiable. All the sites are located within the country including the Wichita Mountains and the headwaters of the Arkansas, Cimarron, and Canadian rivers. In titling these stories, I found it possible to record year counts in the field from three informants and to check them against Mooney's record of Anko's year count made in 1892. While a few discrepancies had crept in, the accounts were surprisingly consistent (see appendix). The subtitles used were taken preferably from Mooney's account; where that had a less direct bearing on the story to be told, from the record of Kiowa George Poolaw, who had copied the original Anko account and who continued the record until his death in 1939. The figures used as decorations for chapter openings are adapted from Mooney's reproductions of Set'tan's and Anko's drawings for the years before 1893; the drawings used for later years are based on the Kiowa pictographs but are not copied from them.

The sketches that follow were collected mostly in the summers of 1935 and 1936. Other events were recorded in the following eight years. It was my good fortune to work with two very old people, both now dead, whose memories spanned the period of the white conquest of the Southern Plains. In talking to them and to some of the older people, it became evident that I could not generalize about the life of the Kiowa tribe during this period. Each request for general information brought a specific reply, and many times the replies contradicted each other. It was plain that, in a period of such great stress, no general rules could have been made to apply. While each person acted within the general pattern of the culture he knew, the pattern itself was changing too rapidly and too radically to be absolutely defined.

Each of the sketches, therefore, represents Kiowa behavior under given circumstances at a given time. In many cases the individual behavior described would be that of any Kiowa under like conditions; in some, it would not. It is only that no one but a Kiowa would have behaved in that way, at that time, under those conditions, that links the sketches. Each sketch may be taken as an eye-witness account of the event related, and where the feelings of a person are described, it is only because he himself said that he felt that way that the feeling is put down. I have tried to tell these stories as much as possible as they were told to me.

Names of living persons and of their recently deceased relatives have been changed at the request of the families interested.

The names of the two principals have been changed slightly since their deaths. Spear Woman was originally named Lance Charging Woman. Eagle Plume was named Down on the Breast Plume of the Eagle. I have made these changes as a mark of respect which they would have felt they were entitled to receive.

These two persons were met first through the late George Hunt, of Mountain View, Oklahoma. He and his daughters, Mrs. Ioleta Hunt MacElhaney and Mrs. Margaret Tsoodle, were my principal and almost my only interpreters. On Mrs. MacElhaney fell the burden of the work, not only as interpreter, but as contact woman. Her great knowledge of both English and Kiowa and her painstaking care in translation made it possible to be sure of accuracy of spirit, as well as meaning, throughout the work. The translation of Sitting Bear's song which is used is hers.

My other informants were the late Kiowa George Poolaw, of Mountain View; the late Henry Tsoodle, Senior, of Carnegie; Sanko, or Prickly Pear, who is now dead; and Mr. and Mrs. Tahbone, both of whom are still living. Working with all of these people was a pleasure and a privilege.

In my own culture, I have others to thank. Forrest Clements first suggested the work, and made it possible by securing funds from the University of Oklahoma. Leslie Spier, Frederic H. Douglas, René d'Harnoncourt, and J. Joe Finkelstein helped many times in many ways. In the field I received full co-operation from W. B. McCown, superintendent of the Kiowa Indian Agency, Gordon McGregor, and other men and women of the United States Indian Service. Edith Mahier, Frances Mahier Brandon, and Ruth Kimbrell worked harder keeping me at work than I did in writing. Elizabeth Stover and Donald Day, of the S. M. U. Press, published earlier versions of two of the sketches in the *Southwest Review*. Finally, to Marjorie O'Maher and to my mother, Sydney C. Marriott, I am indebted for patient, enduring, and long-continued editorial assistance.

ALICE MARRIOTT

Oklahoma City, Oklahoma
December 6, 1944

Contents

The Ten Grandmothers

PART I : *The Time When There Were Plenty of Buffalo*

The Bear

The Year that Red Sleeve Was Killed (1847)

THERE WAS NEVER MUCH STIR IN THE KIOWA CAMP BEFORE war parties set out. For one thing, their going was never told until the night before, even though everybody was sure that some chief was getting things ready. You felt uneasiness running through the camp and prickling your skin, and that could only mean that excitement and adventure were stirring, but you couldn't know for sure until the last minute.

Sitting Bear was a young man, but he was already a chief. He had power for medicine and power for war, and power to make women love him. He had four wives, and they all had children. Their tipis were clustered around a bigger tipi for him. Not many men had tipis of their own, but Sitting Bear liked to have a place where he could sit with his society in the evening, without having any women or children to bother him.

Halfway past big day, in summer, the shadows began to slope across the red hills and slide down into the green valleys. The country curved south and west from where Sitting Bear sat in front of the tipi. In mid-spring the grass was green here, with many flowers speckled through it. Then, the green covered up the red of the hills for a while and smoothed things out until even Saddle Mountain looked rounded instead of sticking up stiff.

Usually the camp stretched along a creek, where there was shelter from the wind, pasture for the horses, and water for everybody. But when the Kiowas camped here near the hot springs, they put their tipis on flat places on the hillside, and the tipis were more scattered than they were at other camps. You couldn't line them up on a hill so that every tipi sat flat and faced east. The camp looked fine though, with the white tipis and the brown and white and yellow buckskin clothes of the people moving around among them.

The Kiowas were all moving all the time, these past few days, because the stir and excitement of getting ready to go on a raid kept them from staying long in one place. Even the women felt the tense-

3

ness. They kept working, but you had a feeling that they were thinking up things for themselves to do, instead of keeping at something that had to be done. You could tell that something was going to happen, all right.

Sitting Bear just sat there, watching the camp and thinking. After a while his second wife, with her baby, Eagle Plume, in her arms, came and sat down beside him. She was a fine woman, though he didn't love her as he did his first wife, and he made room for her. They sat together and watched the shadows soak into the light farther and farther up the hill facing them.

"Something is coming across the flat," said Sitting Bear.

"Looks like men on horseback," added his second wife.

"Looks like Comanches," said Sitting Bear.

They watched the long, thin Comanches on their long, thin horses shape up from lines to people, coming towards them. Sitting Bear thought how ordinary the Comanche clothes and saddles were. Everything the Comanches had was plain; the only trimming was fringes. They never had beadwork or silver ornaments, as the Kiowas did.

This time most of them didn't even have fringes. Nearly all of them were young men, dressed in their breechclouts and moccasins, and some of them were riding bareback. Just starting out for an enemy, they looked. They weren't starting for the Kiowas, because the two tribes had had peace for a long time, and anyway their faces weren't painted yet. They rode into camp and stopped before Heap of Bears' tipi.

Sitting Bear and Heap of Bears were related in a medicine sort of way. They were both named for the bear, the most powerful animal there was in a medicine way. Unless you were named for the bear, or were speaking to somebody that was, you mustn't even say the word *bear*. It was that powerful. Bears could drive you crazy, just for saying their name, and to look at them could almost kill a man. Nobody knew what would happen if you killed or ate a bear. People were too afraid to try.

Because they had the bear name together, Sitting Bear had the right to go into Heap of Bears' tipi as if it were his own, and sit there and advise with him as if they were brothers, even though Heap of Bears was older than he. He got up and said to his second wife, "I guess I'll go and find out," and walked over to Heap of Bears' tipi.

The Comanches were all sitting around when he got there. Their leader was getting out his pipe and tobacco as Sitting Bear came in. That looked strange, because it was Heap of Bears' right to put up the tobacco. He was the host. But Comanches were different; they had their own ways.

The Comanche lighted the pipe and handed it to Heap of Bears. When they both had smoked, it went to Sitting Bear. Then it went around to the other men. Heap of Bears spoke in sign language so that the Comanche could understand.

"Where are you going?"

The Comanche put his pipe back in its long bag before he answered. Then he said, "Over into the Ute country."

"What are you going for?"

"We heard those Utes have some good horses. They have young women, too. We need horses. Young women can help. They are good to wait on older women. We are going over to the Ute country for those things."

Heap of Bears sat and thought. "Those are good things, all right. A man can use those things."

The Comanche nodded without saying anything.

"Why have you come here first?" Heap of Bears asked. "What do you want us to do?"

The Comanche rubbed his hand back and forth on the earth in front of him. "This is what I've been thinking. This is what came into my mind. For a long time Comanches and Kiowas were fighting. Then they made peace."

"That's right," said Heap of Bears.

"That's all right. They are getting along all right now, but that peace may not last. Sometimes it doesn't. I have been thinking. I have been thinking we ought to do something to make that peace stick."

"That's right," said Heap of Bears.

"I think that if we go out together to fight the Utes, that's what will make that peace stick," said the Comanche.

All the Comanches nodded their heads backwards and then forwards, and said "Haw!" when he had finished.

Heap of Bears sat and thought for a while. Comanches could make up their minds quickly to start something, but Kiowas took more time and thought everything over. Finally Heap of Bears said to Sitting Bear, "Please tell my dancing society to come here."

Sitting Bear belonged to another society, himself, but he went out and found the speaker for Heap of Bears' society just outside the tipi, and told him. When the speaker went away, Sitting Bear came back and sat down, and they all waited until the society came in. It was the Gourd Dancers' Society.

The Gourd Dancers sat down and listened while Heap of Bears

told them what the Comanche had said. Then he added: "Now this is what I think. I think maybe this Comanche is right. I think maybe the two tribes ought to work together to prove they have a peace. I think we ought to go out with the Comanches on this raid."

One of the younger men spoke right up. "The Comanches are going for horses and girls," he said. "Horses are all right, if we get enough to go 'round. If we don't, the Comanches can have them. We got plenty of horses anyway. We don't want Ute girls. They're fat and ugly, and they smell bad. The Comanches can have those. What are we going for, then, if the only things we get are things just the Comanches want?"

Everybody nodded his head and said "Haw," and waited for Heap of Bears to speak again.

"There's something else we're going for," he said. "We're going for revenge. I guess you all remember when Eagle Heart's brother was killed last year. Well, that's what we're going for. To get revenge on the Utes for killing him."

That made it all right. They had a reason for going. Somebody said, "When are we starting?" and the Comanche leader replied, "To-morrow morning, if you can get ready."

They all went off laughing behind their faces. That was just like the Comanches. They decided things in a hurry and then were slow in getting ready. Kiowas always made plans ahead and thought about things, so that they were ready on time. They could leave tomorrow morning, all right. They didn't have much to do.

Sitting Bear went back to his own tipi. His first and second wives were both waiting there for him. The shadows had soaked up all the sun, now, and the valley curled down in front of them like a dog letting all its muscles go just to rest. Both the green and the red were turning blue, but it looked as if their colors had gone up in the sky, where the red and green sunset was wiping out the day's blue. All the light was yellow, and all the colors were so mixed that you couldn't tell where one ended and the next began.

Sitting Bear sat down and watched the lights turn color for a while before he spoke to his wives. "Heap of Bears is joining up with the Comanches," he said. "They're all going out to fight the Utes."

His wives waited.

"They want revenge," Sitting Bear went on. "They want revenge for the time when Eagle Heart's brother got killed by the Utes."

"Are you going?" asked his first wife.

Sitting Bear nodded. "I guess I am," he told her. "I thought a lot of Eagle Heart's brother. We were young men going hunting together. I guess I want revenge."

Both the women nodded. The second wife's baby began to cry, and she took him out of his cradle and began to feed him, swinging her whole body above the waist to quiet him. It was a good thing she had had her baby a month ago and was all right now so that she could take care of herself and him. The first wife was going to have her baby soon, and Sitting Bear kept the others busy waiting on her. He thought a lot of her. He was always thinking that something might happen to hurt her.

He sat now and watched the black cover up all the colors before he spoke. "Somebody's got to go with me. I've got to have somebody to take care of my shield."

Most times he would have taken his first wife, but they all knew she shouldn't go now. They were wondering who would be chosen.

"I guess you'd better go," he said to his second wife, and she nodded her head. Sitting Bear looked at the baby in her arms. "I guess you can take him, too," he added.

Then they all got busy, putting Sitting Bear's things together so that he would have everything he needed. Just this past year there was a new soldier society, the Crazy Dogs, to which he belonged. It was a society for the bravest men, and only ten could belong. It had different rules from the other societies, and those rules were hard. One was about a spear that the society had. The man who carried it wore a sash over one shoulder, and when he went into battle, he put the spear through the end of the sash and into the ground. That meant he had to stay where he was and fight until killed, unless one of his brothers or another society member ran up and pulled the spear out of the ground and said to him, "Go forward." Then he could retreat. That was another rule of the society. The men who belonged to it gave their orders backwards.

In a way, having the sash and spear was like having a war bonnet, but in Sitting Bear's family it was worse, because Sitting Bear had a war bonnet, too. He was double-hobbled. He couldn't desert his spear and he couldn't shame his war bonnet, no matter how fierce the fighting. He just had to stay there ahead of the other men and fight as if he were trying to get himself killed. Of course, somebody else could always release him, but sometime his people might not be able to get to him to set him free.

There was a shield, too. That was the sign that Sitting Bear belonged to a special society. It was called the Eagle Shields, and it was very special. The shields had to be taken care of in just certain ways.

It took so much time to keep one right that a man wouldn't do it for himself. That would be up to one of his wives.

It was a good thing for a man to have more than one wife. Especially if he had power things to be taken care of, there was more to be done than any one woman could do. All those things had to be done just so, and if they weren't handled right, the power might get angry and kill the man or the wife who had neglected them. That was one thing about power. It could do a lot of good for people, but you had to treat it just right. It could turn around and make everything go bad for you, too, easy.

All of those power things that Sitting Bear had must go with him. Most times his wife would carry them on her own horse, but this time she had the baby. The baby might do something wrong, through not knowing, so it was better for her to carry him and load the wonderful things on a pack horse. Then she could lead the pack horse and carry the baby, and everything would be safe.

The only time that women were supposed to go on a raid was when they went to take care of their husband's things. Sometimes a couple that was running away would go out with a war party. Then, if they got back safely together, they were married. If the woman had been married before, her first husband would not claim her any more.

They were three-fourths of the way through the moon; it was late when it rose. The light from it was red and then yellow and then white; and when all the color had gone from the light, the men in Heap of Bears' tipi began beating tipi-stakes together and singing. That was the sign that it was time for the war party to begin getting together.

Most of the men who were going had already made up their minds, and all they had to do now was go over to Heap of Bears' camp and say so. Some of them were young men, but there were many older ones, too. Everybody had respect for the way Heap of Bears managed a war party. He was wise, all right. He never stayed and lost men if the fighting went against him. He knew enough to retreat before his young men could get hurt. That night everybody felt safe and believed the war party was going to be victorious. People sat and stood in front of Heap of Bears' tipi, and some of the old men beat the tipi-pegs together, and everybody sang. It was all warlike. Eagle Heart came over and joined the singing.

Soon Heap of Bears held up his hand for quiet. Everybody stopped singing.

"I have something to say before we start out," said Heap of Bears. "This is something everybody ought to know. We are going out with the Comanches to fight the Utes. That's good. It makes us better friends with the Comanches, and we may kill some Utes. The Comanches say they are going for horses and girls. That's all right. They can have those things if they get them. If we get some, we maybe can use them, too. But that's not the main reason we're going. That's different. The main reason we're going is to get revenge. Eagle Heart's brother was killed by the Utes. That's the reason we're going. We want to get even. That's why I want to say this thing. I want Eagle Heart to go with us. I want him to go as one of our leaders, because it's his brother got killed. I want him to be just as important as anybody, because it's his revenge we're going to take."

Everybody cheered at that, and Eagle Heart said, "Thank you for honoring me," and came up and sat by Heap of Bears beside the fire. The dancing and shouting and talking started up all over again.

Sitting Bear went away and stretched out on his back in his own tipi, with his knees crossed up in the air. He had said he was going and he had to go, but he thought something might go wrong. Two leaders on a war party were bad. It never would work out. You had to have just one man whom everybody respected and looked up to and took orders from. You couldn't have two sets of orders being given at the same time. The thing that made it worse was who the two leaders were. Heap of Bears would always be careful and make sure of everything, but Eagle Heart was always rushing things. He never took the trouble to be certain of them first. If he made up his mind to do something, that was what he did right away, and nobody could stop him. Those men were too different to go on the same war party anyway. They shouldn't both be leading it.

Right there Sitting Bear made up his mind. He decided that he was going to do what Heap of Bears said to do. This was Heap of Bears' war party. He was the one the Comanches went to in the first place, and he was the one who had called everybody together. That was the way it ought to be. The man who started something should be in charge until he finished it.

Some of the people were going to bed now, and the singing and shouting weren't so loud, but others were still up. They must have stayed up all night, because when Sitting Bear waked, the singing was still going on. The women brought him water to wash his face and a bundle of broom sedge to brush his hair smooth. They started to bring him his paint, but he shook his head. There was no sense in painting your face when you were just starting out. It was better to save your paint until you came up with the fighting, and then use it to scare the enemy.

The Ten Grandmothers

The three horses were ready. Sitting Bear mounted his big grey stallion, and he and his second wife rode over to Heap of Bears' camp and joined the other Kiowas.

The Comanches were still eating. Comanches were always hungry and took a long time over their food. Kiowas would eat sitting on their horses when they were starting out like this. Just some water and a handful of dried meat was enough for them. When the Comanches had finished, they got on their horses. Everybody was all ready to start. Sitting Bear looked around. It was the greatest war party he had ever seen. There must have been over a hundred men ready to go. It was about the greatest war party anybody had ever heard of.

They rode out of camp with all shouting and waving their bows and spears over their heads, but as soon as they were down the slope and headed south across the flat, they settled down and rode easily. You couldn't ride too hard when you were just starting out. That wasted the horses, and it might tire the men, besides.

They went south and west towards the Wichita Mountains. Everything seemed to start at the Wichitas. If you crossed them and went south, you were on your way to Texas and Mexico. If you stayed north of them and followed along them west, there was good grass and camping, mesquite trees and water, and after a while you came out on the Staked Plains. It was hard traveling across there, but if you knew the water holes you could make it. Then you came in sight of the big mountains, and if you stayed on the east of them and went north, you came into the high mountains, and that was the Ute country. There were other ways to get there, but this made the easiest traveling, even if it took longer.

It was a good day's ride from the hot springs to Saddle Mountain, when you didn't push the horses. Kiowas were in their own country or on the edge of the Comanches' all the time, too; they could travel easily and stop to rest and eat when the sun was directly overhead. There was not much shade, and it was warm in the middle of the day. Sitting Bear thought some about the baby, but he slept easily and ate all right. After all, he was a month old, and by that time a baby was able to travel anywhere.

It was making dusk when they reached Saddle Mountain. There was not the color in the sky that there had been the night before, and the red-black mountain looked bare after the green around the springs; but there was a wide meadow with a little creek on the north side of the mountain, and there they camped. Because they would have to sleep out in the open, it was a good thing to find pasture for

The Bear

the horses. That way it would not be hard to find them in the morning. There were deer in the meadow, but, when they saw people coming, they ran back towards the mountain where the horses couldn't go. Some of the men turned their horses loose and started after the deer. It was better to eat fresh meat while they could get it and save the dried meat for later.

The Comanches made their camp a little south of the Kiowas, near the mountain. The wind was down now, sinking with the sun, but it would come up with the clear dark, and here it always blew from the south. The Comanches would get it first, but in spring you didn't need the wind as much as you would later in the summer. Anyway there was always enough wind to go 'round.

Sitting Bear didn't go off hunting with the other men. He stayed and hobbled the three horses; and then, while his wife went to look for firewood, he played with the baby. He took Eagle Plume out of the big day cradle and held him in his lap, where he could kick and stretch and grow. Once Sitting Bear turned his son over and looked at the back of his head. It would have a good shape when the boy was grown.

Everything was easy and quiet in the camp, waiting for the young men to come back with the deer meat. The woman returned, built up the fire, and fed the baby; and they sat and waited for the hunters to come in. There were stars all over the sky when they heard the voices of the young men. They must have gone a long way up the mountain, hunting. At first there were just little sounds of them, but when the sounds grew plainer, you could tell that something was wrong. Sitting Bear got up and went over to where Heap of Bears was waiting. Soon the young men came. They were carrying two deer, which they laid down in front of Heap of Bears.

"Thank you for the meat," Heap of Bears said. He took out his knife and got ready to skin and cut up the deer by firelight.

The young men still stood there. They were waiting for something more than their share of the meat.

"What is it?" Sitting Bear asked them. "What happened?"

One of the young men spoke then. "The Comanches went hunting, too," he said.

"Didn't they get anything?" Heap of Bears wanted to know. He thought maybe they were supposed to send some meat over to the Comanches. That would be hard. Two deer were not enough to go around in their own camp. Some Kiowas might have to eat dried meat as it was.

"They killed something," said the young man.

11

"What was it? What did they kill?"

"It was a medicine animal. It was that animal you and this other man are named for."

They were all quiet, thinking it over. Then Heap of Bears said, "Did any of our young men help kill it?"

"No," said the young man. "We didn't even see it killed. We heard them shouting, and we knew what had happened, so we came back right away. We didn't even look for anything else for ourselves."

"That's good," said Heap of Bears. "That's the only safe way to do."

The young man went on talking. He was too much worried to show the proper respect. "They are bringing it down to camp," he said. "I think they are going to cook it."

Heap of Bears turned to Sitting Bear. "I guess we'd better go over there," he said, "I guess we'd better find out what's happening."

The Comanches had just come in with their game when the two men arrived. The bear lay like a man that has been killed and gone back to being a pile of bones and rags. That was partly why the Kiowas were afraid of the bear. It was like a man. It was like something that might have been their own ancestor.

Only Sitting Bear and Heap of Bears had come over. Since they had the medicine name, they were safer than the others; but they didn't know how safe. They didn't want to go too close, just to find out.

The Comanche leader had his knife in his hand and was getting ready to skin the bear.

"There you are, friends," he said. "This is a good time to come. We have plenty of meat here."

Heap of Bears walked around south of the bear, so that the rising wind would blow from him to it. "We don't eat that kind of meat," he said.

The Comanche looked at him.

"We don't kill that kind of meat," Heap of Bears went on. "That's sacred. We're afraid to be around it."

"Comanches are different," said the Comanche leader.

"That's what we know," replied Sitting Bear. He was standing beside Heap of Bears. "That's why we came over. We want you to leave that meat alone. Throw it away. Get rid of it, and don't eat it. It isn't safe for us to have that kind of meat along."

The Comanche was trying to understand; you could tell that. "It won't hurt you," he said. "You're not going to eat it. We're the ones who are going to do that."

"All the same it isn't safe for us," said Heap of Bears. "We can't be around where that kind of meat is being eaten."

The Bear

The Comanche started skinning the bear just the same. "My young men are hungry," he told them. "This is good meat for them. You'd better go back to your own camp if you're afraid."

Sitting Bear and Heap of Bears went back. They began to move over to the west, where the smoke wouldn't blow straight from the cooking fire to them. Others followed them, but Eagle Heart stayed where he was.

"That's strong, all right," he said, "but I'm not afraid. This isn't the camp where they're cooking that animal. We're not going to eat it. Just the Comanches are. We all know about them. We know they've done that before. One more time won't make any difference."

Some of the young men admired Eagle Heart and felt as he did. They stayed where they were, too.

The Comanches cooked their meat and ate it and went to bed early. They felt all right. They were doing what they had a right to do. None of the Kiowas could settle down very easily. They were all restless and upset, and they sat around and talked things over.

Heap of Bears made up his mind about what he was going to do. "I think we'd better go back," he said. "It isn't safe to go on a war party that has power working against it."

That settled it for Sitting Bear. He had made up his mind to follow Heap of Bears, and that was all there was for him to do. He told his wife to get ready, and the young men who had moved with them began to get ready, too.

The wind blew all night, down the red-black mountain and across the Comanche camp and into the camp where Eagle Heart and his young men were. By morning they were all soaked with that smoke. It smelled different from other cooking smoke, heavy and greasy with the fat of the bear. The grey light edged over the rim of the earth and spilled into the sky and along the ground, and, when it came, Eagle Heart could see the other Kiowas getting ready to go back. He left his own group and came across to Heap of Bears.

"What are you doing?" he wanted to know. "You can't turn back now."

"I think we'd better," said Heap of Bears. "I don't think this is a good raid to go on."

"I think it's all right," said Eagle Heart. "I believe we'll make out."

"Nobody can make out with power against him," retorted Heap of Bears.

"We're going to risk it," said Eagle Heart.

That should have been all there was to it, but it wasn't. Some of the young men who were going back had brothers who were staying.

They argued and pleaded with them, and tried to get them to go, too. Some gave in, but others wouldn't, and it looked as if this would even break up families. It was bad.

When Heap of Bears and his group rode off, they put the whole thing behind them. They would go home and try to get themselves clean. Then, when they couldn't smell the bear cooking, things would be all right. They could start back again and make another raid against the Utes.

"There were too many for good fighting, anyway," said Heap of Bears.

Sitting Bear answered, "That's what happens when you have two leaders. You have to have just one man in charge to make things go right. He's the one that's got to be responsible."

They came up with their camp, and they moved with it away from the hot springs. Then the Taime keeper sent word around that it was time for the Sun Dance, and they all started to move again. They went west, to End of the Mountains, to hold the Sun Dance that year. All the time they were wondering what had happened to Eagle Heart and the young men who went with the Comanches into the Ute country.

There were just four young men who came back. The Sun Dance was over, and the bands were scattered out again. Heap of Bears and his band had camped on the Washita, in the Big Bend, when the young men came in and found them.

"Where are the others?" everybody wanted to know. "Where are Eagle Heart and the other young men?" They couldn't believe that just four had returned.

"They all got killed," the young men said. "The power was too strong for them. We found the Ute camp and attacked it. Everything seemed to be going all right. Then one of the Utes shot that Comanche man, the Comanches ran away, and we charged. Then the Utes shot at us. They shot everybody except the ones you see here. We had fast horses. We got away."

Sitting Bear sat down and looked at his two sons, one from his first wife, now, along with Eagle Plume. "You'd better remember that," he told them, as if they were grown men. "You'd better be careful. You've got to have power working with you all your life, or everything you do will go wrong."

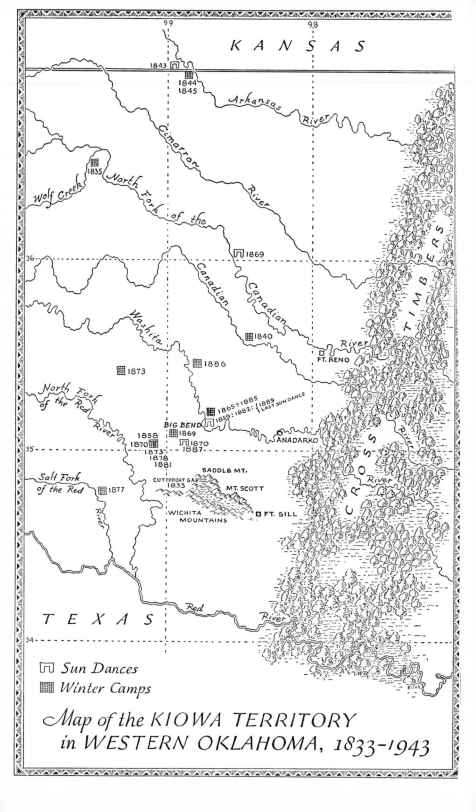

K A N S A S

99

98

1843

1844
1845

Arkansas River

Cimarron

River

1835

Wolf Creek

North Fork of the

36

1869

Canadian

Canadian

1840

Washita

River

FT. RENO

1873

1886

North Fork of the Red River

1865 ÷ 1885
1859 : 1882 : {1889 LAST SUN DANCE

BIG BEND
1869
1858
1870
1873
1878
1881

1870
1887

ANADARKO

Salt Fork of the Red

1877

SADDLE MT.
CUTTHROAT GAP
1833

MT. SCOTT

35

River

WICHITA
MOUNTAINS

FT. SILL

Red

River

T E X A S

34

🏠 *Sun Dances*
▦ *Winter Camps*

Map of the KIOWA TERRITORY
in WESTERN OKLAHOMA, *1833-1943*

C R O S S   T I M B E R S

The Traders

*The Year of the Horse Sacrifice
Sun Dance (1861)*

THEY WERE CAMPED ON THE WEST SLOPE OF SADDLE Mountain, above the springs that fed the creek in the valley below. Later in the year the springs and the creek and the valley would all be dry, but now, with the redbud and the wild plum running up the slopes like young colts, there was fresh water everywhere.

Spear Girl's mother had put her tipi on the edge of the camp, near enough to the springs for her daughters to carry the water easily. It was hard for little girls, just twelve and ten years old, to bring water. It was better to have some dust blowing through the tipi from the paths people had tramped to the springs and to be where the girls could get to the water easily.

Sitting Bear's camp was not far away, with its five big tipis, and men came and went all day and on into the night. Men were always visiting Sitting Bear's camp, planning dances or battles with him, or just talking and being fed. Nobody ever went away without eating. Sitting Bear was a real chief.

It was young morning, and already there was a big crowd of men at the tipi. They had all gone to see Sitting Bear, because they were all in one cluster, like wild bees getting ready to fly, and they were talking about one thing. Spear Girl's mother, who wasn't near enough to hear them, wondered what was happening.

"You go and see," she said to Spear Girl and Bow Girl.

As Spear Girl was the elder by two years, she had to look out for her little sister. She took hold of Bow Girl's hand, hard; and walked her over towards the crowd of men. She could see Big Tree and Big Bow and Little Bluff and Stumbling Bear in the crowd, and since they were all important men, she didn't want to go too close. Sitting Bear's first wife saw the children, though, and spoke to them politely, because they were visitors in her camp.

"Get down, sisters," she said. She always called them "sisters" because her mother's mother and their mother's grandmother had been sisters. It was hard to work the relationship out in your head, but it did seem to make them all sisters.

The Traders

Spear Girl said, just as politely, "Here we are, older sister," and they went across to the woman's tipi and sat down just outside the door. They could see the men from here and hear what they were saying. Their older sister gave them each a wad of meat and marrow on a stick to chew while they looked and listened. The meat was good, but listening was not good, because what the men said didn't seem to mean anything. They were talking about white men. About white men with mules. It was puzzling for a while. Then Spear Girl began to understand. The men must mean people with their faces painted white, like dancers. She understood that, but she didn't like it. The children were always afraid of the dancers. She listened some more.

Big Tree said the white men had camped last night on the other side of Cutthroat Gap. That showed they came from a long way off, because nobody who lived around here wanted to camp at the place where the Osages had cut off the Kiowa women's heads and left them in their own cooking-buckets for their husbands to find. Only strangers who didn't know about that would camp near there.

Little Bluff said the strangers had many pack mules besides their saddle horses, and that they had silver bridles even on the pack mules. That meant they were important. Only big men had silver bridles, and not even Sitting Bear had a silver bridle for his pack mule. They must be rich.

What came next Spear Girl didn't understand. It was about trading with the Comanches last year and the Mescaleros the year before. Sitting Bear said, "They may have better things than the Pueblos." Spear Girl had heard about the Pueblos. Her mother had a shell necklace that she had got from a Pueblo man for four buffalo hides. They were good hides, but the necklace was white and blue and pink and black, and four hides didn't seem too much to give for it.

She wondered who had traded with the Comanches and the Mescaleros. Not the Kiowas, because they had all the things the Comanches and the Mescaleros had, and more, too. Those people had nothing a Kiowa would want. They had a lot of silver, and they made bridles, belts, bracelets, and earrings out of it, but the Kiowas could make them, too, when they had the stuff to work with.

The girls had eaten all the meat and marrow and had thrown away the sticks. Bow Girl was beginning to get restless. She was still a very little girl. "Let's go home, sister," she begged, so Spear Girl got up and said, "Thank you for food, older sister," to Sitting Bear's first wife, and they went back to their mother's tipi.

"What are the men talking about?" their mother asked.

"White men," said Spear Girl.

"What kind of white men?" asked the mother. It didn't seem to puzzle her to hear about them.

"Strangers, I guess," said Spear Girl. "They camped over near Cutthroat Gap last night. They don't know much, or they wouldn't camp there."

"Where did they come from?"

Generally mother didn't ask questions at all, and she had taught Spear Girl that it was not a polite thing to do unless you just had to. Spear Girl felt embarrassed because her mother was being rude to her. She thought she had better tell everything at once; then her mother wouldn't have to be rude any more.

"The men talked about white men. The white men camped in Cutthroat Gap last night, so they must be strangers. They came from a long way off. They had saddle horses and pack mules, and they had silver bridles on the horses and on the mules. Then one man said something about trading with the Comanches and the Mescaleros last year, and Sitting Bear said they would have better things than the Pueblos."

"Thank you for telling me," said her mother. "That is what I needed to know."

Spear Girl felt better. She guessed her mother had been rude to her because she needed to be. It was because that was the quickest way to find out what she wanted to know.

"Come and help me," her mother said then. "I want to get some things out to trade with."

She seemed excited and in a hurry. She went back into the tipi and began to drag the rawhide cases out from under the beds. They were big cases, and they were fairly full, because all three of them worked hard all the time, and they had plenty of pounded meat and tanned hides to put in the cases.

Spear Girl was surprised, though, when she saw the one her mother was opening. It was a big, old one, so old that instead of having painted patterns on it, it had designs drawn in white. Her mother kept their best things in it: the shell necklace and her silver belt, with the strip of leather that had silver slides on it and hung from the belt and sang when she walked. There were other things in the case, too; but the best and the ones they had the most of were painted deerskins. They were tanned soft, with the hair off, and made up with square and diamond-shaped designs for little girls' robes, just like grown women's buffalo-skin robes.

All of these good things were in that one case. Spear Girl watched her mother take them all out. The belt, the pendant, and the shell necklace she put right back, but the little, painted deer hides she laid on the bed and looked at. There were six of them.

"Come here," she said to Spear Girl. "You pick one you want to keep. Tell your sister to come, too. She can pick one."

It took them quite a long time to choose, because the hides were all beautiful. Spear Girl chose the one with the most red on it, finally, and Bow Girl took the one with the most blue.

"That's the way it is," said their mother. "I bet you marry a Comanche," she told Spear Girl, "always picking out red. Now your sister here will have to marry a Kiowa. Nobody else would stand for all that blue."

Spear Girl laughed. Her mother was joking with them, so she could joke back a little. "Maybe you knew some Comanches sometime," she said. "You painted that red robe."

Her mother laughed, too. "I don't know Comanches," she said. "I just painted it that way so I could trade it to them."

They went out of the tipi and piled the things beside the door. Then Spear Girl looked around. She had been so much interested in what they were doing, she hadn't been noticing, but now she saw that every woman had a pile of things by her door. All must be getting ready for trading.

After they were all through, the women started to cook. It was like getting ready for a Sun Dance, in a way, because everybody was working hard, but it felt like a good time coming up from underneath. Spear Girl worked, too, helping her mother; and she began to wonder when the good time would get all the way to the top.

"How long will it be?" she asked, and her mother told her, "It takes them all day to get here from Cutthroat Gap."

Dusk had slid down into the valley and almost up the slope to the camp before anything happened but cooking. All at once, away off, Spear Girl heard pieces of metal striking against each other. They had a good sound, like singing, and they kept time with each other, like drumming—like men's singing and playing the drums to practice before a dance, but higher, like women's voices, and far off and a little lonesome, like children's.

"What's that noise," asked Bow Girl, and her mother said, "Bells. Little metal rattles they hang on their bridles."

Dark had come all the way before the sound of the bells came into the camp. It had got nearer and louder, but it was different from singing, because it never got deeper or stronger. It was a strange sound, because you always knew that it came from metal striking metal, and that nothing else in the world could make it.

The Ten Grandmothers

Sitting Bear, Little Bluff, Big Tree, and Big Bow went towards the sound to meet the strangers. Everybody else stood off and watched. The white men had a funny shape in the firelight, because of the things that they had on their heads—slanting-up and sweeping-out things, which they took off and held in their hands when they talked. Spear Girl was glad they took them off, for then she could see that their heads were shaped like anybody else's and that their skins were an odd color. They must have washed the paint off, because they weren't white at all. They were a peculiar, grey sort of red, not brown like Indians. Maybe the paint had stained them and had made them that color.

Sitting Bear was talking to them in sign language. They knew sign language, all right, and they used some of it, but the way they used it was as funny as their skins. They made big, wide swings with their arms, moving them from the shoulders and holding them clear away from their bodies, instead of keeping them close to their sides and moving from their elbows. If they had had robes on, or had needed their knives in a hurry, they'd have had a hard time getting their arms down.

One man was pointing to a tipi, and then back to the mules, which stood with the metal on their bridles picking up sparklight from the fires, and the metal of their bells making sparks of sound. At first Spear Girl thought this man was making a new sign that nobody had ever seen before, because he pointed with his forefinger at the end of his arm, instead of with his lips and chin as other people. Sitting Bear seemed to understand, though, because he pulled his chin around to show a clear space on the east side of the camp, where the strangers could go.

The strangers nodded, pulled their horses around, and went off to the place. Spear Girl wondered what they would do about making a camp. They didn't seem to have any women with them. This time of year it could be cool at night. Even the young men, coming back from raiding parties, sometimes said they needed tipis at night and wished they had women along to put them up.

These strangers must have been used to not having women, though, because they began putting up their houses, not regular tipis, but square-sided things, made out of soft stuff that folded up, like the red cloth that Sitting Bear's war-bonnet tail was made of, except that these were white.

"It is rude to stare," said her mother, and Spear Girl went into the tipi and went to bed and covered up, head and all, because she was ashamed of staring.

The Traders

In the morning light the straight-sided tipis looked queerer than ever. Spear Girl could see them out of the end of her eye as she helped her mother get breakfast. They didn't have much breakfast, because they were all too excited to eat. By the time they had finished, everybody was going over to Sitting Bear's camp; and as soon as they had things put away, they all three went over there, too.

People were sitting around, looking down at the ground, waiting. Once in a while some one of the men spoke, and after waiting politely, somebody else answered him. Then the bells began to strike each other again, and the strangers came across the camp, leading their mules. There were big loads on the mules' backs.

They talked for a long time to Sitting Bear in their sign language. Spear Girl stopped being polite and just watched them. It was all right, because you had to watch sign language to know what people were saying. Everybody else was watching, too.

The strangers said they had come from a long way off, to the south. They had been four sevens of nights on the way, so you knew it was a long journey. They had brought many things with them. They would give the things to the Kiowas, if the Kiowas would give them hides and pounded meat and earth paints. Those were all the things the Kiowas had that they didn't have. Sitting Bear asked them what they had. They signed that they had many different things. Then Sitting Bear told them to unload the packs so that the people could see what was in them.

Unloading took a long time. The packs were tied on the mules' backs, instead of being dragged behind on tipi-poles, and it took a great deal of work to untie all the knots used to fasten the bundles. It made more work than the Indian way of packing. If you tied a load right, all you did at night was unfasten one knot and everything came loose right away. You didn't have to yell at your horses the way these people did, or stir up a lot of dust and then throw things down in it.

When everything was unloaded, the Kiowas began to go up to look. Sitting Bear's first wife went first, because she had the right. Then his other wives followed her, and then all the women began to look. The men stood back and waited. There were guns on one of the mules and lead and powder on another, which were all the men wanted anyway. They didn't have to look at the other things to know that.

Once the women began to look, everything was fun. There were big rolls of red and blue cloth. There were many sheets of silver. There were bunches of little, shiny, bright-colored beads. And there were sacks of other things. When the women asked what was in the sacks, the strangers made signs for food.

Spear Girl and Bow Girl stood back with the other children and watched their mothers. One of the men held out the red cloth to Sitting Bear's first wife, and measured out a piece as big as a buffalo robe. She took off her robe and held it out to him, and the man signed "Two" with his fingers. Sitting Bear's first wife shook her head. The piece of cloth would make a good robe, but she had a good robe. One was worth as much as the other. The man held up the red cloth and let it run over his arm like water running over a red rock. It was beautiful. Sitting Bear's wife watched it for a while. Then she turned around, went off to her tipi, got another robe, and gave the man the two. He handed her the red cloth. She took it, folded it around her shoulders, and did a few steps of a dance to show off. Everybody laughed and made the war-whoop. They were making fun of her, but she didn't care because they were all having a good time.

The trading went on like that for a long while. Each woman exchanged robes for what she wanted, red cloth or blue cloth or beads. Light-Eyed Woman didn't want any of those things. She wanted the bells from the mules' bridles. At first the man didn't want to let her have them, but finally he gave up. He gave her all the bells from one of the mules for four robes. Even Sitting Bear looked disgusted with her.

"What do you want with those old things?" he asked.

Light-Eyed Woman replied, "I'm going to put them on my son's dance costume."

Her son looked surprised, as if he didn't like having a costume different from everybody else's, but he said, "Thank you for the bells, my mother," the way he should.

They got through with all the big things after a long time, and then the strangers began to open the sacks with food in them. Spear Girl and Bow Girl and the other children began to move closer. They wanted to see what these people had to eat. It was odd-looking stuff. There were green-colored beans in one sack; that is, they looked like beans, but the men had a different name for them. They called them coffee. Spear Girl wondered what they would taste like. She knew what beans were. The Caddoes and Wichitas raised them, and sometimes gave them to the Kiowas. And there was corn meal, such as those people pounded up, in another sack. One time the Kiowas had found the spot where the Wichitas had hidden their food for the winter, and had broken the caches open, and taken the corn meal. It was fairly good, if you boiled it with pounded meat. Then there was

The Traders

some white dust in another sack. It looked like paint. Maybe it was what the strangers had used to make their skins white. In another sack there were big, dark-brown, clear-looking hard lumps of stuff.

The man who was opening the food sacks looked younger than the others. He smiled at the children and beckoned to them, but they hung back. Then with his knife handle he broke off some scraps of the brown stuff, and held it out to them in his hand. Eagle Plume, Sitting Bear's older son, and Young Sitting Bear, his brother, went up and grabbed pieces and ran away with them. When they were out of reach, they put the stuff in their mouths and began to eat it.

"Nah!" said Young Sitting Bear suddenly. "This stuff is good, like honey. All sweet. You better get some."

The other children went up to the man then. He stood, holding out the sweet stuff and smiling, and let them take it from him. Spear Girl and Bow Girl hung back until they were the last, and there were just two little bits of pieces left. The man smiled at them, and came over and put the little pieces in their hands, one for each of them.

Spear Girl tasted the stuff with the tip of her tongue. It was sweeter than any honey she had ever eaten and it had a different taste, but it was good. She put the whole piece in her mouth at once and smiled back at the man. He took his knife handle and broke off two big pieces and gave them each one.

"Thank you for honey," said Spear Girl. She didn't know what else to call it, even if it wasn't honey.

The man smiled again and said something that sounded like *"Sta wano,"* so she guessed that was his name for it. She said it after him, *"Sta wano,"* and he nodded and smiled again. Then the women came over and began to trade for food. Spear Girl's mother got a whole double handful of the green coffee beans. They seemed to be the most valuable, because the man took a good tanned buckskin to pay for them.

Spear Girl stood on the edge of the crowd and thought. The sweet stuff was better than any beans she had ever eaten. It must be valuable, too. The man had given her two pieces, a big one and a little one. Then he would want to trade for them. She began to wonder what she had better give him.

Spear Girl didn't own many things. Her two dresses and three pairs of moccasins and her plain deerskin robe were about all. She needed those things. She wore them all the time. She needed her awl and her sinew thread, the little case they went in, and the belt the case hung from. She needed just about everything she had. Then she re-

23

membered. She had one thing she didn't need. It was the painted skin her mother had given her the day before.

She went back to the tipi, got the skin out, and looked at it. It was beautiful. She hated not to have it, even if she didn't need it. But the man who had given her the sweet stuff would expect something for it, and the skin was all she had. He had given Bow Girl some of the *sta wano*, too; but Bow Girl was little, and maybe she didn't understand. The skin grew more beautiful as she looked at it. Maybe the man would understand about Bow Girl. Maybe this skin would be enough for both of them.

She folded the skin up carefully, and put it under her arm, where it wouldn't show, with long fringes of her sleeves falling over it. That was the way to carry things you were going to give. You didn't want to show off with them until the right time came. She went back to the man, holding the painted skin tight under her arm.

The women had gone off to their camps to cook the new foods, and the stranger was beginning to wrap and put away all the things that were left. It looked odd to see a man doing that. Maybe that was why the men had such a hard time with their loads. Packing was women's work. Men didn't really know how to do it.

The young man looked up and smiled at Spear Girl. He showed her that all the *sta wano* was put away and ready to load on the mule. Spear Girl shook her head. That wasn't what she wanted. The skin she had would be just enough for what he had given her and Bow Girl. She took the skin from under her sleeve and shook it out in front of the man. He doubled his legs under him, sitting on the props under his heels, to look. Spear Girl pointed to Bow Girl and held up two fingers. Then she pointed to herself, and held up two more. That made four. Then she made the sign for eating, and the sign for all gone, and held out the hide. The man sat for a long time and looked at her. He seemed puzzled. He looked at Bow Girl, and he looked at the hide. Then he laughed.

Spear Girl decided he hadn't understood. She made all the signs again, and when she finished she said, *"Sta wano,"* and held out the hide. The man touched the hide and said, *"Sí, sta wano,"* but this time he seemed to mean the hide instead of the other stuff. It was all very strange.

Spear Girl made all the signs again, while the man watched her. She made the signs for eating and all gone, hard, so that he would understand just what she meant. This time the man seemed to see. He shook his head and smiled a good smile, as her uncle did when he was pleased.

The Traders

Then the stranger took the hide. He folded it all up, not the right way, but as a man would, and gave it back to her. Then he gestured back to the tipi, and made the sign for a present.

This time Spear Girl stood and stared and stared at him, until he made the sign three more times. That was it! The sweet stuff was a present! He was all right, then. He was a good man. He knew what children wanted, and he would give it to them. She signed, "Thank you for the present," and ran off to the tipi. She wanted to put the hide away before her mother saw it was out of the case.

That night Spear Girl's mother cooked the new coffee beans. She had got some of the white dust, too, and she made it into a paste with water and wrapped it around sticks and cooked it over the fire. They all sat around and watched the things cook, and wondered how they would taste. The beans smelled funny; not like other beans cooking, and in cooking, the paste turned brown all over the outside.

It was long after dark when they tried to eat the food. The white stuff had cooked hard, and eating it was like trying to crack pecan shells with your teeth. When you got a piece broken off and chewed, it had no taste. At least, you could taste pecans when you got them out of the shells.

The beans were worse. They were as hard as the cooked paste, but they were not tasteless. They were strong and bitter. Those beans puckered your mouth all up when you tried to eat them. They were bad.

Spear Girl's mother took all the new food out behind the tipi and threw it away. Then she got out some good pounded meat that she had fixed with berries, and they ate that.

"This is what we need to eat," she said. "This is what is good for Indians. We don't need any of that white man's food."

She hadn't tasted any of the *sta wano,* though, or she might not have talked like that. Spear Girl went to sleep wishing she had another piece of the sweet stuff.

Hunting

*The Year of the Horse Sacrifice
Sun Dance (1861)*

YOU NEVER REALLY KNEW WHAT A MAN WAS LIKE until you knew how he acted when hunting. That was the way to see what there was inside him and how it was going to come out. You might think lots of men were good if you knew them just around camp, but after you saw them hunting, you found out something. Even in the case of a young man on his first hunt, you'd know.

Sitting Bear's oldest son, Eagle Plume, was alone with his mother. Sitting Bear had taken some young men and gone down into Texas, and another son, who was named for him, had gone with him. Eagle Plume was at home. He was fourteen, and he could have gone with his father, but Sitting Bear said he wanted to train his sons one at a time in fighting.

Eagle Plume liked being the only man at home. He could sleep late, and when he waked, his mother would have meat roasted for him, not boiled. Then he could take his time eating it, and when he had eaten, he could rest for a while. Afterwards he might go to work making himself some arrows. He was almost out of arrows, and Standing Wolf was teaching him how to make them.

"You may be old sometime yourself," Standing Wolf had said. "When a man is old, that's when he needs to know how to make arrows. That way he can always get himself something to eat."

Eagle Plume went to Standing Wolf's tipi now that he had eaten. He took some of the roasted meat with him, and the old man said, "Thank you for food," and put it back until he was ready to eat it. They sat in the door of the tipi, where the spring sun fell full on them and the south wind blew on them crosswise, and worked on the arrows. It was still early, and their fingers made long shadows on their work, winding the sinew around the feathers.

Lone Bear came by and saw them there.

"There you are," he said. "Two old men sitting in the sun, when everybody else is going hunting."

Eagle Plume looked up at him. He had never been on a hunt alone yet, and he had no buffalo horse. The only horse he had was an old, bob-tailed, yellow one.

Lone Bear saw the look, and a good smile came into his eyes. He let it slide over towards Standing Wolf, and said, "I think one of the old men can still sit on a horse."

Standing Wolf was pulling the sinew tight with his teeth, but he nodded his head back and then forward.

"I think that old man who can sit on the horse has some new arrows," Lone Bear went on, and Standing Wolf nodded again. Eagle Plume could feel his own eyes getting big in his head and his own breath getting big in his heart. Lone Bear looked straight at him.

"Go get your horse and come with me," he said. Eagle Plume went home, then, as if somebody had shot him out of a bow.

The old, bob-tailed, yellow horse was grazing a little apart from the herd. Eagle Plume had been riding that horse for a long time and had trained it himself. It would stand where he told it to, and he could guide it without a rein, just by pulling on its mane. He jumped on its bare back, and headed it for Lone Bear's tipi.

This wasn't like one of the big hunts, when everybody went and the soldier societies had charge of things and you had to obey strict rules. This was just a few men, about six, going hunting to get something to eat. There were some more boys about Eagle Plume's age with them, and they were all riding easily, talking and singing and enjoying themselves. They went west from the camp, and the prairie swung and rose and fell away beneath the horses' hooves as if it were alive. There was a ridge behind the camp, and when they passed it, there was nothing but men and horses and the good smells of day in the world.

Lone Bear rode over close to Eagle Plume. He had a pinto for a buffalo horse. It wasn't very big, but it was light and quick, a nervous sort of horse, but strong. It was all excited now, so excited that it didn't want to come too close to the bob-tailed yellow.

"Remember these things," said Lone Bear. "There are rules about hunting, just as about fighting. When you see the herd, you don't want to rush at them. Wait until somebody older than you are gives the signal. Don't kill more meat than you think you can skin and your horse can pack home. That way it won't be wasted and lie around rotting. If things get bad and there's an old bull after you, let your horse go. Let him run away. He knows more about hunting than you do."

The pinto was dancing up and down like a painted dancer by that time, so Lone Bear let him run. It was better to quiet him in that way than to make him more nervous by whipping him.

One of the other boys saw Eagle Plume and called to the rest, "Look at the old man arrow-maker! Look at his bob-tailed horse!"

They all came riding around him then, everybody laughing and making fun of the yellow horse. The horse knew it too, and he didn't care, but Eagle Plume cared for him.

"That's all right," he said. "Anyway, I'm riding my own horse. I didn't have to borrow one from my father's herd. Does your father know where his horse is now?"

That turned the laughing away from him and started it at the boy who had first been making fun of Eagle Plume. Everyone began to tease him about riding somebody else's horse and forgot about the bob-tailed yellow. It didn't matter if he had borrowed a horse, because many men who weren't young lent their good hunting horses for a share of the meat the borrower killed; but riding along with the morning running over their bodies, the boys liked having somebody to pick on.

Lone Bear went up a rise ahead of them, stopped the pinto, and held up his hand for everybody else to stop. All waited there behind him, until he rode back and told them, "There's a herd there around the spring. Everybody come on when I give the signal."

He rode back up the hill and sat looking out at the herd, while the hunters all bunched their horses together behind him and waited for him to give the word. The men were still and the horses were still, and Lone Bear up ahead was stiller than all the rest. It seemed as if he had to be very solid to hold the pinto there where it ought to be. Then his arm went up and down, and they all went forward without knowing whether they started the horses or whether the horses saw the arm move, too.

Eagle Plume was riding with the main group. Two of the boys who had teased him were ahead, shouting and running their horses, but the men around him were riding quietly and letting the horses do the running. He tried to do the way the men did, because he knew that most of them were good hunters.

The ground went backwards between the yellow's feet as if it were afraid of being kicked, and Eagle Plume went forward along the yellow's neck, with his bow in his hand and an arrow on the string. There was a calf ahead, a yearling, and he turned the yellow towards it. The horse ran up facing the calf and stopped. The calf just stood there looking at them.

Eagle Plume raised the bow and shot. He aimed for the spot between the shoulder and the ribs where the arrow would go into the heart, and he hit it, too, for he saw the arrow sticking out, but the calf just stood there. He tried again, for the eye this time, and hit the calf in the forehead between the eyes. The arrow hung down there like a dancer's headdress ornament.

He was out of arrows. He had just had two. The others must have fallen out when they were chasing. Here he had the calf, and the calf was shot; but it wasn't dead, and he didn't have another arrow to kill it. He tried to think what he had better do.

He slid off the yellow's back, and took his knife out of his belt. He hadn't lost that, anyway. If he could get close enough to the calf, he might be able to get one of his arrows back. The one in the forehead looked pretty loose. Maybe he could even get close enough to cut the calf's throat. He could try. He left the horse, and it stood there watching him and the calf.

The calf had its feet spread wide apart, and it let him get up close enough almost to touch the arrow. Then it jumped, and started after him. He ran back towards his horse, but before he could get close enough to mount, the yellow horse turned around and kicked backwards. It kicked the calf in the head, and the calf dropped and lay as if it had been killed.

Now he was glad he had his knife out. It was ready for the skinning. Somebody was shouting behind him. It was Lone Bear, riding down to find out what had happened. He jumped off the pinto and started over.

"You got one already," he was calling. "That's good. That's the way to do when you go hunting." He was all excited and pleased as he came towards Eagle Plume and the calf.

That calf was as mean as a bear. They both thought it was dead and were all ready to skin it when up it jumped. It chased Lone Bear, who was so surprised that it knocked him down. He lay there on the ground where he had fallen and the calf came up and began licking him all over. They never found out what it meant, acting like that.

It might go on licking him all day, or it might get tired and want to do something else. Eagle Plume thought he'd better make sure it didn't do anything else. He took his knife and got on the side of the calf opposite Lone Bear. Then he slit the yearling's throat. It turned around once, so that it faced east instead of west, fell down, and really died this time. It always happened this way. Buffalo always died facing east.

Lone Bear got up. There was so much blood on him you would have thought he was killed instead of the calf, but he wasn't even hurt.

The Ten Grandmothers

"That's the way," he said. "That's what you've always got to do. Always remember if you help people in time of danger, they'll help you out when you need it. It's that way in life, not only in hunting. People who try the most deserve the best. That way everybody knows they're good, and they get the best, too."

He went over to the calf and got ready to help Eagle Plume skin it. "If a man helps his friends out and his horse out, why, then, they'll help him out, too. That way he will live like a good man with his friends and his horses and get a lot more from both of them. Always remember, hunting is like fighting and like living."

First Fight

The Year of the Raid into Texas
(1862)

FOR ALL OF THE YOUNG MEN, THERE WAS ONE THING THAT WAS important. That was the first time they went on a raid. Going on a raid to fight, not just to help out with the cooking and hold the men's horses, showed you were a man. It showed more than that; it showed you were ready to take a man's part and do the things that belonged to being a man.

Hunting Horse waked to the sound of drums. They were in the air and all around him. They even seemed to come out of the ground where he lay. They were heavy, pounding drums, and as soon as you heard them, you knew they were men's drums, with nothing to do with women at all. He lay and let the drumbeats run through his blood and into his bones, and their steady upward pounding lifted him out of bed and towards the door of the tipi. As he went, a woman somewhere began to cry.

It wasn't late, for a first-quarter moon still showed the edge of its thumbnail against the west sky. The drums were pounding at Sitting Bear's camp, and he went across to see what the matter was.

Sitting Bear was sitting on the ground in front of his tipi. His blanket was drawn up over his shoulders and his head was bowed forward as if he were thinking. Two of his wives stood behind him. One held his yellow shield, with green birds painted on it, which showed that he belonged to the Eagle Shield Society. The other held his war bonnet and the long red sash that showed he belonged to the Crazy Dogs. Those two societies were the highest ones to which a man could belong. Nobody else had ever belonged to both of them.

There was a big crowd of men around, showing plainly in the firelight. Their wives were behind them in the shadow, and the mass of the women and the way they moved just a little was like the mass of big woods against the sky. You knew they were there, thick, but you couldn't pick out any one of them by her looks.

There were children hanging to their mothers and listening, where you couldn't see them at all, and over beyond the men, between them

31

and the women, were the very young men and the older boys. That was where Hunting Horse went. That was the group he belonged to. They were all in the Herders Society together.

Bird Tied to His Head was the one who was beating the drum. It was a piece of rawhide laid flat on the ground in front of him. Some of the other men were beating tipi-pegs together. Bird Tied to His Head wasn't singing when Hunting Horse came up, but just afterwards he began to sing the *Journey Song*.[1]

> *Going away on a journey,*
> *That's the only thing.*
> *That's the only way there is,*
> *For a young man to make himself rich and famous.*

He sang it four times, and the other men began to take it up, but Sitting Bear never moved. Hunting Horse felt something moving in his throat. It was his own voice, coming out of his mouth with the *Journey Song,* deep and strong, like a man's voice. It had never felt that way before, hard against the inside of his throat.

Bird Tied to His Head put down the bow he was beating the hide with, and began to talk.

"This is what I have to say," he began. "This is the thing I have been thinking about. There are getting to be too many white people around here. They're filling up all this country. It used to be that they just came once a year. Once a year they would come with things to trade to us. Now they're around all the time. They build wood houses and live in them. They stay there. They even put fences around land and run the buffalo off. I don't like it. Now's the time when we've got to do something about it. There aren't too many of them, and they're all down there in Texas. Last year the Comanches went down. They killed a lot, and ran the rest off, in one place. But now other places are filling up. I think we've got to stop them soon. If we don't run them off, they'll be all over the place. That's why I'm starting this war party. It's open to everybody. Anyone who wants to join me in going to Texas to fight the white men can come in now."

Bird Tied stopped talking and began to beat on the drum again. It was a different song from the *Journey Song,* a quick, exciting song, that made fun of the white men and dared them to fight.

> *You call yourselves white men,*
> *But you all have red faces.*

[1] Several slightly different versions of this song are known. The wording changes with the singer; therefore slight variations are used in this book.

First Fight

Come out and fight with us,
And we will see if your blood is red all over
The way it is in your faces.

The song went quicker, and more of the men sang it. They began to come forward and stand beside Bird Tied and Sitting Bear, to show that they were ready to go. Hunting Horse stood there listening, and the quick, excited song seemed to come behind him and push him forward into the group behind Bird Tied. He was standing to one side, then he was standing in the group, and he never knew how he got there.

When the song was over, there were about forty men all bunched up behind Bird Tied and Sitting Bear. That was a lot to go on one war party. Usually there were about half that many. People were whispering and talking around them, because there were so many. It must have been that they really wanted to run the white men off, because not many men would follow Bird Tied at one time. He was too reckless.

Sitting Bear lifted his bent-down head and looked at them.

"There are a lot of men there," he said to Bird Tied.

"Yes," said Bird Tied. He sounded proud of having so many men follow him.

"There are a lot of young men there," said Sitting Bear.

"That's right," said Bird Tied.

"You better be careful," said Sitting Bear. "We don't want to lose all those young men. You better not be too reckless. We're going to need them."

That was a funny thing for a Crazy Dog to say, because the Crazy Dogs were the men who had to stay in one place and fight in a battle until they were killed or until one of their fellow-members released them. Crazy Dogs were supposed to be braver and more reckless than other men.

"I'm going to be careful of the young men," was all Bird Tied said.

They scattered out then, and began to get ready. There was always a lot to do, getting ready to start on a war party. It kept everybody busy all night.

Hunting Horse didn't have any parents of his own. They were both dead. He lived with a woman who was a distant cousin of his mother's and her husband. They were fond of him and good to him, but it wasn't like having their own son leave them. They helped him to get everything ready, and his cousin's husband told him what to take and what he had better leave behind.

The Ten Grandmothers

It turned out that he was leaving practically everything he owned, except four pairs of moccasins and his bow and arrows and quiver. He wanted a gun, but as he didn't have one yet, he still had to shoot the old-fashioned way. A gun cost a great deal, between four and eight horses, depending on how good they were. Just before he was ready to start, his cousin's husband handed him something else. It was a stone hammer, like the ones the women used for pounding dried meat, but instead of a wooden handle it had a rawhide one with lots of spring in it. The end of the stone head was pointed and sharp, and with the spring of the handle and the drive of a man's shoulder behind it, it would be a fierce weapon.

"It doesn't look like much," his cousin's husband said, "but you take it. You may get to fighting so close you'll need to use it."

It didn't weigh much, so Hunting Horse hung the hammer on the other side of his belt to balance his paint bag and knife, got his horse, and rode off. Just before he left, his cousin put her arms around him and held him. Her face was wet on his bare shoulder, but all she said was, "Come back to us safe." Then she let him go.

He had expected Sitting Bear to go with them, but it seemed as if he weren't going. He was still sitting bent over the fire, and his wives were still standing behind him holding the things that were weapons fighting for him instead of weapons for him to fight with, and it looked as if none of them had moved all night. Bird Tied and the men who were going with him were beginning to gather again, ready for the parade through camp before they started. When they were all there, Sitting Bear stood up.

"There you are," he said, "all of you together and all ready to start. That's good. That's the way it ought to be for the young men. You are going to Texas to fight the white men. They aren't very bad enemies now, but I think they will be worse later. There are a lot of them and they come on fast, like the Navajo. I think fighting them will be like fighting the Navajo. There will always be more of them after while to fight." He stopped and looked around at all of them. "Now I am going to sing my song," he said. "I'm going to sing my Crazy Dog song. That will let you know that I think you all ought to fight as bravely as Crazy Dogs, whether you belong or not." He pulled in a deep breath and began to sing that song.

I live, but I will not live forever,
Mysterious moon, you only remain,
Powerful sun, you alone remain,
Wonderful earth, you remain forever.

First Fight

Then the women made the war-whoop in the backs of their throats that fairly lifted the young men into their saddles and drove them out of the camp, and they were all gone away into Texas, riding with Bird Tied.

There were certain requirements that always belonged with going on a war party. There had to be the meeting the night before, to call the men together and decide who was to go. Then there had to be a buffalo doctor along, to take care of anyone who got wounded, because buffalo doctors had the power to cure anything where the blood flowed. There had to be an owl doctor along, too, because owl doctors had the power to tell what was going to happen. Some of the older boys who were just beginning to be men accompanied the party, to help with the cooking and to hold the horses if the older men were going to fight on foot. Sometimes a woman sneaked off from her husband and went with some other man, if she was in love with him. Sometimes a woman would go with her husband, to take care of his shield and other equipment.

This time there was an owl doctor and a buffalo doctor and some of the older boys, but there were no women. The party was all men. They were on their best horses, and they headed south across the prairies, with the coming day rolling the mountains up out of the earth behind them. That was one good thing about camping south of the mountains. It made it easier to get down into Texas.

The morning rolled the mountains up and made them big, and midday rolled them away, so that all day they got smaller behind the war party. The men rode without much talking, steady and quiet and all set on where they were going. They went forward all day except for a stop in the middle of the day to rest and water the horses. At night they found a grove beside a spring, and some of them wanted to camp in the grove, and some wanted to light fires to cook their meat. At first Bird Tied wouldn't let them, but when he saw a small buffalo herd, he gave the signal, and two of the men slipped out and shot a cow with arrows, so as not to make any noise. They came back with the hump and the tongue and the paunch. Bird Tied let them light a little, clear fire, and when the paunch had been emptied and cleaned and filled with water, they hung it over the fire and cooked the rest of the meat in it. Then they put out the fire and covered it with earth. They covered the earth with twigs and grass, and then they were ready to sleep.

In the morning nobody wanted to take time to light the fire. They all washed in the creek and came back and ate the cold meat that was left over. They had mesquite meal and dried meat with them, but

Bird Tied wouldn't let them eat that. He made them save it until they were nearer to the enemy they were going to fight.

That day the mountains were far behind them, and the only time they knew they had been near mountains at all was when they looked back from the top of a rise and saw the world in the north rolling and broken. By night they couldn't even see that much, and they knew they were well on their way.

That evening they killed a deer and cooked it over the coals on sticks, because the paunch was too small for boiling. They slept and washed and ate again, and started on across the earth that got flatter and flatter, with no more sudden dips and swells to hide them from anybody that might be looking. They saw nobody, because they were staying away from places where people would be until they reached the place where they were going.

They were four days on the way, with the world flattening all around them, and late on the fourth evening they saw something begin to shape up. It was south and a little west of them, and it was a wooden house. As they went on, others shaped behind it. "That's the place we started for," said Bird Tied. Hunting Horse wondered some whether that was the place they had started for, or whether Bird Tied had just decided that it would do as well as any other place. But you didn't say that when you were a young man going out on your first real war party.

They ate mesquite meal that night. It was dry and tasteless, and it didn't fill you up, but you could keep going a long time on it. It was the strongest food there was, and it was better than dried meat on a war party, because it didn't take up much room and was light to carry around.

After they had eaten, Bird Tied called them all together and told them his plan.

"This is the place we were coming to," he said. "This is where we're going to fight. There are a lot of white men here. Some of them have their women and children with them. They have built houses, and they have their horses and cattle here. This is what I want to do. Early in the morning we will attack. We want to get the horses and burn the houses. If we can, we ought to kill the men. It's a long way back to where we came from, so we won't take any prisoners. We'll just let the women and children go. We won't even try to hurt them unless some of the women start fighting us. But the main thing is to burn down the houses they live in and run off their horses and cattle. That's what we've got to try to do."

They all went to bed then, but Hunting Horse didn't sleep much.

First Fight

He kept lying awake and thinking about the fighting tomorrow. Those white men had good guns, and they were good fighters. Some of the Kiowa men were going to get hurt. Maybe even some of them would get killed. Something went crawling along his backbone like a worm inside the bone, and then it crawled around and around in his stomach. He thought it must be fear. His mind and his heart weren't afraid, because this was what a man had to do and what he had come out to do, but his backbone and his stomach kept crawling with the fear inside them. It kept him awake for a long time.

Somebody touched his forehead with a hand. It was Bird Tied waking all the men. They turned and stretched and got up without talking, because they all knew what they were going to do. Now was the time when you couldn't get ready. You had to be ready now, or you shouldn't have come at all. The boys brought the horses up, but Bird Tied sent them back.

"This time we'd better fight on foot," he said.

The only thing you had to do when you were getting close to an enemy was not make any noise. They all got across the ground in the dark that seemed to lessen with every movement that they made, and their silence hid them as the light would show them. There were fences that they crawled under, and gates that they went around. Once they stopped in a corn field and Hunting Horse heard someone near him whisper to himself, "Here is the fruit. The fruit that looks as if it were beaded," and it came into his head that *Fruit That Looks as if It Were Beaded* would make a pretty name for a girl. Some day he would have a daughter and name her that, he thought. Then Bird Tied gave the word, and they all yelled and ran forward.

The white men were surprised, all right, but it didn't keep them from fighting. They had good guns, and as they were inside the house, they could hide when they shot. The Kiowas couldn't hide, but that wasn't the most important thing. The horses lived in a house as the men did, and Hunting Horse was one of those who went to open the horses' house and let them out. There was a lot of hay piled up inside, and it caught fire easily. The others threw sparks around, turned, and ran out, but Hunting Horse stayed for a moment to make sure all the horses were gone, because horses were afraid of fire. Then he turned and ran out, too. Right in the doorway he came face to face with a white man.

They just stood there and looked at each other at first, they were so surprised. Then they both yelled. The white man jumped at Hunting Horse's throat, and they twisted their arms around each other and stood there wrestling. It was while he was holding on and being held on to that Hunting Horse remembered his hammer. He got his arm free and reached down to his belt for it.

He never afterward remembered just what happened or even how he felt. His hand was empty, and then it held the hammer. His arm was down at his side, and then it was raised. The white man was facing him and grunting, and then he was on the ground, twisting before he was still, and the end of the hammer was smeared. Hunting Horse cleaned it on the earth before he went to see what the others were doing.

The fighting seemed to be all over. The houses were burning, and the women and children had run away. The horses and cattle had been driven off, and daylight was there to put out the light of the fire. They had done what they had come to do. Two of the Kiowas had been killed, and some of the men picked them up and carried them off. Several more had been shot and were being carried or helped back to the buffalo doctor. He could make them well if anyone could.

Hunting Horse found himself going back to the horses beside Bird Tied. "So that was your first fight," Bird Tied said.

"Yes," answered Hunting Horse, "I've been in my first fight now."

"That's something a man never forgets," said Bird Tied. "Did you fight with anybody?"

"There was one white man ran up to me and tried to stop me, just after we turned the horses loose," said Hunting Horse.

"What did you do to get away?" Bird Tied asked him.

For a minute Hunting Horse couldn't think. Then he held up the little stone hammer, and Bird Tied saw that it had been cleaned with earth and saw a smear that Hunting Horse had missed.

"That's close fighting," was all Bird Tied said.

They started away as quickly as they could. They laid the dead men out on the earth and piled rocks over them, so that the coyotes wouldn't get them. They tied the wounded men on their horses, and then they started back. They had to travel all day and on into the night, for fear other white men would get on their trail and follow them. The boys had rounded up the captured horses and brought them along, so that the white men would have a hard time starting after them, but nobody wanted to take any chances.

Going back was different from going out. They had to be more careful, and they had to go slowly because of the wounded men. But it was worth it, because none of them died. Every night the buffalo doctor would go to work, using his power to cure them. Every day they seemed to be getting better. But it was slow, all the same. It wasn't until the third day that the mountains began to shape up ahead of them, and it wasn't until the sixth day that they knew they were near their own camp.

That night they camped just out of sight of the main group, and the scouts went ahead to let people know that they were coming in. The war party slept some, but a lot of the time they spent getting ready to go in. They all painted their faces black, because they had won the fight, and the boys rubbed the horses with bunches of grass, so that they would look fine. They waited until full daylight before they rode into camp.

The people were all in their tipis, but they were expecting the war party, and when they heard the men coming in shouting, the whole camp ran out. Two families who came out saw that their members had not returned. They went back into their tipis, and you could hear the women starting to wail. But the others were all happy. They carried the wounded men into their tipis and made them comfortable, before they began to sing and shout and get ready for the victory dance that night.

Hunting Horse rode into camp with the rest, and when the first rush of excitement was over, he went off to his cousin's tipi. That was where he belonged, but he was ashamed to be going there. He had been in a fight and had killed a man, but he hadn't brought back any horses. That was wrong. When a man went on his first war party, he ought to bring back something to show for it. He went into the tipi and sat down beside his cousin's husband. They knew he hadn't brought any horses, but they were glad to see him. His cousin gave him food, and nobody said very much until that night. Then they all went over to the victory dance.

There was a big fire going in the middle of the camp, to make light for the dancing, and everybody made a ring around it. Four of the old men had a big drum by the fire, heating it to make the tone sharp and clear for the dancing. The women were gathering around. Some of them were carrying spears, and the few whose husbands had the right to them were wearing war bonnets. Everybody was excited about what was going to happen next.

Before the dancing started, Bird Tied made a speech. He told where they had been and what they had done. He told who had gone with them, and he left out the names of two of the men, so that everybody knew that those two were dead. He told them that there had been one young man with them who was going on a war party for the first time.

"This is a fine young man," he said. "He is brave. He is generous. He turned all the horses loose so that the others could catch them.

He didn't try to grab one for himself and get it away. He was thinking about doing his duty all the time and not about getting something for himself. When a white man grabbed him, he fought with him. He killed that white man with a hammer, close to. That's why I say he's brave. I want everybody to know I honor this young man and have respect for him. I want him to have two of those horses that he turned loose for the others. I want him to have two mares. That way he will have the start of a herd."

His cousin pushed him on the shoulder, and Hunting Horse went up and got the bridle reins of the two horses in his hand. He said, "Thank you for mares," to Bird Tied, and then he walked back to where his cousin was standing. She made war-whoop for him and hugged him. "You'll have to start thinking about a wife," she said, "now that you're going to have a way to take care of her."

He knew he couldn't take care of a wife for a long time, but it made him feel good to have the right to start thinking about one.

Hunting for Power

The Year of the Sun Dance on No Arm's River (1863)

SITTING BEAR WAS A STRONG MAN AND A FAMOUS MAN. He had war power; when he took parties out, they were always successful. He was one of the ten famous warriors who formed the Crazy Dog Society and who were so brave they were almost sacred. They wore long red sashes, and when they got into battle, they stuck the special sacred spears they carried through their sashes and stood there facing the enemy. They were all ready to fight until they died. If one of them fought until the others thought he was going to be killed, then they would yell at him, "Stay there! Stay there!" and he would pull up the spear and come back, for they talked by contraries. Or if one of the other members wanted to do a brave deed, he would ride up, pull up the spear, and let the man go.

That was one kind of power that Sitting Bear had. Another kind was peace power. Everybody in his band looked up to him and respected him. He was a good man, besides being a fierce one. When people quarreled or wives were angry with their husbands and wanted to leave them, the person who was hurt would go to Sitting Bear to get things made right.

If the quarrel wasn't very serious, Sitting Bear would just talk to the ones who were fighting until they felt better about it and were friends again. Maybe he might make a person who had hurt somebody else give him some horses. But there wouldn't be anybody concerned except just those two and Sitting Bear.

If something more serious was the matter then Sitting Bear would use another one of his powers. He would go to the Grandmother bundle that hung at the west end of his tipi and untie the old black pipe that belonged to it. He would take the pipe and make the two who were fighting smoke it. If they once took it in their hands together, then they had to stop fighting, even if they didn't smoke it. Just touching it was enough, it was so powerful.

Sitting Bear had other power for other things. He belonged to the

41

Eagle Shield Society, and that was for magic. It was as strong as the Crazy Dogs. All of the members had shields painted alike with birds and guns, and they wore special crow-feather headdresses when they were in meetings. They could change feathers into knives and back again into feathers, and if anybody dropped a knife in a fire, point down, they could never eat anything that had been cooked over that fire. That was their rule.

All these powers Sitting Bear had obtained after he was a grown man. They had come one at a time. Some of them, like the Crazy Dogs and being able to settle disputes without the Grandmother, were more honors than powers. But he had them all because when he was a young man he had gone out on a power hunt and had found power.

Nobody but Sitting Bear could know what had happened to him then. For anybody else to know what had happened would have spoiled all of it. But the power that Sitting Bear had received was a power to get more power from many places and be able to hand some of it on. To show his power he had a little, black, stone arrowhead, which he wore tied to his scalp lock, and most of the time his hair hid it. Just once in a while, when he was dancing with the Crazy Dogs, he would let it show.

Sitting Bear was worried about handing on his power. He had four wives and many children, but only three sons.[1] The second son was named for him and was his favorite, and he was the son Sitting Bear would have liked to give the power to. He was the bravest son. He had gone on many war parties already. His whole family and everybody else in camp did him honor. It was a credit to them to have a young man like him around, and they were careful to give him the best of everything, because he might get killed and then they would miss him and feel sorry, thinking of the things they hadn't done to make him happy.

The oldest son was Eagle Plume. He was just like everybody else except that he looked like his father and was ugly. He was the son of Sitting Bear's second wife. He had been on two war parties and had brought back four horses each time, a number which was about right for a young man of his age. Most people did that well. Nobody made any fuss about what he had done, and Eagle Plume didn't care. He was proud of his brother, too, and he liked to show off his brother. It gave him credit to do that.

All of these things were all right. What was wrong was that none

---

[1] Sitting Bear's youngest son, Joshua Given, received a white man's education in the East, and later returned to the tribe as a missionary. He is generally better known than Eagle Plume.

of Sitting Bear's sons had power. They had not been out to hunt for it, and they had not had any power dreams that just came to them. If some older man wanted to teach them, they could learn that way, but it looked as if nobody had been instructed to teach any one of them. They could not just go to somebody and say, "Give me your power." They had to wait for a dream that would give them permission to ask, or for a man to come to one of them and say, "My power wants you to take part of it."

Sitting Bear had all that power himself, and he wanted his sons to have some of it. But he could not give it to them without having some sort of sign any more than anybody else could. He had waited until two were grown men, thinking that something would come, and he was growing old and impatient. He had to have somebody to whom he could hand on the Grandmother bundle. It had always gone from father to son in his family, and it would be a disgrace if he had to leave it outside.

He had thought about it for a long time—when he was sitting in his tent smoking and when he was out on his horse riding, sometimes when he was alone and sometimes when other people were there. Finally, one day he saw what he had to do. He went to the door and called to his two older sons, "You come in here now."

They came in and sat down and waited for him to talk. He smoked out his pipe and told them, "You're both grown men now. Soon you'll be getting married."

"That's right," said Young Sitting Bear.

"That's the way things ought to be," said his father. "It's good. It's the right way. But there are other things. There's more to being a man than hunting and fighting and marrying, other things that a man has to do."

Eagle Plume looked at the ground between the fire and his feet. He thought he knew what his father meant, but he wanted to be sure.

"There are some things I have to do," went on Sitting Bear, "some things I have to take care of. There are some of them that are old things and some of them that are new things. I have them, and they can't be thrown away. When I go, somebody else has to take care of them. I have to have somebody to hand them on to."

"Who will that be?" asked Young Sitting Bear.

"I don't know yet," said his father. "That's what I'm trying to work out in my mind. I have to have somebody in my family. It ought to be my son. But anybody that takes care of these things has to have power of his own first. He has to go out and hunt for it and find it."

Young Sitting Bear let his eyes jump up to the Grandmother

bundle for a moment. "That's pretty hard to do," he said. "A man has to feel just right, to do that."

"I've been thinking about that for a long time," said Eagle Plume. When the other two talked, sometimes they all three seemed to forget he was there, and everybody was surprised when he spoke. "I've been thinking about power. A man needs power to get along. I've been thinking I ought to go out and hunt for some."

"You better both go," said Sitting Bear. "That's the best way, if you both go. Then maybe I can divide my power. Give some to one of you, some to the other. That's the way we'll fix it. You both go."

The Kiowas were camped at End of the Mountains, and there was no good place to go for power anywhere near. Of course, you could get power anywhere you were, if the power wanted you to have it, but if you weren't sure, it was better to go to a place that was well known, where many other people had found power before. There was power stored up and waiting at those places, for people to come along and take.

Eagle Plume sat down in front of his mother's tipi and thought. He watched the sharp, red walls of the bluffs going up and up and making a quick line where they met the blue sky from the east, and he knew that was the way he ought to go, east and a little south. Something was telling him to go that way. He stood up and got ready to start.

There were four things you had to have if you went to look for power: a buffalo robe with the hair on, a bone pipe, tobacco, and flint and steel. Eagle Plume gathered all these things together before he went to bed. He drank some water, but he didn't eat anything. You did not have to start fasting until you reached the place where you would wait for the power, but it wouldn't hurt anything if he began ahead of time. It would help to get his mind clean.

The next morning he waked early. The sky was black through the tipi ears, and the stars were set against it like little dark dull sparks, so he knew it was near morning. He got up quietly, put his things together, took off all his clothes but his breechclout and moccasins, and started.

He had gone a long way, he thought, when the dawn wind began to run along the earth as if it were trying to catch the night that was going away. But when light came, he could look back and still see little bumps on the earth that were tipis. He knew he hadn't gone nearly far enough. It was hard to find a place that was far enough off that people wouldn't come bothering you, and still near enough to camp that you could get back when you hadn't had anything to eat or drink for four days and nights.

He stopped four times during the day. Each time he rested and smoked and prayed. The smoke seemed to stick in his throat like something hard, and he tried to swallow it and then he tried to cough it up, and still it stuck there. He went on with the smoke ball still in his throat.

It was late evening when he found the place he wanted. There was a mesa that didn't look very high until he started to climb it. Then its red sides became steeper and slicker and redder even than the cliffs at End of the Mountains, and he thought for a while he was never going to get to the top. He did, though, and lay and panted and looked around.

He could see clear away to the east, to where the night was running under the day and turning the whole sky dark. To the west he could see all the different lines of colors of sunset, melting and mixing into one another, and they seemed nearer and closer than the night when he looked at them, and farther away than the camp when he looked to the east. South and north the two were fighting for the sky, but it was night's turn to win, and soon the dark blue got between him and the light colors, and the day was gone.

He wrapped himself in the buffalo robe and lay there, watching the colors fight and the dark win, watching the first big, bright stars come out so near he could put out his hand to touch them, and feeling the dryness in his mouth and the lump still in his throat. Something warm and soft was coming over him, starting with his feet, and he knew it was sleep. But there was one thing he had to do before he could rest.

He got up, filled and lighted the pipe, and blew the smoke to the east, then south, then west, then north, then up, then down. When he blew smoke to each of the earth corners, he prayed. He prayed for health and long life. He prayed to live to see his children and his children's children. Then he prayed that power be sent to him and that it might be good power and that he might use it right.

When he lay down again, the lump was gone from his throat, and he could swallow; but the warmth was gone from his feet, and they hurt with cold. He slept a little and waked after a while, and smoked and watched the stars. When he smoked, he prayed again, for the same things he had prayed for before.

He went on like that all night. Four times he waked. Each time he was cold, and it seemed as if nobody could go on being that uncomfortable without having something happen. The excitement that had kept him going hard all day was gone now, and he was hungry. All of these things came into his mind, but he threw them away from him. If he was going to find power, now he was out hunting it, he would have to forget he was a body and just remember the place inside his heart where he could think.

When the light came, as if the sunset had slid around to the east from the west, he sat and watched the colors win their fight with the dark, and lose it again to the light that was without any one color but was all colors. Lightness poured over the earth like water, and he tried to think about something else, because to think about water was to become nothing but one big thirst.

It was not until the next day that day and night began to run together for him, and he began to wonder if he could ever tell one from the other so as to know them apart. There were flashes of brightness against the dark, and sometimes the lightness went black in the daytime, and he began to wonder whether he could tell when he had been there four days. Perhaps not. Perhaps he would lose count and come down too soon. Then everything would be spoiled. It might mean that he never would get power.

But he waited. He had lost track of the number of smokes, but he still knew the directions. Whenever he roused enough to know, he smoked and prayed. Sometimes tears were running down his face when he was praying; sometimes his eyes were dry and burning, and there seemed nothing left in the world but him and the heat of the sun that was sucking him dry.

It was just at daybreak that he heard the voice—daybreak that was coming very slowly, not shoving the night aside like the earlier dawns he remembered at this place, but trying to slip past the darkness and get into the world without being noticed.

The voice was like the light. It slipped into his mind from somewhere, and it seemed all around him yet nowhere. At first he thought there were two people talking; then he knew there was only one voice. It was saying something to him, but not in words he knew. He had to work hard, trying to make his mind make words of the tiny sounds. At last they came.

"Look down," the voice was saying. "Look in the grass at your feet. That's where a man must look for power. He has to make himself humble before it will come to him."

It seemed hard work to pull his eyes down from the edge of the world and the seeping light to the ground directly in front of him, but he did it. The grass was smoothed down and trampled where he had lain down to sleep and had stood up to pray; there were little heaps of ashes from his pipe all around, and at first he could see only those things that he had already seen before. He had to hunt with his eyes through the grass before he saw something else.

It was a mountain boomer. The little lizard was stretched out in front of him, its head on its little paws, like a sleeping child. While he watched, it sat up and waved those paws at him, like a man talking sign language.

"There you are, Eagle Plume," it said. "You came a long way to find me."

"It will be longer if I start back," said Eagle Plume.

"You won't find it so long," said the lizard. "I'm going back with you, and I can make it short for the man that has me. The way I run over rocks and hide, that's the way the man who has me can run and hide over the earth. Nothing will hurt him, because he can make himself so that he won't be noticed. He can be just like anybody else, so that he won't be noticed in camp. He can be just like anything else that grows, so that he won't be noticed out of camp. People will pay no attention to him, but they will go on talking and teaching him, and that way he will come to be wise."

"That's a strong power," said Eagle Plume.

"It's about the strongest power there is," said the mountain boomer, and it began to make itself grow bigger. "It's a power that gathers other power to it. The man that has it will never lose it. Instead, he will get more and more. Other powers will come to him from other people, without his going to hunt for them."

The mountain boomer was standing up on its hind legs now, with its face even with Eagle Plume's, and its big black eyes, like his father's, staring into his.

"Are there any rules that go with this power?" Eagle Plume asked.

"Not that go with my power itself," said the mountain boomer. "The other powers that will come to it will bring their own rules. You can paint your face the way your father does when he isn't wearing his society paint. And you can eat whatever you like, but not fish. Always mix sumach bark with your tobacco. Those are all things everybody does anyway. Nobody will notice much if you are doing them. The fourth thing you are to do, I will show you. There is something you must wear tied to your scalp lock. I will go back to camp with you, and show it to you on the way. You'd better get ready to start now."

Eagle Plume began to get things together. He gathered up the pipe, tobacco, and flint and steel and tied a buckskin string around them. Then he tied the string to his belt, so that he wouldn't lose those things. He got his buffalo robe and wrapped it around him. He felt strong, now, and sure of what he must do. All the weakness he had been feeling was gone.

The mountain boomer stretched itself out along the earth in front of him. "Get on my back," it said. "I'll carry you down."

He got on its back, and it started running down the slope that was higher and steeper than Saddle Mountain. As they went down, the lizard grew smaller and smaller under him, but he knew it was still there. Then they were at the bottom, and he was sitting on the bare earth.

"Look on the ground at your feet," said the mountain boomer's voice. "The thing you must wear can hide itself so that only the one that's meant to have it can find it."

The ground was as red as blood, and the little black thing showed plainly, sticking up in front of him. He put out his hand and held it. It was a little, black arrowhead like the one his father had. He just sat there and looked at it.

"Take a piece of your string," said the voice, "and tie that to your scalp lock."

He did. It seemed to take a long time, but times were running together so that he couldn't be sure.

"Now you can go home," said the mountain boomer. "You won't be able to see me, but I'll be with you all the time from now on. Sometimes I'll talk to you, and then you'll know what you must do. You'll know how to make decisions. But I'll be all covered with the red earth and you won't be able to see me. You'll just know I'm there."

Eagle Plume looked down. He was covered with red earth himself. He must have got it riding down the slope on the mountain boomer's back.

He started towards the camp, walking in the direction from which he had come, west by north. He went more slowly than when he had gone out, but something inside of him was carrying him along. He had forgotten what it was to be hungry or thirsty, and the lump had gone from his throat since the first morning. When it was dark, he lay down and slept; and when he waked, it was full light again, and he got up and went on.

The camp surprised him by coming out of the ground in front of him about midday. He had forgotten about the camp. The thing inside was still carrying him along, and he knew he had to go where it took him, but he had forgotten what that place would be. Then when he saw the camp, he remembered. The place where he was to go was his father's tipi.

Hunting for Power

He was right in the camp before he saw any of the people. They were all busy around him, doing regular everyday things, all except his brother. Young Sitting Bear was running. He came to Eagle Plume and put his arms around him and wept. It was as if they had been apart for a long time. Then they went to their father's camp.

Sitting Bear got up when he saw his son, and looked at him sharply. Then he got a cup of water, not full, just the bottom of the cup covered, and gave it to Eagle Plume. Then he sat down.

"You've been gone a long time," was all he said, and Young Sitting Bear added, "Seven days and seven nights."

Eagle Plume was wondering what he had better do. They would want to know if he had got the power he had been hunting, but they couldn't very well ask him. Unless the power told him, he couldn't talk about it to anybody himself. Then he knew what he must do. The power was helping him make the first hard decision. He turned his head, so that his scalp lock was towards his father, and raised his hair with his hand. Just for a moment Sitting Bear could see the little, old, black arrowhead tied to his son's hair in the place where he always wore his own. Then he knew.

"Your brother is tired," he said to Young Sitting Bear. "He needs to sleep. Take him to his mother's tipi."

When they had gone, Sitting Bear sat there alone and thought. This wasn't the way he would have wanted it, but you couldn't tell power what to do. The power was always there to tell you. If it came to one son instead of the other, that one was the son who was meant to have it. His son who was named for him was honest. He would not go out to look for power unless he knew there was a chance that he would get it. And he would not say that he had power if he didn't have it. If it came to him, he would let his father know.

This was how it was going to be. In a way, it made things easier. There was somebody now to whom he could leave the Grandmother bundle. It could go on, handed down from father to son. It didn't have to go to an outsider. And the power that would be guarding it would be the same mountain boomer power as his own. He was sure of that. That part would be all right. He didn't have to say anything about it to anybody now. Later on, if power came to his son who was named after him, then he could change. Nobody but himself and his two sons would ever know, and what he did would always be right with both his sons.

The Sun Dance

The Year of the Big Bend Sun Dance (1865)

I

THE BANDS CAMPED APART DURING THE WINTER AND came together in the early summer for the Sun Dance. This was the best time of the year in the prairie country; the grass grew long and thick in the flats and up the rises, and the leaves did not yet seem to shrink along the stems that held them to the trees.

All the people had come in as they were called up, and the big circle made a ring around the flat bottom that seemed to go for a long way in the bend of the river. It had to be big to hold five thousand people. In the center was the cleared space where they would put up the dance lodge, but it was not set up yet. Later in the day they would go out to cut the center pole, and when that was in place the building could begin.

It took a long time to get the people together. The old man who looked after the Taime had to ride out first and find all the camps and visit them. The leaders of the men's societies went with him, and some young men, who were getting ready to join the societies, went, too. They showed respect for the old man and the society leaders by dressing up, and they carried their bows and arrows, but they did not shout and yell when they found a camp; they waited for Taime Man and the older men to lead the way to it. Then they followed quietly and sat on their horses, not looking around, but with their eyes down, quiet and respectful.

After all the camps had been notified, the people began to get ready to come. The dance was in a different place nearly every year; one big camp would use up the pasture and the wood, so that they could not come back for a few years. Every year they waited to see where they would go this time. It was a long trip for some of them; the People Who Lived Way Out on the Prairies always had a long way to travel and were the last to come in. But the Big Shields, who were the Taime Man's band, always knew first where they were to go and were there waiting for the others.

The Sun Dance

Yesterday the last of the True Kiowa People band had come in to the Big Bend of the Washita and had filled in all the space that was left for them between the Big Shields and the Male Elk band. Now everybody was here, and things could begin.

All these things Spear Girl knew as well as she knew her own horse; she knew them so well she didn't even think them as she stood and looked at the Big Circle. They just were, like the sun and the rain, and nobody had to think about them. There was a lot more thinking to do about pasture for the horses, and about the brush arbor her mother was planning to put up back of the tipi, so that they could have a cool place for people to sit when they came visiting.

At that, thought Spear Girl, as she picked up her rawhide wood rope, they didn't have as much to do as some people. Sitting Bear's women, now. They had a lot to see to: a tipi apiece for the four of them, and another for Sitting Bear himself, to say nothing of a big brush arbor. Then there had to be a little shade over Sitting Bear's shield, and another for the Grandmother God that he guarded. There were all those horses to take care of; Sitting Bear had over a hundred horses. Two of his young sons also wanted a tipi apiece, though probably only Young Sitting Bear would get one. More than likely Eagle Plume would have to sleep in his mother's tipi—unless he was out scouting around for some girl's tipi to crawl into now he was thinking about getting married. Spear Girl said, "Na-na-na-na," under her breath, because she disapproved of Eagle Plume and didn't care who knew it, even if he was her cousin on her father's side.

"What's the matter, friend?"

She looked up, but didn't recognize the young man on the horse, although she knew he belonged to her band by the way he spoke.

"Get down, friend."

When he stood beside her, she knew him. He was Hunting Horse, and now he was a good young man. Just a year ago he had been a crazy boy, and her mother had chased him away for upsetting the wooden water buckets with his lariat when he rode by her camp.

"There is too much work to do, getting ready for Sun Dance."

Hunting Horse had got suddenly busy with his horse's girth, but he said, from under his arm, "Not so much, I think. Camp goes up pretty easy."

Spear Girl felt very wise, and somewhat sorry for anybody who knew so little. "It looks easy for you. You got your cousin to do all the work. You just ride around and watch the tipis go up. Women have to make them go."

Hunting Horse turned around and looked at her straight for a glancing moment. Then he got busier than ever with his headstall. "You are a woman, friend. You have grown up."

"I was born the year of the Antelope Driving Winter. That was sixteen years ago. Sixteen years make a woman. Not Miss Little Girl, but Miss Young Lady."

"Miss Young Lady." He looked at her again for a second, "Will you ride behind me tomorrow when they bring in the green boughs to cover the Lodge?"

It was while Spear Girl was trying to decide, because, after all, no one had ever asked her to ride with him before, that her mother came out of the tipi and found them.

"Where are you going, friend?" she asked Hunting Horse, and Hunting Horse got on his pony and said, "To my cousin's camp," and rode off in a great hurry. Spear Girl's mother watched him out of sight.

"Well," she said when he was lost in the crowd, "am I going to have to start watching you now? It's bad enough to have you grown up and thinking about men when you don't know how to make a tipi by yourself, but why don't you pick out a fullblood Kiowa when you do start? His mother was a Wichita, and don't you forget it."

"She grew up as a Kiowa," said Spear Girl. Last year she had hated Hunting Horse for upsetting the water buckets, and now she felt sorry for him and wanted to say kind words about his mother. It was strange.

"Well, she wasn't," said her mother. "Those people who brought her up may have been good to her and treated her as a favorite child because they hadn't any of their own, but she didn't belong to them."

She picked up her own rawhide rope. "Come on, now. We've got to get brush for the arbor. What would the sun say, lazy girl, if he saw you poking around all day?"

Spear Girl very nearly sighed as she followed her mother. It was almost like quarreling, the way her mother had spoken to her. That was strange, because she felt like quarreling, too, and with her mother, of all people! You didn't quarrel with your mother, especially at Sun Dance time. You did as she told you and learned what she taught you, and showed respect for her every way that you knew.

All morning they dragged brush with the ropes, and by noon there was a big pile behind the tipi. Her mother's brother came along with a buffalo shoulder, and her mother made him sit down while she cut off thin slices and cooked them on wooden forks over the coals.

"Uncle," said Bow Girl, Spear Girl's little sister, "when are they going to cut the center pole?"

"Right away," said their uncle easily, "just as soon as everybody eats and rests a little. Then they go out to cut it."

"Can we go?" Spear Girl asked.

"I guess so," said her uncle.

"I guess not," said her mother. "I need somebody to help me cut up this meat and dry it. I don't even have drying-poles ready. It's hard, not having a man alive. Then you have to do everything yourself."

Her mother was always saying that, thought Spear Girl. Men never helped with cutting meat or getting drying-poles, but whatever her mother had to do, she said was harder because she had no man. Spear Girl sighed, because she still felt like quarreling with her mother. It was very bad.

"I guess they better go," said her uncle, unexpectedly. "I guess you better go, too. Everybody ought to be there when they cut the center pole. That meat will keep if you hang it in a tree."

Spear Girl felt warm inside because of her uncle. He was good to them, she thought. Not many uncles took that much trouble for their nieces. Because of him, her mother was cutting a slit in the piece of meat and hanging it in the fork of the tree behind the tent.

When the uncle had eaten and they had eaten, and he had smoked and they all had rested, he got up. "I guess they're about ready to start, now," he said. "Come on. We'll go over to Taime Man's tipi."

People were beginning to move across the circle towards Taime Man's tipi, slowly and gatheringly, the way the shadow of a cloud moves across the prairies. Their white and brown clothes, just mixed with each other, were like the colors that grasses make when they turn over in the wind. There was nothing bright and sharp; everything was as soft as the colors of the world itself, where the only bright color was the sky. They gathered in front of Taime Man's tipi and waited, and after while he came out.

He was an old, old man, and just by looking at him you knew that every year he had more wisdom, like a good herd growing more colts. He was kind, too; even a child would know that he could tell stories and give extra bits of food if it were hungry any way at all. Just now he looked wise and kind and good; but he looked strong, too, as if all the power that was inside him had been gathered together in his heart and showed through his face. He raised his arms with the green and yellow paint along them, and prayed for a long time, and more and more power seemed to come into his face under the rabbit-fur cap.

When he had prayed, he let his arms fall to his sides, and stood waiting. Then a family came out of a tipi beside his and led a young woman up to him. She was a captive woman, a Mexican, and she was dressed beautifully. Her buckskin dress was painted with yellow and green, and the parting of her hair was painted yellow. Her metal belt and the pendant that hung from it glowed. She had to be a captive, because what she was going to do was dangerous, and you could not risk one of your own women to do it; she had to be dressed beautifully because what she was to do was a great honor, even if she died doing it.

The captive woman followed the old man to where two white horses, painted green and yellow, were tied beside his tipi. They got on the horses and started to ride, and all the people followed them.

They went clear around the camp to the east opening, and from there they rode all the way around again—the south side, the west, the north, and the east. The same way you go around a tipi, thought Spear Girl, as she followed them, four times around. All the people were very quiet; no one was saying anything. Then the old man turned and rode down into the woods along the river.

He did not go a long way. Quite soon he stopped and pointed. Then with a shout, the young men rode as fast as they could past the people on foot, and as hard as they could to the tree that he pointed out. That was the way they rode on a war charge, and they struck the tree, as if it were an enemy, with their bows or spears, or the special crooked spears some of them carried for striking the enemy. Four of them hit the tree almost at once. Spear Girl could see their faces: Young Sitting Bear, White Bear, Sun Boy, and Little Bluff. It was Young Sitting Bear who hit the tree first, and his mother and her sisters made the war-whoop for him. Eagle Plume's mother, Old Sitting Bear's second wife, didn't made a sound. She would have liked her own son to be first, but he never was when he and his brother rode together.

The Taime Man got off his horse, and the young men fell back and were as quiet as the other people. The old man took an axe, and handed it to the captive woman.

It took her a long time to cut down the tree. The family that had brought her up had made a favorite of her, and she was not used to work. But at last the tree was down, and she turned and gave the axe back to the old man. When she had done that, the men who were leaders of the societies came, and with their own axes stripped away the leaves and the branches and the bark. Then the old man reached into his saddlebag and took out a paint sack, and the captive woman painted four red stripes around the trunk of the tree, just below the fork. The men put ropes around the trunk and tried to lift it. They tried three times, without moving it, and then, on the fourth try, they raised it from the ground and started back to camp with it.

The Sun Dance

The way seemed longer going back than it had coming out, for the tree was heavy and the men went slowly. Sometimes one dropped out and a member of his society took his place, but they never stopped, and they never let the tree touch the ground until they came to the hole that had been dug for it in the center of the circle. There they laid it on the ground, with the painted end pointing east, stood back, and waited.

Taime Man stood at the east end of the pole. He raised his arms and prayed, and then he tried to step on the pole. On three tries he failed, but the fourth time he made it and ran all the way along the log like a young man, not slipping or falling off once. Everybody shouted, because they knew now that it would be a good Sun Dance.

Buffalo Hunter came forward then. He had the right from his father, who had learned this part of the ceremony from the Arapaho,[1] who gave the Kiowas the Sun Dance. He rode in from the east side of the circle, with the hide and head of a buffalo across his saddle. He had been out all morning hunting for the buffalo, because it had to be a young bull and he had to kill it with just one arrow. He rode up and laid the hide on the ground in front of Taime Man, who tied it between the forks of the pole.

Then Taime Man took off a big pearl-shell button which he wore on his scalp lock, and tied it in the buffalo's nostrils. His wife came and tied to the pole four new, freshly tanned hides. The captive woman and her family tied on all the fine clothes that she had worn, and she stood there in an old, smoked, skin dress that she had been wearing underneath. Then everybody else came and began to tie on presents. Last of all, the Taime Man took two little rawhide figures and tied them on. One was like a buffalo and was painted black. The other was like a man and was painted red. The buffalo figure stood for all the earth spirits, and the man figure stood for all the man spirits.

After that, the men came up again and began heaving at the pole to put it in place. They heaved three times before it would stir, and the fourth time it settled into place, and they began to pound the earth in around it to hold it. When it was steady, the Taime Man sent them away to bring the other poles for the lodge.

It took a long time to do things just right, thought Spear Girl. It had taken all afternoon to get just this one pole up, and the men worked until dark bringing in others. But it took a lot of poles, and men weren't used to that kind of work. It would go quicker if they let the women do it. Things took so long that they didn't get any more

---

[1] Arapaho Man, who had first given the Sun Dance to a Kiowa man to show friendship.

building done, and it was dark when they had a pile of poles ready to start with in the morning.

Spear Girl almost expected that Hunting Horse would ride by that evening, but she had seen him helping the Herders Society men carry the pole, and when she heard the Herders Society begin to sing its initiation song that night, she knew he was not coming. She helped with the cooking and went to bed so quietly that her mother felt relieved, and decided that maybe she wouldn't have to watch her daughter after all.

II

All the next day was taken up in stripping the bark off the other poles and setting them up, and the work might as well have gone on at End of the Mountains for all Spear Girl saw of it. Her mother kept her busy that day with poles of their own, drying-poles for the meat. While her mother and Bow Girl cut the meat thin, Spear Girl was building the rack. She had to look hard for poles, too, but not as hard as she would after tomorrow, when most of the little wood would have been used to cover the Lodge.

Covering the Lodge was the best part of the Sun Dance, she thought, tugging at her rope with the bundle of wood at the end. Then all the people would have cedar crowns on their heads and cedar and willow branches in their hands. They would ride out, singing and waving the branches, to gather big, leafy limbs for shade. When they rode back, dragging the big limbs, they would wave the branches in their hands and sing.

It was exciting, too, because men and women rode double that one time of the year, the women behind the men; their arms around the men's waists. You were supposed to ride only with your brother-in-law or with a man that you were going to marry. In fact, if you rode behind a man who wasn't your brother-in-law, you just about had to marry him. Or if you had been married a long time, you could ride behind a man who belonged to your husband's society, because he was almost the same as your brother-in-law, anyway.

That was what was so exciting about having Hunting Horse ask her to ride with him. He wasn't her brother-in-law; he couldn't be, because Bow Girl was younger than she, and couldn't be married for quite a while yet.

About this time she arrived at the tipi, and her mother told her to wake up and start putting up the drying-poles. That was better, though, than being off in the woods getting them. She could look over her shoulder sometimes and see how the men were getting along putting up the frame of the Lodge. It went up quickly. At midday there was a ring of poles standing in the ground around the center pole, and they were connected by poles laid across them from one fork to the next.

Her uncle did not come to see them then; he was too busy working with the men at the Lodge. They had broiled enough meat so that they would have it if he did come. When he didn't, her mother called little Wood Fire, an orphan boy who strayed around from one camp to another because he didn't like to live with his grandmother, the only relative he had. He was glad to get the meat.

"It's pretty good," he told them. "I just ate some with Sitting Bear's wife, but this is pretty good."

"What do you want with two lunches, little Dirty Nose?" Spear Girl's mother asked, and the child answered, "Maybe us men'll be too busy to get any supper. It's Rabbit Dance tonight."

Spear Girl felt sorry for the child, because without any parents to give things for him so that he could be an honored member, he would just have to sit and watch the other boys dance. Maybe at the end, when they threw the circle open, he could get in and dance for a little while. All the little boys could belong to the Rabbits, but unless their parents could give a feast for the others, they could never be honored members.

"Well," her mother said, as the child ran off, "maybe 'us men' are having Rabbit Dance tonight, but that one will more likely be borrowing things out of other people's tipis. His grandmother ought to talk to him good. She needs some man to talk to him."

"Maybe some of the young men could," Spear Girl ventured, and her mother gave her a quick look and said, "Some young men who are only half-Kiowa. Anybody else knows better than to scold other people's children."

They had the Rabbit dance that night, and Spear Girl and Bow Girl looked on and laughed until they hurt at the sight of the little boys hopping up and down and flopping their hands beside their faces like ears. The littlest girls danced, too, in a ring behind the boys, like grown women, and the old men took turns drumming and singing for the dance. When it was all over, Big Tree's wife invited all the members, their sisters, and the men who had sung for them to feast in honor of her son, and they all went off to her arbor. Somehow it made Spear Girl feel good to see Wood Fire going off with them.

It was when she was turning away and starting back to her own tipi that she felt someone beside her, and Hunting Horse said in her ear, "Will you ride with me tomorrow?"

"I want to," she whispered back, "but my mother won't let me."

"Miss Little Girl," he told her, "always scared of what her mother will say! Anyway, I'll ride by your tipi when we're ready to start."

He was gone before she could say or do anything, but as it was before her mother could turn around and catch her, that was all right.

Her mother let her sleep late the next morning. It seemed as if she didn't care if the sun came up and caught her daughter asleep, because that was what happened, all right. From then on, Spear Girl was behind with everything all morning. It seemed to take her longer than usual to dress, longer to brush her hair and smooth it over her shoulders, even longer to eat. She had just come back with the fire wood when she heard the singing start at the Lodge. All the people were gathering with their horses and their willow and cedar branches, all ready. And she was down here at the tipi, and hadn't done one thing to get ready yet. While she stood and watched and wished she had waked up early, she saw one horseman separate from the group and ride towards her.

Her mother saw him, too, and she took a firm grip on Spear Girl's wrist and began to pull her into the tipi. Hunting Horse stopped in front of them and began to laugh.

"Miss Young Lady!" he said. "Your mother won't let you!"

"I will not!" cried Spear Girl's mother, and pulled harder than ever towards the tipi. He just sat and laughed, and Spear Girl wanted to cry. Before they knew what he was going to do, he reached down and caught Bow Girl's arms and lifted her up behind him. "Don't worry, Miss Little Girl," he called back, "I'll take good care of our little sister."

It was then that Spear Girl stopped pulling against her mother, and turned and ran into the tipi and lay down on her bed. She wanted to laugh and she wanted to cry, but mostly she wanted to laugh, because that was just the same as saying that he was going to marry her anyhow.

III

It was noon when the people got back with the branches, and after they had eaten and rested, it took them a long time to put the branches on the Lodge. Spear Girl's mother went around with a face like a thunderstorm. She said very little to Bow Girl, who returned singing and waving branches with the rest of them, and nothing at all to Spear Girl. When Bow Girl said, "Hunting Horse sure does ride well," her mother retorted, "It's the only thing he's any good at," and Spear Girl wanted to run away into the tipi again.

In the evening her uncle came to see them. He sat quite still for a long time, and then he said, "My sister, there is a man who wants to marry your older daughter."

"That no-good!" said Spear Girl's mother in a voice that seemed to carry clear across camp. "Half-Wichita and only owns three horses. And as often as not when he goes hunting, all he comes back with is the horse he started out on. Hunting Horse is a good name for him! That's all he is, just a man hunting for his horses!"

Her brother waited for her to stop. It was no good interrupting an angry woman. When she was quite through, he said, "Not Hunting Horse. It's Crow Necklace. Hunting Horse spoke to me, but I told him nothing. He is too young to marry. But Crow Necklace is an older man. He's steady. He has lots of horses, and he knows where they are. Besides, his wife is getting old, and he needs someone to help her around the camp. He will give you four horses and me four horses. That's what he thinks your daughter is worth. Eight horses."

Spear Girl sat down hard on the floor of the tipi, and Bow Girl sat down beside her.

"Crow Necklace is an honorable man," their mother said slowly. "He asks for my daughter the honorable way."

Bow Girl began to cry a little. "What are you going to do, sister?" she sniffled. "I don't want you to marry him. Hunting Horse is fun. We could have a good time with him."

"I won't marry Crow Necklace," said Spear Girl. "They can't make me marry him. I don't want him. I'm going to marry Hunting Horse."

"How, sister?" the little girl's eyes were wide in the dark. "How will you?"

"I'll run away," said Spear Girl, and when she said it, she knew she would, even if people wouldn't think it was the right thing to do. "I'm going now to tell him."

"Let me tell him," said Bow Girl. "Please let me. If you go away, they'll guess. But they won't notice me."

"All right," Spear Girl whispered back, and Bow Girl rolled under the turned-up back wall of the tipi, just as their mother called to Spear Girl to come out and hear the news.

She sat very still while they told her, and when they had finished she began asking questions. She wanted to give Bow Girl plenty of time to find Hunting Horse and tell him. She asked so many questions they had to tell her all about it four times over before she finally understood.

"It is a good marriage," her mother said finally. "He is a rich man, and you won't have much to do. His first wife can teach you a lot.

He's a fullblood Kiowa, and not part something else." She felt a little sorry for Spear Girl, after all, because she wasn't getting just what she wanted. She felt sure that Spear Girl was getting what was good for her, though, and that was the important thing.

"When I was a young man," said her uncle, "no girl would think about marrying a man who couldn't give horses for her. That is the honorable way to be married. It shows respect for the girl's people. Nowadays men and girls just seem to run off and get married, but it looks to me like the wrong thing to do."

"Yes, uncle," said Spear Girl.

"That's all right, then," said her uncle, getting to his feet. "I'll tell Crow Necklace he can bring his horses over tomorrow, and you will go home with him."

"Not tomorrow," said Spear Girl's mother suddenly, and Spear Girl felt all soft inside with relief. "I have to get some things ready for her first. It isn't honorable to let a man give horses for a girl, and not give anything back to his people. Tell him to come the last day of the Sun Dance."

"All right," said the uncle. "But I better tell him now. He might change his mind. He was thinking about another girl, too, Ute War Bonnet Girl, but I don't think he spoke to her people."

Just worrying about his horses, that was all, thought Spear Girl. Nobody was worrying about her. Just their old horses. And she was the one who would have to marry that pock-faced old man, and put up with his deaf, cross old wife. Well, she wouldn't do it. That was all there was to that. But she sat quietly, with her head down, because she had heard Bow Girl come back into the tipi.

Bow Girl didn't get a chance to tell her anything until they were in bed. They had to wait a long time for their mother to go to sleep, too, and it was hard to keep awake so long, even if they were excited.

When they knew their mother was asleep, Bow Girl put her mouth close to Spear Girl's ear and whispered, "He says he wants to run away, too. He says he has to, because he hasn't enough horses to give any away. He says tomorrow night, when everybody goes to watch the dancing start in the Lodge is the best time. He says to stand on the outside of the circle, and when the dancing is going good, get away and join him. He'll have the horses and meet you down at the picket lines. Then you can go away to the hills and come back the last day of the Dance, and everything will be all right."

"All right," said Spear Girl. She wondered how she would manage about her clothes. She'd just have to leave them, that was all. If she tried to make a bundle of them, her mother would notice, and that would spoil everything. She gave up thinking about what she would take with her, and just hoped that Hunting Horse would have something for her to sleep on, and went to sleep for that night.

IV

It was hard keeping a secret, she discovered. She felt as if it must show on her, like face paint. She knew it, and Bow Girl knew it, and of course Hunting Horse knew it, so she felt sure that her mother and her uncle could find out just by looking at them. But nobody seemed to guess, and the day went along like most days.

Her mother would want to see the dancing start, because she always did. Everybody would be there, and she didn't need her brother to tell her to go. They had to make the ceremony to open the Lodge first, and before that was the Mud-Head parade. Everything they owned had to be gathered up and put away before that started, because the Mud-Heads would grab anything that was left outside the tipi and tear it up or spoil it. All the meat had to come off the drying rack and go into the tipi, although it was not yet ready to eat. It took them all morning to get every single thing they had picked up and put away, and for once in her life Spear Girl was glad they didn't have much.

It was noon when they heard shouting and looked up to see the Mud-Heads charging away from the Lodge. Nobody knew just who the Mud-Heads were, because they were so smeared all over that you couldn't tell. They took off all their clothes but their breechclouts and coated themselves with mud. Some of them sat on each other's shoulders and rode as if they were on bucking horses. The men who carried them tried to throw them off. One was pretending to be a woman, with a bundle of rags in her arms for a baby. She had a make-believe husband, who whipped her, but it wasn't make-believe whipping. As the Mud-Heads came through the camp, you could hear the people shouting and running and grabbing up their things and trying to get out of the way. Bow Girl and Spear Girl stood inside the tipi and watched. They were safe there, because it was the rule that the Mud-Heads couldn't come in.

But one of the Mud-Heads came close to the door and said, "When they start the fourth dance," and then let out an awful whoop and began to chase their mother. It was the last time he could do anything like that, Spear Girl thought. A man had to be very respectful to his mother-in-law.

All the rest of the day, after the excitement was over, they went around quietly, and the secret was somehow easier to keep. It was dusk before they ate supper, and clear dark, with stars but no moon, when they crossed over to the Lodge. Bow Girl and Spear Girl kept dropping a little behind their mother, but as she was always stopping and waiting for them to catch up, they gave up trying to get lost.

There were crowds of people at the Lodge when they got there, and the men were trying out the drums, warming them, and then tapping them a little to see whether the tone was right. Then they would warm them some more. It took a long time to get started. All the while, Taime Man sat quietly at the west side of the Lodge, behind a little screen of willow boughs. He must have just eaten, and it was the last time he would eat or drink for four days. That was one thing men could do that was harder than anything women had to do, Spear Girl thought. To go four days without eating or drinking—that would be too hard for her to do.

At last the drums were warmed just right. The men stopped tapping and began to beat. The young men who were going to dance stood up in their places, and the people crowded up closer than ever. Even their mother pushed forward, and Bow Girl and Spear Girl stood still and let people come between them and her.

At the end of the second song, they were on the outside ring, and more people were still pushing past them. At the end of the third song even Bow Girl became excited and began to push forward. That was when someone came behind Spear Girl, took her wrist, and said, "Now."

They turned and ran together away from the Lodge, away from the fire and the music and the people, and the music seemed to catch them by the ankles as they ran and try to draw them back. They ran away from it, and Spear Girl asked, "Why aren't you down by the picket lines?"

"I sent Wood Fire," said Hunting Horse. "Keep running. Hard! He knows my horses. He'll have them for us."

Spear Girl ran harder than ever. Wood Fire might know the horses, but he might make trouble, too, and tell on them. Still, it was better to send him than someone who might be missed. They were outside the tipi circle now, and the only light was that which the earth reflected from the stars. They were near the picket lines, too; she could smell and hear the animals, moving and grazing in the dark.

"Over this way," said Hunting Horse, and he guided her off to the right. He was so sure, she thought. Just like a full blood. He knew just which way to go. He was a good man. He was just young, that was all anybody could have against him.

"Here," said a voice almost at their feet, and they stopped. Wood

Fire came up out of the ground in front of them. "I could just get one. The others got scared." He didn't sound very sorry for it, Spear Girl thought.

"We'll ride double, then," said Hunting Horse. "They'll miss us in a minute. We've got to hurry." He swung himself up, and pulled her up behind him strongly. She clutched him around the waist, and he kicked the horse.

"Hee Haw!" Hunting Horse stopped kicking. "What's the matter with this horse? This isn't my horse!"

"Hee Haw!" The noise was coming from beneath them. The animal was running, but not like a horse.

"This isn't anybody's horse," Spear Girl gasped. "This is Wood Fire's grandmother's old donkey!"

"Hee Haw!"

"He'll get everybody down here!" said Hunting Horse. "Wait a minute. I can find my horses in any dark."

"We can't wait," said Spear Girl, "Look! Everybody's looking around to see what the trouble is now."

"All right." Hunting Horse gave the donkey a hard kick and it started to run. "But when we come back," he said between his teeth, "I'll catch that Wood Fire, and I'll show him the difference between a horse and a donkey. I'll let this old burro kick him!"

Oh, dear, thought Spear Girl. She knew what her mother would say. It was bad to run away to get married; worse to run away with a half-Wichita. But worst of all was running away on a donkey that wanted to tell everybody about it while it was going on. At that, she reflected, hanging to Hunting Horse's belt, it wasn't as bad as just walking across the camp and putting her clothes into Crow Necklace's tipi.

The First Tipi

The Winter Little Bluff Died
(1865–66)

IT WASN'T REALLY VERY DIFFERENT, SPEAR GIRL THOUGHT, BEING married and not being married. You worked just about as hard, and the great difference that you had expected—not having your mother boss you—hadn't happened at all. They were all at home in the old tipi: her mother and sister, and Hunting Horse and herself, and they just went on doing the same old things the same old way. It wasn't much fun.

Bow Girl came and sat beside her, to pack the pounded meat into rawhide cases. They were quiet for a long time, because, being sisters, they didn't need to talk with their voices. After while their uncle came and sat down with them.

"Where is your husband, niece?" he asked Spear Girl.

"At Sitting Bear's camp. They are making a feast for the Herders Society because that is Young Sitting Bear's society."

"That is your husband's, too."

"Yes, it is his."

Their uncle took out his pipe. It was old, a little short section of the big leg-bone of a deer. He didn't smoke it in the evenings, when all the men gathered around, smoking, because he had a big red pipe that he liked to show off with. But when he really wanted to think, he got out the little old bone pipe.

"Your husband goes to society meetings as if he were not married."

"He likes to be with other young men, uncle."

"That's all right. Men like to be with each other part of the time. But part of the time they should be with their wives, too."

"My husband is with me a lot when he isn't working."

"He would be with you more if you had your own tipi."

Spear Girl felt ashamed. They were poor, and they had always been poor, because, until she married, they had no man to work for them all the time. Her uncle was rich, and he helped a lot, but that didn't take the place of someone working all the time. She didn't like to say so to her uncle, because he was good and generous, and helped them more than he was obliged to, as it was.

The First Tipi

He shook out his pipe, now, and turned to face her directly. "I've been thinking a lot. Hunting Horse has nobody to help him get started. You have your mother and sister, and that's all. Somebody has to help you two. I guess I'd better do it."

Spear Girl just sat and stared at him. It was like her uncle, but still she hadn't expected it. She didn't even thank him. She just stopped pounding down the dried meat and sat and stared, and Bow Girl stared, too.

"I don't want to give you everything to get you started." Her uncle was putting his pipe away now, because his thinking was over. "I'll give you what you need to make things out of. We won't make a give-away out of it, or have any ceremony. But you'll have what you need to work with. You two will have to do the working yourselves." Then he got up and walked off, and Spear Girl and Bow Girl just watched him go.

It was very late when Hunting Horse got home. The Herders Society members had danced a long time, and then they had eaten a big feast, and he was tired. He just flopped down and started breathing deep, and Spear Girl knew there was no use trying to tell him anything then.

She waked early, with her skin prickling all over, wondering what it was that was going to happen that was so big and good and exciting. Then she remembered. This was the day that they were to get their things to start living with. She punched Hunting Horse in the ribs with her elbow, and he grunted and turned over, and started breathing again. For a minute she started to get angry with him, but the day was too good to spoil, so she got up quietly. She dressed and combed her hair. For a minute she thought about painting her face, and then decided that since it wasn't like getting regular wedding presents, she would look foolish if she did it. Instead, she went out and helped her mother get breakfast.

They had all had breakfast, even Hunting Horse, and the newness had rubbed off the day and most of the excitement was gone, when she saw her uncle coming across the camp. He was leading a horse, piled high with all sorts of things, and behind him came his two wives, each of them leading a horse with a big load. They stopped in front of the tipi.

"There you are, sister."

"Get down, brother."

Her uncle tied the horse, and stepped back into the shade beside the tipi. His wives tied their horses, and began to unload them. Spear Girl started to help them, but her mother called her back.

The Ten Grandmothers

"You don't unload your own wedding presents, daughter."

She wanted very much to see what they were. But she would have to wait until every single thing was off all three horses before she could look. She got a dipper of water for her uncle, and he drank the water and handed the dipper back to her.

"I'm glad you like to use gourd dippers, niece. I have brought plenty of gourds for you to make them out of."

Well, that was fine. The gourds had got all sun-scorched that summer, and there weren't enough to make dippers for everybody. Even people who had got tin cups from the traders still kept some gourds around, and used old-time dippers for themselves. They just got the tin cups out when they had company and wanted to show off. Spear Girl knew how to make good dippers.

"Thank you, uncle," she said.

"There is everything there that you need to work with," her uncle said. "We have brought hides for a tipi, and willows for beds, and robes and deerskins to make bedding out of. All the hides are dried and rolled up. You'll have to tan them and cut them yourself, but there are a lot there. How many buffalo hides are there?" he asked his first wife.

"Thirty-two," she answered. "Enough for a big tipi. We have logs for tipi-poles over at our camp. Your husband will have to trim them down and bring them over himself."

Spear Girl wasn't paying much attention to the tipi-poles. She was thinking about the cover. Thirty-two hides were a lot, when they had to be tanned, and she had never cut or sewn a tipi-cover. Not very many people tried to cut their own. There were some women who were good at it, and they did that kind of work for everybody. But they wouldn't do the tanning.

Her mother was looking off across the camp, as if there were something she wanted to see on the other side. "My daughter's husband hasn't much to do," she said. "I guess he can start work on the tipi-poles right away."

Spear Girl heard that, and it turned her mind away from the tipi-cover. Her mother shouldn't speak like that, even about her son-in-law. It made her feel queer, and without looking at Hunting Horse she knew it made him feel queer, too. But he didn't say anything. He took his axe and started across to her uncle's tipi.

Everything was all unloaded now. It made a big pile in front of the tipi. People were coming up to see what was happening.

"That's a lot of hides," said Grass Woman. "Who's going to tan all those hides?"

66

The First Tipi

Spear Girl straightened up and stopped thinking about what a lot of work it was going to be.

"I am," she answered. "I want to tan the hides for my own tipi."

Bow Girl was standing beside her. "I'm going to help my sister," she added. "We always do everything together."

Nobody said anything, but Spear Girl felt better. The people around her felt better towards her. They must have been afraid she was going to let her mother do all the tanning.

Bow Girl brought water to her uncle's two wives. "That was hot work for you, all that loading and unloading," she told them, and her aunts said, "Yes, it was hot work, all right. Now you can get to work and get hot, too."

That was all right. You ought to get hot, working on your own home. Spear Girl didn't mind it. Grass Woman spoke again. She always had something to say. "That many hides takes a lot of brains for tanning. A hide needs all its own brains to tan itself. I have some brains. My man killed three buffalo this month, and I dried the brains and saved them. I'm going to make rawhide. I don't need them. You can have them."

Spear Girl was feeling better all the time. The newness seemed to be coming back to the day. "Thank you for the brains," she told Grass Woman.

"I have brains, too." That was Pond Woman. "I don't need them. Four buffalo brains."

It was like a give-away, then. It seemed as if every woman in camp had been saving brains. They all wanted to give some away, and they all gave them to Spear Girl. Grass Woman and Pond Woman got their brains, and then the others went for theirs, too. Spear Girl stood and watched flat cakes of dried brains pile up beside the buffalo hides, and felt more and more excited. It was going to be all right. Now she could get to work right away, without waiting for Hunting Horse to finish the poles and then go buffalo hunting and bring her back the brains, one at a time. This way they would finish their work on the tipi almost at the same time. That was right, too. They ought to work together, making their own home.

She said "thank you" to everybody, and when all had seen all the hides and the gourds and the willows for the beds, they went off to their own tipis, and Spear Girl could begin to put things away.

That was harder. There was just the one tipi for four of them, and they had it full already. While she was trying to bring in all the things that rain could spoil, her mother was sitting inside the tipi thinking. Spear Girl felt a little strange about her mother. Everybody else had given her things and had been encouraging, and wanted to see her get ahead, but her mother had hardly spoken all morning. Spear Girl didn't like it. It tied up a knot in her insides. She knew, suddenly, how her mother had felt the night that Spear Girl ran away with Hunting Horse, but knowing didn't make her feel any better now.

Finally her mother got up and came outside the tipi. Spear Girl and Bow Girl had everything picked up or covered up, and the camp looked nice again, with everything where it ought to be. Her mother looked at it all for a moment, with her eyes as if she didn't see.

"That's all right," she said, then. "I guess everything's the way it ought to be."

She was talking about the way the camp looked, but she was talking about something else, too. Spear Girl didn't exactly understand, but she knew that what her mother said went deep; down under the neatness and rightness of having everything where it ought to be.

Her mother sat down beside the tipi, with her legs folded sideways under her.

"I've been thinking a lot," she said. "I think I ought to do something for you, too."

"You don't have to," Spear Girl told her.

"I have the right to," said her mother. "I need to do something. That way I show respect for my daughter and the man she married. If I don't show respect for them, soon nobody's going to respect them. They'll just give things because they're sorry. That's not right. Nobody ought to have people feeling sorry for her."

"That's right," said Spear Girl. "That's what my uncle has said, lots of times."

"I can't do much," her mother went on. "We never did have much. But we have some things. What I'm going to do, I'm going to have the woman come to cut out your tipi. Then I'm going to have more women come to help sew. Lots of women. We'll give them a feast, just the women. That way, your tipi will be made right, just like everybody else's. But you got to tan your hides yourself. Just your sister can help you."

Spear Girl felt better than she ever had in her life, but what was odd about it was that feeling good made her cry. It was good crying, and she didn't mind it, but it was strange to cry just when you felt better than you ever had before. She turned to ask her mother about it, and her mother was crying too, but she was smiling at the same time.

"That's all right, daughter," she said, "You're just a young girl yet. You don't understand things. But feeling good just does make you cry sometimes. You'll know about it all when you get more grown up." She stopped crying and smiled all over. "When you get a home of your own," she added. That was funny, too, because while Spear Girl and Bow Girl talked without words more than they talked with them, neither of them had ever been able to do it with their mother before.

It was a lot of work, getting ready to cut and sew the tipi. Spear Girl and Bow Girl worked and worked with the hides. They wanted them all smooth, scraped down to the same thickness all over, and white; and it took them a long time to get thirty-two hides just the way they ought to be.

All the time that they were working with the hides, Hunting Horse was away all day. One day he worked on the tipi-poles, and the next day he went hunting. Their mother needed a lot of meat for the feast, and as he was the man of the family, it was up to him to get it.

When everything was all ready, Spear Girl laid the hides out smooth, one on top of the other. Everything they had was full of pounded meat, some of it pounded with berries, and some of it plain; and her mother had borrowed extra kettles from their uncle's wives. Even then, there weren't enough to cook in, and she had cooked some of the meat over coals, on sticks, and some of it she had boiled the old-time way, in the skin of a buffalo's stomach. Bow Girl thought that was very funny. "Just like men eating out on a war party," she said, and giggled.

Spear Girl dressed. She put on her best white buckskin dress, with beadwork instead of painting on it; and she braided her hair and painted the parting red, and put a red circle on each cheek. It was too bad to dress all up like that just to sew hides, but as everybody did it, she had to do it, too. Stepping carefully, so as not to get grass stains on her high white moccasins, she went over to Navajo's Eye Woman's tipi to tell her to come and start cutting the cover.

Navajo's Eye Woman knew she was coming and was all dressed up in her best clothes waiting for her. "Get down," she said. Spear Girl sat down beside her and drank the water Navajo's Eye Woman gave her in a tin cup. All her gourd dippers were ready, she remembered. She'd made them by the firelight in the tipi, when it was too dark to tan outdoors.

Navajo's Eye Woman listened to Spear Girl's invitation without saying anything. Then she put her robe around her, got up, and led the way out of the tipi. She had worked so much with hides that many people called her Hide Woman, even if that wasn't her name, and she was bent all over and walked with a stick, from stooping over so much, scraping. Spear Girl hoped she wasn't stooping herself, from tanning thirty-two hides, and straightened up as stiff as she could, following Navajo's Eye Woman back to the old tipi.

Navajo's Eye Woman looked over all the hides very carefully. She turned them over from one side to the other, and she felt over the whole surface to make sure they were all even. Spear Girl was glad they had worked so hard with them. She would have hated to have Navajo's Eye Woman find a poor one. Finally Navajo's Eye Woman finished.

"Spread them all out smooth on the grass," she said. "They are all good. I can use every one."

Spear Girl and Bow Girl tried not to show how proud they felt, spreading the hides out flat on the grass. While they were doing it, Navajo's Eye Woman gave each woman a handful of sinew thread, and she asked each one if she had her awl. Every woman did, and Navajo's Eye Woman nodded. "That's good," she told them. "Bad luck if somebody forgets her awl."

Then she walked around and looked at all the hides carefully, to make sure she got the right one to start with. When she had picked it, she moved it off to itself, took her knife from its sheath at her belt, and began to cut. She cut the ears at the top of the tipi first, and gave them to the two oldest women to sew, because they were the hardest part.

Spear Girl and Bow Girl were the last to get their sewing. It was just part of the bottom, next to the ground, because they were the youngest there, and that was the easiest part, but they worked hard, because they wanted it to be as right as all the rest of the cover.

They all sewed all day. None of the men came near them. Most of the men were in Sitting Bear's camp talking, because all the women were working on the tipi-cover, and there wasn't anything much for the men to do, or anybody around to tell them to do it.

There was a clear space between the rim of the sun and the ground when they finished, but not a wide one. All the pieces were sewed together, smooth and even, and Spear Girl wondered if she would be able afterwards to remember what woman worked on what piece; the work all looked so much alike. Navajo's Eye Woman looked around for her, and Spear Girl got up and went over to the old woman.

"Where are the poles for this tipi?" asked Navajo's Eye Woman.

Spear Girl stood up straight. She and Hunting Horse had made their plan that morning, early, before anybody else was awake. Now she stood up and faced towards Sitting Bear's tipi, and raised her arm straight up in the air.

The First Tipi

Hunting Horse saw her. He had his horses all ready, all three of them. Two of them were loaded with tipi-poles, but the other one had presents on it, the best they had, out of the things Spear Girl's uncle had given them. A buffalo-hide robe with the hair on, a deerskin tanned white, a heavy smoked buckskin, bags of paints, and a gourd dipper—all women's things, that Spear Girl had made herself. Women's things to give to the woman who made the biggest woman's thing.

Hunting Horse led the horses up to the group of women. He dropped the lines, and let the pack-horses stand with the tipi-poles, while he gave the other horse's lines to Spear Girl. She led the horse to Navajo's Eye Woman, and Hunting Horse stood on the edge of the group of women to watch her.

"My husband and I want you to have these things," Spear Girl said, politely.

"That is good. That is kind," Navajo's Eye Woman said. She took the lines, and tied the horse to a tree behind her. "Thank you."

Spear Girl's mother began to set up the tipi-poles. Her brother's two wives came to help her, and they got the job done quickly. You could still see half of the red sun above the red earth.

Navajo's Eye Woman went and stood between the door-posts and raised her arms and prayed. She prayed for long life and good health for the people who would live in that tipi, and she prayed thankfully for the buffalo and the hides that made the tipi. Then she dropped her arms, and some of the women raised the tipi-cover and spread it over the poles. It just fitted.

They had the feast in the new tipi, after Spear Girl had lighted her first fire with coals from her mother's. All the women sat inside in the firelight while the dark grew around the outside, and their shadows grew bigger and bigger on the new white walls. Then they took what food was left—all a big lot of it—and tied it up in bundles to take home and make a feast for their husbands. Each one, as she went out, said, "Thank you for feasting," and every time Spear Girl replied, "Thank you for working."

When everybody else had gone, Bow Girl came and stood beside her, and they looked around at the new, clean, white walls. "I know what you're thinking," said Bow Girl, at last. "You're thinking that now when Hunting Horse comes home, you can put the beds in and have everything ready to start living here."

And that was odd, because Spear Girl wasn't thinking that at all. She was wondering if her mother ever had felt just the way she did right then. Now being married was beginning to feel really different.

The Household

The Year of the German Silver Sun Dance (1866)

THE SUN RAN OVER THE PRAIRIE, PUSHED BY THE WIND behind it, and the new day crawled to the tipi door and peered in. Spear Woman stirred in her sleep and tried to push the day away, but that didn't do any good. The day kept coming and coming until it came into the tipi, and she had to get up and do something about it.

The first thing she had to do was take care of the baby. He was wet and crying. It seemed as if the first thing she always knew now about the new days was a wet, crying baby. It made her tired just to think about him that way, without having to do something about it.

She lifted him out of the cradle and laid him on her lap and pulled away the soaked rabbit-skin and sage-brush padding between his legs. He was a long baby, but he was round, too. He was strong, and he could already throw himself about in her lap. It tired her to hold him.

She threw the padding in the fire, and pulled a fresh supply from the case under the bed. When she had made the baby comfortable, she tied him in the big cradle, with its long, protecting horns and wide, protecting hood, and carried him out and leaned the cradle against the tipi. He looked the morning over while she washed her face, decided he liked it, and went back to sleep so as not to get too much of it at one time.

It seemed to take her a long time to get breakfast. She spilled water down the front of her dress, and had to clean it off. The fire smoked, and she couldn't get it to burn clear. When it finally did burn, it was too quick and hot, and the meat was scorched all over. Pulling the meat back from the flames, she dropped it in the ashes. While she was trying to get it out without burning her fingers, Hunting Horse came out of the tipi and told her he couldn't find his lariat.

That made her angry. It was a new rawhide lariat, one she had made herself. He had needed one for months, but she couldn't braid rawhide before the baby came, for fear of winding the cord around its neck and strangling it. The first thing she did, while she was still in bed, was to braid that lariat, and it was a good one. Now he said he had lost it.

"Get away from here!" she told him. "Go look for it yourself! Don't you see I'm busy?" She burned her fingers on the meat again, good.

Hunting Horse went away and looked for the lariat and thought things over. It had been getting like this for a long time now, three weeks at least—might be a month. Ever since she got up and began moving around and taking care of him and the baby herself. It had sounded fine to be having a baby, and he had been pleased with himself and the rest of the world, but it hadn't occurred to him that he wouldn't go right on living with Spear Girl the way he had for a whole year, baby or no baby.

Soon she called him to eat. The ashes were blown off the meat, and the scorch was scraped off, so that it looked all right. She put it in front of him, in a wooden bowl, with a handful of wild plums, got her own breakfast, and sat down with him.

"Did you find the lariat?" she asked.

"No," he said.

"When was the last time you saw it?"

"Right after we ate last night."

"Was that before you turned the horses out, or after?"

"I think it was after."

"I thought you turned them out before we ate."

"Well, maybe I did. Anyway, I had the rope when we ate, because I saw it on the bed beside me."

Spear Woman reached down behind the bed, and picked up something. "Is this it?" she inquired.

He looked at it and looked at it, then said, "Where did you find it?"

"Right where you left it. Right there by the bed. Next time you better be more careful. Takes a long time to make a good rope. Don't know when I can make another one."

Hunting Horse took the rope and started to say something, but the baby began to cry, and Spear Woman went off to give him his breakfast. It was time for Hunting Horse to go after the horses.

Things were like that most of the time now. Hunting Horse and Spear Woman weren't actually quarreling, but they might as well have been. They were both unhappy and they never seemed to have anything pleasant to say to each other. It was too bad. Hunting Horse wondered if they would go on like that. It was bad for the baby, to grow up in a house where there was quarreling. He wouldn't be a very happy baby, if all he heard was fighting all the time.

The Ten Grandmothers

The sun was way up when he found the horses, and it was big day when he got back with them. Spear Woman had cleaned up the breakfast things after she had fed the baby. She had cleaned the tipi and had put the bedding out to air, washed her face again, and was sitting down making her husband a pair of moccasins. Life was strange. Only a short year ago she had been running around like a young girl, going to dances with him and having a good time, and now look at her. The only times she ever sat down were when she was going to make something. She was always busy, and much of what she did turned out like the breakfast that morning. She did too many things at once, and nothing was done right.

Just as Hunting Horse came up, the baby began to cry, and Spear Woman dropped the awl and moccasins and ran for him. On the way she saw Hunting Horse.

"There you are!" she said. She sounded angry. "What are you doing?"

"Why, not anything right now," said Hunting Horse. "I got the horses and brought them up, and now there isn't anything to do. We got plenty of meat. I don't have to go hunting."

"All right," said Spear Woman. "You can take care of your son then."

She fairly threw the baby at him, cradle and all. That scared the baby, and he began to cry harder. Spear Woman started off to get the meat to cut for drying, but the baby had scared her, and she began to cry, too. Hunting Horse looked at them both and decided it was easier to stand just one of them at a time. He took the baby over to Little Bluff's tipi.

Little Bluff's wife had been an adopted sister of his mother's. She took the baby, unlaced his cradle, and changed him, using some rabbit skins of her own. The baby shut up, looked around, and went to sleep. Everything was so quiet that Hunting Horse couldn't believe it for a minute.

"How long have you been married?" asked Little Bluff's wife.

"A year," said Hunting Horse.

"How old is your woman?" she wanted to know next.

He had to stop and remember before he could answer that, but then he said, "Seventeen."

"How many women were there in her home?" demanded Little Bluff's wife.

He wondered what she meant, because she knew the answers as well as he did. "Three. And no men." He would answer that question before she could ask it.

The Household

"And now there are one woman and two men," said Little Bluff's wife.

"That's right." It was odd. He hadn't thought of his son as a man before, but he was one, of course. He would be more and more of a man as he grew older. Hunting Horse began to get proud of the boy and of himself again.

"That means one woman has more to do than three women had before," said Little Bluff's wife.

"What do you mean?" he asked.

"A woman takes care of herself and her own things. When there are three women, each one just takes care of things for herself. But a man doesn't take care of anything. The woman has to look for things for him and cook for him and clean up after him, while all he has to do is go hunting."

"I'm looking after the baby to help," said Hunting Horse. He felt he had to say something for himself, because after all he hadn't been able to find the lariat that morning.

"Did you offer, or did she tell you to take care of the baby?"

"Well, she asked me to. She kind of gave him to me to take care of."

"And then you brought him over here, and I changed him."

"That's right," said Hunting Horse. He felt ashamed of himself now.

"Well, it's not right for her," said Little Bluff's wife. "One man always takes a woman to look after him. When you got two men, you got to have two women."

"I don't know," said Hunting Horse. "I don't know if I want somebody else around."

"You got to quit thinking about yourself so much," Little Bluff's wife told him.

Hunting Horse picked up his son and wandered off. He was thinking. He was disturbed, because there was a great deal of truth in what the woman had said. There were two men in the family now. That meant there was much work to do. What was more, Spear Woman never seemed to get it all done. As he came in sight of the tipi, he thought even it was getting dirty and ragged. They would be needing a new one soon, and that would mean additional work for Spear Woman. He shook his head, went and sat by the fire, and leaned the baby against the tipi.

Spear Woman hung the last piece of meat on the rack and asked, "Are you hungry?"

He didn't especially want to eat, but he didn't want not to eat. He was thinking. She gave him cold meat and some more wild plums, took some herself, and they sat and ate it quietly.

Then he said, "Do you ever get lonesome?"

He thought he was ready for anything, but he wasn't ready to see her cry again. The big tears came into her eyes and rolled down her face. She didn't even try to stop them. Then she replied, "Yes, I do."

"How old is your sister?"

"She's two years younger than I am. Fifteen."

"Is anybody asking to marry her?"

"I don't know. They're camping with Big Tree's band. I guess not, or I'd know."

"Then I guess I'd better marry her."

Spear Woman just sat and looked at him, with her mouth open.

"I guess we'd better get her here, before anybody else asks for her."

"Why do you want her to come here?"

He couldn't quite look at her, but he could talk. "When we first got married, we had fun all the time. Riding and singing and dancing and laughing fun. Now we don't have fun. We don't have fun together. I think you're too tired to have fun. I think you're lonesome, too. Maybe if your sister comes, you won't be so lonesome. There will be somebody else to help with the work, too. Then you won't be so tired. Then we can all three have fun."

Spear Woman drew a deep breath, that came clear up from the bottom of her toes. "That's right," she said. "That's the way it ought to be. Women need to help each other. They need to help men, too. Now we have two men, we need two women."

She said it so much as Little Bluff's wife had that he wondered if they had been talking things over. But she had turned her head and was listening to see if the baby was crying, and he couldn't see her face.

"All right," he said, "Tomorrow I'll find Big Tree's band and bring back your sister. You want your mother to come, too?"

"I guess so, if she wants to," said Spear Woman. "You'd better see if they have any extra hides. We can make a new tipi, and cut down the old one and give it to my mother. This one isn't big enough for all of us. It looks bad, too."

The Give-away

The Year of the War Bonnet Sun Dance (1869)

NOBODY EVER FORGOT THE YEAR THAT THE TWO WIVES WERE given away. For always afterwards people were telling that story and laughing about it and getting angry over it. Spear Woman was one who became angry. She never got herself to the point where she thought it was funny. She was always too sorry for one of the girls.

It started when Stone in the Pool was killed on a raid in the Ute country. Some of the young men had gone right into a Ute camp to get horses, and the Utes waked up and saw and heard them. They had a fierce fight, and everybody got away but Stone in the Pool, who was killed. Owl's Eye and White Back went back into the camp and got him and carried his dead body away so it wouldn't be scalped. When they were well away from the Ute camp, they buried Stone in the Pool and killed his horse before they came on home.

Everybody thought a lot of Owl's Eye and White Back for that. The Utes didn't eat people they killed, like the Tonkawas, but they might cut up the bodies to get parts for magic uses. Nobody would want that to happen to a person he knew. When Owl's Eye and White Back returned, everybody tried to do them honor at once.

Stone in the Pool had been a young man, but he had two wives. They were sisters, who got along well together and made a nice home for Stone in the Pool. They were both hard-working and industrious, and they were pretty, too. The younger one, Fawn Woman, was one of the prettiest women in the whole tribe. All the people said so. Her eyes were big and open, and her nose was straight, and her mouth was just right, not too big and not too little. She had lots of hair, and she kept it oiled and shiny. The best thing about her was the way she walked. She wasn't a big woman, but she walked tall, and it always surprised you to find how little she was. It was an art, for a woman to know how to do that.

Her sister was Broken Leg Woman. She was pretty, but not as pretty as Fawn Woman. She was a few years older, too, and that made

77

a difference. But they were very fond of each other and had a good time together. When Stone in the Pool was killed, they went home together to their brothers. Their brothers were glad to get them back because they were good workers.

After the family got through mourning and were feeling better, they talked things over. They decided they ought to have a give-away for Owl's Eye and White Back because of the brave thing those two had done in bringing Stone in the Pool back after he was killed. It was in late winter when they decided, and right away they started to get things ready. They were going to have their give-away at the Sun Dance.

Spear Woman thought she had never seen such a big pile of things at a give-away before. They were just stacked up on the ground in the middle of the Sun Dance lodge. It was on the fourth day, just before the chase around the center pole. One of the brothers kept standing up and calling out the names of people to come and get things. First he gave away to all the old people that weren't related to him: blankets and brass buckets, and kettles of food so that they could keep the kettles, and buffalo robes, and horses. Then he gave away to the younger people. Spear Woman and Bow Woman weren't related to him, so they got a blanket apiece. Hunting Horse wasn't related, either, so they gave him a horse. It was a good red horse, and Hunting Horse was so surprised and pleased he almost forgot to say "thank you." The giving went on and on, until the big pile of goods and all the horses were gone. Just the family were left, sitting there together. Stone in the Pool's two women were all painted up to look fine, and they had on their best clothes. Fawn Woman looked as if she had never been married at all, she was so beautiful.

Then their oldest brother stood up again. He made a speech. This was a funny time for speech-making, Spear Woman thought, with the give-away over and all the goods gone. But the brother went right on talking.

"We are having this give-away in honor of these two brave young men," he said. "We want to give presents to all the people here who aren't our relations. Some of you we have had presents from before. We want our presents to you to be as good as yours were to us." Everybody else nodded here, and said, "Thank you," or "That's right." Then the brother went on talking.

"You all know how it is about give-aways," he said. "You're not supposed to give to the person you're honoring. But this time we're going to make an exception. We're going to give to those two brave young men. Our family is going to give the very best they have to those two. These are our presents to them." He stooped down and caught his sisters' hands and pulled the women to their feet. He led Broken Leg Woman over to White Back, and Fawn Woman to Owl's Eye.

"These are our gifts to you," the brother said. "This is the way we show you honor. From now on these are your wives."

Spear Woman was always sure the two women weren't expecting it. Broken Leg Woman took it all right. She let White Back take her hand, and stood there beside him, looking down at the ground politely while her brother finished talking. She really was lucky, to have a brother who would take care of her and get her married so soon after her husband was killed. Lots of men wouldn't go to that much trouble for their sisters.

But Fawn Woman was different. She hung back from Owl's Eye and dragged at the end of her brother's arm. She set her feet hard on the ground, and she threw back her head.

"No," she said, loud, as if she were yelling. "No! I won't! I don't want to marry that old, ugly, heavy-chested man!"

That was what made Spear Woman so sure Fawn Woman wasn't expecting it. If she had been, she'd have told her brother quietly ahead of time. She wouldn't have wanted to shame her whole family in front of everybody. That was why Spear Woman acted as she did. When Fawn Woman jerked away from her brother and started running, Spear Woman shoved the people back out of the way to make room for her, and then took Fawn Woman's hand and ran her over to her own tipi.

Nobody came after them, because they were all too much surprised. It was a lot of fuss to have going on in a Sun Dance camp where everything was supposed to be nice and happy, anyway, so the people just let things go for the time being. It could all be straightened out later. But Fawn Woman didn't wait to get it straightened out. She ran away that night, without even telling Spear Woman where she was going. She just crawled out of the back of the tipi in her good clothes and was gone. That was the end of that part of it for that year, and Spear Woman was glad it ended so easily.

They went along through the rest of the year, with summer settling down into fall, and fall hardening into winter. Then the winter melted into spring, and the spring eased into summer. They were around the year again and back to the time for the Sun Dance. This time they were going north, Where the Wild Rice Grows on Arrowhead River.

That was a pretty place where everybody liked to be. It was a good place for a Sun Dance camp, and it was cool, too. When Spear Woman and Bow Woman had everything ready, they sat down in front of their tipi where they could watch out over the whole camp. That was when they saw Fawn Woman come riding in. She was with Bird Tied on Top, and she was married to him. They could tell that from the way she was taking care of the pack-horse loads.

Fawn Woman made her camp close to theirs. When she had everything set up, she came over and sat down with them. They didn't ask her, but soon she told them.

"I ran away with him," she said.

"Why did you?" Spear Woman asked. She really wanted to know. "That was a fine young man they were marrying you to. He's brave, and he would take good care of you. He never was married before, either."

"I didn't want to," said Fawn Woman. She sat still, with her hair falling like straight leaves on both sides of her face, for long minutes before she went on talking. Then she said, "I didn't want to marry my first husband, but they made me. He was married to my sister, so he had first claim on me. That was why I married him. But all the time the one I wanted to marry was this one I'm married to now. I made up my mind when my first husband died that this was the one I was going to marry or not anybody. That was the way I felt about it."

They didn't speak. If she felt that way about it, she felt she was right, and there was no point in saying anything. They just sat and waited to see if there was anything more she had to tell them. There couldn't have been, because after while she got up and went home without speaking any more at all.

Hunting Horse went off to dance with his society that night. Lots of men, when they got older and married and had children, didn't do things like that. They just went to meetings to sing for the younger men to dance. They said the dancing got them stirred up and excited, and then they were too wild to sleep. But nothing ever stopped Hunting Horse from sleeping when he wanted to, not even dancing. He was just that way.

All the societies were practicing that night. It made a big sound that spread around the camp like the big dark. It wrapped you up and held you in the same way that the dark did, and little things went on inside the dark and the sound. Both of them were too big to touch you, but all the little things seemed to get closer and nearer and more touching, right against your skin.

That was why, even with four societies all dancing and singing at once, Spear Woman could tell when she heard Hunting Horse's voice. If you listened in the big dark to the big sound and the little sounds that made it, you could recognize almost every one of them. Then after a while she recognized Owl Eye's voice and Wood Smoke singing with him. It was a wild sort of singing those two were doing. They were singing dancing-society songs, but they were singing them their own way, loud and high and strong enough to shake the tipi down.

After while the societies broke up for the night, and Hunting Horse came in and lay down and went to sleep, but Spear Woman couldn't do any sleeping. She was wakeful. Bow Woman was sleeping all right, and so were the children, but Spear Woman couldn't. She sat in front of the tipi, and Fawn Woman came and sat with her. She was wearing bracelets up and down her arms, and Spear Woman heard them click against each other in the darkness. After a while Fawn Woman spoke.

"I'm afraid," she said. "That singing frightened me."

Spear Woman nodded, though she knew Fawn Woman couldn't see her.

"It was frightening singing," she said.

They both knew what they were talking about without naming it.

"Where's your husband?" said Spear Woman.

"Up at the lodge," answered Fawn Woman. "He went to help with the pole gathering, and he thought he'd stay and sleep in the lodge so as to be ready to finish tomorrow."

"You'd better stay here," Spear Woman said. "You can sleep in my bed. I have enough robes to sleep all right on the floor."

That was how Fawn Woman came to be at their tipi instead of her own the next morning when Owl's Eye and Wood Smoke came riding up. They were laughing and shouting and singing society songs.

"I've come for my wife," said Owl's Eye. "I've come for the wife that was given to me."

Fawn Woman didn't say anything. She just stood and looked at him, with her head up. Then she put out her hand and pushed with it through the air towards him, and all her bracelets clicked together up and down her arms.

"You're going to come home with me," said Owl's Eye. "If you don't, I'm going to cut off your nose. I have the right to do it, because we were just the same as married, and you ran off with another man."

"No," said Fawn Woman. "No! I never was married to you, and I never would be."

Owl's Eye got down off his horse and so did Wood Smoke.

"You were, too, married to me," said Owl's Eye. "Your brother gave you to me. That makes you my wife. You're just living with that other man, and that's a wrong thing to do. I'm going to cut off your nose for doing it. You're my wife, and that gives me that right to do it."

Fawn Woman saw the knife in his hand, and she turned and ran away from him, without looking where she was going. She ran hard into Wood Smoke, and he grabbed her. She jumped back from him, and he held on to her arm. He was laughing so hard he could hardly stand up, but he still held on to her.

"Run!" shouted Spear Woman. "Run for Eagle Down's tipi! Quick! They can't get you if you are near the Grandmothers."

Fawn Woman was scared, but she heard and obeyed. She twisted her whole arm around in Wood Smoke's hand, and was free and running. When she got to Eagle Down's tipi she didn't speak or call, she just went right inside where they couldn't see her. Wood Smoke and Owl's Eye just stood looking.

"That settles that," said Wood Smoke. "Now you'll never get her."

"I guess I won't," said Owl's Eye.

"There are lots of other girls," said Wood Smoke.

"That's the one I wanted," said Owl's Eye.

"Well, it's too late now," said Wood Smoke. "She'll stay with that Grandmother until they bring you a pipe and you smoke the pipe. Then it will all be over except you may have to give presents to Bird Tied on Top for trying to get his wife."

"He's got my wife," said Owl's Eye. He was being stubborn about it. "He ought to give presents to me."

Spear Woman was tired of listening to them quarreling. She was sorry for Fawn Woman, and she thought nobody would want to be married to a man who acted as Owl's Eye did. It was a shame to make a fuss like that in front of everybody. She wanted to say something quickly, to make them stop talking.

"What's that in your hand?" she asked Wood Smoke.

Wood Smoke looked down at his hand. One of Fawn Woman's bracelets was still in it, and that was the first he'd known about it. He looked at the bracelet, and he looked at Owl's Eye, and then he began to laugh again, harder than ever. He went over to his horse and swung up and got ready to ride off. He was holding the bracelet up the length of his arm above his head, and singing. He was singing the music of one of the society songs, but not the regular words.

Two young men went out to battle, sang Wood Smoke.
They fought a hard fight with a fierce enemy.

The Give-away

It was an enemy that could stab them to the heart.
When they rode away, they had one of the enemy's weapons.

He rode off, singing his silly victory song, and Owl's Eye followed him. Spear Woman turned around and went back into her tipi. All around her she could hear people listening to the song and laughing, but she didn't think it was funny. She felt too sorry for Fawn Woman.

Power Given

The Year of the War Bonnet Sun Dance (1869)

WHAT THE MEN WHO WERE DANCING SAW OF THE SUN DANCE was little. They were too busy; they had to get their instructions and follow them out; they had to have their paint changed every so often, and they had to watch Taime Man closely. Those were the things they had to do. There were things that they had to feel, too; they had to feel hunger and thirst for four days and four nights, and they had to feel the power of the Taime turning the hunger and thirst into power for them.

That was why, four times a day, Taime Man chased them around the inside of the Sun Dance Lodge with his fan of crow feathers. Crow feathers belonged to the Taime and were a sign of it. The power of the Taime could be fanned off the crow feathers into the running men.

On the first day that they were chased around the Lodge, none of the men might fall, but on the second, usually a few went down, and from then on more and more of them dropped out. Some who fell were just unconscious, and when they recovered they knew that they weren't going to get power in that Sun Dance, so they and their sponsors went to sit outside with the other men. But others really got power, and when they roused, they could stay in the Lodge and tell their visions. A good many had visions that were alike. They seemed to see Taime Man growing taller and taller and turning into a Taime that leaned over them and pushed them down into the ground. That meant that the Taime's power had really come into them.

Men danced in the Sun Dance because they had made a vow that they would, to help themselves or somebody else. The persons they helped were usually close to them, parents or children, or maybe brothers or sisters. It was a way of getting captives back from other tribes, or of helping someone get over a sickness. If they vowed for themselves, there were three things they might ask for. Young, single men asked for success in raiding and to bring home many horses. Married men asked for children and that those they had might live. Both might ask to have good health and to live to be so old their ribs would fall in.

84

Power Given

Sitting Bear never made his sons do anything, but he sometimes told them what he thought they had better do. That was his way. Even when his sons were grown up enough to go raiding and do things for themselves, he would tell them sometimes what he thought they ought to do. Most times they did it.

The summer after Eagle Plume got power, the Sun Dance was held on the upper part of the North Fork of Red River. Sitting Bear put his camp on the east side of the circle, with the rest of the Big Shields, and got ready for all the things that went on at the same time as the Sun Dance. He was chief of the Crazy Dogs this year, and they were planning to make themselves new equipment the next year. This time they would have to talk it over and get everything settled and ready. Sitting Bear also belonged to the Eagle Shield Society, a medicine society, something like the Buffalo Doctors, but it was for making magic, not for healing. A Sun Dance was a busy time for Sitting Bear, with all those things to see to.

He took the time to send for his older sons, though, before the dancing and the society meetings could get started. The two young men came and sat with him, and they all thought and waited.

"Which of you has promised to dance in this Sun Dance?" asked Sitting Bear.

"Not either of us, my father," answered Young Sitting Bear. Eagle Plume didn't say anything.

"That's wrong," said Sitting Bear. "One of you ought to be dancing. When I was a young man, I danced in four Sun Dances in a row. That's one way a man gets power."

His two sons nodded.

"I think one of you ought to be dancing," Sitting Bear told them. "One of you has power. Enough power to go on living with. That one wouldn't have to dance. But the other doesn't have any power. He's going to need it to get through this life. That one ought to be dancing, anyway."

They didn't answer him out loud. You really didn't need to say words to Sitting Bear, because he knew fairly well what you were thinking anyway. It was different with what he was thinking. His thoughts went too deep for just anybody to follow them through.

"I think you better get somebody to sponsor you," he went on. "White Bear says he will stand sponsor for the one that doesn't have any power. The other one can get anyone he likes. They'll start getting ready for the dancing tomorrow. I think you'd better be there."

That was all. His sons got up and left, because Anko and some of the other older men were beginning to come in. It was the time of year when they all came together to draw the picture of that year on their record. They would sit and smoke and talk things over, deciding what was the most important thing that had happened, and then Anko would draw it down. Because he drew better than anybody else, he was their record-keeper.

When they got outside, Young Sitting Bear said, "Whom will you get to sponsor you?"

"I don't know," Eagle Plume answered. "I have to think some about it. It isn't so important about me, anyway. You're the favorite son in our family."

"You're going to dance, though," said Young Sitting Bear, and Eagle Plume replied, "Oh, yes, I'm going to dance."

They sat down in front of Eagle Plume's mother's tipi. If they sat in front of Young Sitting Bear's special one, all the young men in camp would be over there right away to sing and talk and eat and smoke. In this place, they weren't so likely to be bothered.

Eagle Plume's mother brought them meat and broth, and they ate and drank while they sat there, thinking about whom to get to sponsor Eagle Plume. They named first one and then another of the older men.

"Little Bluff."

"He's sponsoring his grandson."

"Big Tree."

"He's lame from having his horse that got shot roll on him. He wouldn't be able to make it."

"Kicking Bird."

"He went to chase the Utes and hasn't come back yet. Got to be somebody that we know's in camp."

After a long time, Eagle Plume thought of Bird Rising. He was an old, old man, but he had taken part in many Sun Dances and knew just the way things ought to be done. He could tell you and show you, and you would be all right if you followed him.

They got up and went to Bird Rising's tipi.

"Come in, sons," he told them.

"Here we are, father," they answered.

When they had eaten the meat and broth his wife brought them, they told him what they wanted. Bird Rising sat and smoked and thought it over.

"I don't know," he said finally. "I've about made up my mind not to dance any more Sun Dances. It's pretty hard on a man that's as old as I am. I have what power I need, enough to see me through what's left of my life. I don't want to go spreading it out too much and wasting it."

But he gave in finally, and they went back to Eagle Plume's mother's tipi. "That's all right," said Young Sitting Bear. "You have two horses you can give him, and I'll give you two more. I don't need that bay mare, and the black is all right. I never ride him."

"Thank you," was all Eagle Plume said. He didn't feel quite right taking his brother's horses for his own Sun Dance sponsor, but he had danced last year and wasn't planning to any more for a while. He really needed his brother's help if he was going to dance this year, too.

The men who were going to take part in the Sun Dance didn't help with building the Lodge or with going after the branches. There was a special, big, double tipi put up for them and their sponsors, and they all stayed in there. The sponsors' wives brought them things to eat, but not too much, and the sponsors began telling them what they must do, and showing them how to paint. They stayed there until the Lodge was built and the opening ceremony had been finished. Then they went out, late in the evening, and entered the Lodge for their first dance. After that they were in there to stay. They had to dance all that first night.

The first night was easy. It was cool, and there on the river a little mist ran along the earth and made the coolness softer. After the sun was down an almost full moon came up and made everything clear, with sharp, blue light and sharper, bluer shadows. It was beautiful, and it showed the blue in the paint of the dancers, and made the yellow designs on the blue look white. The paint was so thick and the light was so strong you couldn't tell what color their skin was.

They rested when the stars were right overhead to show the middle of the night, and again when the stars were halfway between midnight and dawn. All the time that they were dancing they stood in a long line and faced to the Taime, there at the west side of the Lodge. With the little fire burning below it, the figure hardly showed; but its shape was enough to let you know that it was there. When they were resting, each man lay down on a sage bed that his sponsor had made for him at the side of the lodge. They kept all their paints and everything else they had brought with them at these beds.

After the second rest they danced steadily. At first the sky was black-blue, because by this time the moon was gone, but gradually the edges of the sky began to soften and grey, and long misty wedges of cloud began to separate themselves from the greyness. When the underneath edges of the different clouds began to turn pink, it was the time for the first chase around the Lodge.

Taime Man got up and took the crow-feather fan from behind

the Taime. He came and stood at the middle of the line of dancers, with the fan in his right hand, just behind the young men. The drummers started the Chase Song, and when they had sung it twice, he began to brush with the feathers at the two men just in front of him. They were Young Sitting Bear and Lone Wolf's favorite son, Wolf Lying Down. They turned at the touch of the fan, and began to run to the left.

"Huh! Huh! Huh! Huh!" called Taime Man, and all the young men began to run. Their sponsors stood up beside the sage beds and watched them, because if a man fell down in the chase, it was up to his sponsor to get him out and over to his bed and stretched on it as soon as he could.

Nobody fell down in the first chase. That was what was expected. It took a while to get worked up to the point where you would get power or would lose consciousness. At the end of the dawn chase, all the young men lay down on their beds and rested. Some of them smoked, and it was all right for them to talk to each other, but it was a few minutes before they felt much like talking.

Eagle Plume was on the north side of the Lodge, and Young Sitting Bear was on the south side. Each of them was in the place where his sponsor had danced when he had power. If either of them ever sponsored a man, he would have to go to the same place. Because they were on different sides of the Lodge, it was hard for them to talk to each other, but they could see each other plainly.

Eagle Plume watched his brother during the rest of the dancing. He felt it was important for his brother to do things just right, and get power this way. Sitting Bear would certainly feel bad if his favorite son never got power. It meant a lot to him, being able to hand things on to his favorite son. He would hand them to Eagle Plume without feeling bad, because that would keep them together in the family, but he would feel better if they went to Young Sitting Bear.

It was on the third day that Eagle Plume began to worry about his brother. Young Sitting Bear had always had courage that was stronger than his strength. Now his courage was holding him up but his strength had about given way. His eyes were on the Taime all the time, even when he wasn't dancing, and when he was dancing, he swayed back and forth with his steps, and seemed to be jerking and leaning towards the Taime more and more.

He got through the day all right, though, until they came to the end and it was time for the sunset chase. The sun was level with the western edge of the world and was bright red, and the way the men were dancing they stared past the Taime and straight into the sun.

Young Sitting Bear hardly seemed to know when it was time for the chase to begin. Taime Man had to hit him hard with the crow-feather fan, and then he ran four steps forward—little, jerky steps—and went down flat on his face. It was all the men running behind him could do to keep from falling over him. White Bear ran out and grabbed him and laid him on his bed.

By the time the chase was over, Young Sitting Bear had his eyes open. Eagle Plume looked across at his brother and wondered what had happened during those minutes when there was nothing in front of the eyes that man could see. Probably he never would know. A man had to be going to hand on his power, or share it with someone, before he told what he had seen in a vision.

Young Sitting Bear must have had a vision and not just been unconscious, because he stayed right there in the Lodge the rest of the time, and he kept on fasting like the others. The only difference was that he lay stretched out on the sage bed and rested. You could tell his father was worried about him. Sitting Bear had kept away from the Lodge most of the time until his son fell, but now he stayed there. He sat on the outside of the willow screen, just behind where his son was lying. All that last day, whenever Eagle Plume raised his eyes, he could see the two of them there with the screen, like their different thoughts, between them.

There was no power for Eagle Plume in that dance. He went through to the end of it all right. He didn't even feel very tired. There was nothing inside him that was stretching out and pleading and gasping and reaching for power the way there had been that time when he went out alone. This was different. He was in the dance and he did what he needed to do, but he was just letting things go on around him, and he knew it.

When the last chase was over, and Taime Man had driven the dancers clear out of the Lodge and around the outside of it, Eagle Plume went home to his mother's tipi. She gave him broth and some meat, and he stretched out and slept. The rest of the camp was getting ready for the big feast that night, but the young men who had been dancing wouldn't take part in the feasting. They were too tired for celebrating, and if they tried to eat much after fasting four days and four nights, it would make them sick. This was one feast that the young men didn't mind missing.

Everything was quiet in the camp when Eagle Plume waked. The little cool wind was running along the ground again, the moon was gone, and the sun was coming. He lay still and felt the earth, seeing and hearing and smelling and tasting all making one feeling in him.

Then he rolled over and looked out of the tipi past his mother and saw his brother sitting outside the door wrapped in a new red and blue strouding blanket. Eagle Plume got up when he saw that and went out.

They sat there beside each other the way they used to do when they were little boys. Children could sit beside each other without talking, and so could old men, but young men were usually afraid of their thoughts and tried to put them into words so as to get away from them. Now they had gone back to childhood or on to old age, and words were something that they didn't need.

"You came to tell me something," said Eagle Plume when the light had turned yellow and covered the whole earth.

"It's something pretty important," answered his brother. "It's hard to put in words. I have to tell you a vision I had. I never had a vision before, and I'm not sure I know how to tell about it."

They sat some more and waited for words to come. Day was strong around them, now, but the camp was tired from the overnight dancing, and they were free from touching other minds yet awhile.

"When I fell down in the chase," said Young Sitting Bear, "I saw the things lots of people say that they see. I saw Taime Man. Then I saw him turn into the Taime. He was behind me, and I could feel him hitting me with that fan, but at the same time he was ahead of me, too, and I could see him running. He was so old his ribs had fallen in, and he was holding himself up with a stick."

"That's like what people see and not like what people see," said Eagle Plume.

"Well, it's a lot like what they say they see," said Young Sitting Bear.

"I think some of them see it because they expect to," said Eagle Plume.

"I saw this," his brother insisted. "I know I saw it. I'm sure it was there because it was like and not like."

"That's good power, there," said Eagle Plume. "That means you're going to live to be old, old, as old as Taime Man."

"Well, but that isn't all of the vision," said Young Sitting Bear.

"What happened then?"

"Then all the time that I was running and falling and Taime Man was running ahead of me with his stick and brushing my back with his fan, he was talking to me. Telling me things. Some of them were wonderful things, and some of them were terrible things."

"What did he tell you?"

Young Sitting Bear began to pick up handfuls of earth from beside him, and let them run through his fingers to the ground. "This is what he told me: 'Power comes to the man who can use it, whether he looks for it or not. If it is meant for him to have, he will get it. There are some men who are meant to have power and some men who aren't.'"

"That I know is true," said Eagle Plume. "That I have seen."

"Then he went on: 'This power is being given, but it is given to you to hand on, not to keep. There is something that is going to happen to you and to that other favorite son who is dancing beside you. Something is going to happen so that you won't need this power, this power of living to grow old.'"

"That's bad," said Eagle Plume. "I never heard of anything like that before."

"Then he kept on talking. He said: 'Your brother has some power already. He is meant to have more. He is going to live to see a lot of things happen, and he will need all the power he can get to help him through them. That's why this power is given to you. So you can pass it on to him.'"

"That's not the way it is with power," said Eagle Plume. "You don't pass it on until you're an old man and getting ready to die. You can share it with somebody, but that's different. You're not supposed to pass it on when you've just got it."

"That's the thing about this power," said Young Sitting Bear. "It's a different power. It's not to be used like other power. Taime Man said other things to me, too. He said: 'When your brother has this power, he will know how to use it. It is not just power for living a long time, it is power for making other people live long, too. It is healing power. Tell your brother this is what he must do. He must get one of those big pink shells from the traders when they come into camp day after tomorrow. That is to hang around his neck in front. Then he is to get one of those little pink shells from them. That is to tie on his scalp lock beside what he already has tied there. And when he is going to heal, he must take things from the people who come to him. But he mustn't keep them. They are to give to the women in his family. He is to take four sevens of things seven times. Because this power comes to you to give him through the Sun Dance, there must be no Sun Dance colors on the things. They must be any colors, but not blue or yellow or green. If your brother does these things just right, added to the power he already has, he will be able to cure people of sicknesses inside of them. One thing he must never do. It will ruin his power. He must never castrate a grey horse.'" Young Sitting Bear poured the earth from one hand into the other. "That was the end of my vision."

"I don't understand," said Eagle Plume. This was the hardest thing he had ever heard of. It wasn't like any power-giving ever before.

"This is what I think," said Young Sitting Bear. His eyes had gone across the camp to his father's tipi, and he was looking at it the way he had looked at the Taime that last day in the Lodge—at it and into it and through it and beyond it. "This is the way it seems to me. You are our father's son and I am his favorite son. That means that I have lots of things as a young man. You don't have so many. But things balance out in this life. You are meant to have lots of things in your old age."

"Then I'll take care of you," said Eagle Plume. "That's my duty, to take care of you and keep you still the favorite."

"That's why I think you got this power," said Young Sitting Bear. He sat up straight in his new, bright blanket and began to fuss with it just a little, making its folds fall right. "A man with power can stand to live to be old, because the worst things that can happen to him can't come near enough to touch him. But a man without power had better die young, because something is going to get near enough to hurt him after while. It might hurt his body or it might hurt his mind. It's easier to stand if it's his body that's hurt."

He got up and stood like a man who has just put down a heavy load and stretches to know he's free of it. "That's the way it is with me. Power is hard. It's hard to have and it's hard to keep. All our lives we've seen our father worrying about taking care of his power. All that it's done has been to keep him alive to old age. It's hard work for him. It doesn't make him happy." His arms went out with his hands on the ends of them, reaching. "That's not the way I want it to be with me. I want my life now while I can enjoy it. I want to get what there is out of it while it can make me happy. You're different. You're like our father. You're not afraid to be old. You even want to be old. Here is this gift that I can give you. It will give you what you want, and still it will leave me free to have what I want most. That is sharing. That's the way it ought to be between brothers."

People were moving around and coming out of their tipis now. The brothers had been alone in the world that was the earth, and just for a moment they were still alone but in a world that was people's world. Then Young Sitting Bear let his arms fall inside his blanket so as to hold the folds just right, and started off.

"I'm going to see our father," was what he said. "I'm going to tell him he just has one son that's meant to have power."

PART II : *The Time When Buffalo Were Going*

Playing Camp

The Winter the Bugle Was Blown
(1869–70)

THE CHILDREN PLAYED DIFFERENT GAMES AT DIFFERENT TIMES OF the year. In summer when the Kiowas were moving around and there was the Sun Dance and the dancing societies were meeting, they played games of traveling. There were Rabbit Society dances then that imitated the grown men's dances. In real winter they slid on the ice with their feet, or they slid downhill on buffalo-rib bones. If it were so cold they had to stay in the tipis, they made string figures in quiet. For all the times of the year there were different kinds of play.

Now they were between summer and winter, and play was between, too. All the Cold Weather Band people had come in and camped with the Male Elk Band, and together they filled the whole of the big northward curving bend of the Arrowhead River. It was a good place to be; the camp was out at the end where the land bent northward, and the horse herds were in the deep grass where the peninsula joined the bank. Between was a level space that the children took for their own.

Because they had just come in and made a big camp with a visiting band, they played camping and that a visiting band came. It was a good play because there was a part in it for everybody. Hummingbird Girl got ready to leave her uncle's tipi, where there was too much talk about white men and fighting, to join in the playing.

First, she got her own big old yellow dog. It had been a puppy when she was a baby, and now that she was a girl growing up, it was getting to be middle-aged. But it still played with her and came when she called it, not running wild in a pack around the camp as so many dogs did. It was just the old, yellow dog. She had never given it a name, the way old people who kept dogs instead of children did.

The big old yellow dog came when Hummingbird Girl called it, and stood quietly as she tied the poles of her play-tipi along its back. The tipi and all that went with it were made up in a pack to tie to the poles. Hummingbird Girl got them all fastened together and called Paint Girl to get up on the pack. They always tried to go into

95

camp that way in style, with Paint Girl riding on top of the load to show what a strong horse they had.

This day the dog didn't run away, and they went from the big camp to the little one without any trouble about his chasing rabbits or ground squirrels. They had to belong to the visiting band, since the others were there already; but when everybody turned out and welcomed them and gave them pieces of dried meat, they didn't mind.

It was a long, all-day play, that one with the tipis. Hummingbird Girl's tipi was a good one. Her mother had tanned buffalo-calf hides especially for it, and her uncle had cut her own cedar poles for her last year when the people went up in the mountains for poles for the big tipis. Hummingbird Girl was proud of her household. You had to have a hard-working mother to have a tipi that was your own, and not a big old one cut down.

At first the children's camp was very busy, with everybody putting up tipis and building sunflower-stalk fires and turning horses out to graze. You had to hobble dog-horses just like real ones, because they were worse about running away, and the dog-horses would get into real fights. While the girls were getting the camp ready, the boys were off on a play of their own that was a special part of the other play. The boys pretended that the big camp was an enemy camp, and they raided it for food. They came back with enough dried meat for everybody to have plenty. They had taken it off their relatives' drying-racks.

After they had eaten, the boys began to get restless.

"We ought to play having a raid," one of them said.

"Whom are we going to raid?" asked another.

"I'm going off after the Utes," said the first boy. "Anybody that wants to go with me can come along."

All the boys wanted to, and they all began ganging up for the raiding party.

"You can't do that," said Hummingbird Girl. "You can't just go off and leave the women all alone in camp. Somebody's got to look after them."

"Well, we all want to go," replied the boys.

They talked it over for a while longer, and then decided they would dig a ditch and pile up a dirt wall to protect the camp with the girls in it. They dug a deep ditch right across the end of the peninsula, between the camp and the horse herd. The wall they piled up on the inside, nearest the camp, came up over the middle of Hummingbird Girl's chest. Even if it weren't a very thick wall, it was good and high.

Then the game changed. The boys played they were attacking an enemy camp, and the girls were enemy fighters. They had played that way before, and someone had been hurt, so when they played attacking enemies now, they couldn't use their bows and arrows. Now, when they had a pretended battle, they could just throw dirt, and it had to be dirt without any rocks in it. Both sides threw, and the dirt made smoky puffs in the air, like guns firing. It was a fine battle, because everybody could have a gun. They scooped out good deep holes in the ground where they took up the dirt to make their gun-fires. They played that game until the little dark began to slide up the sky and cover the big day. Then it was time to go home. The sun-flower-stalk fires had gone out, and everybody was getting cold.

Even with the cold slipping and sliding around her body, Hummingbird Girl took time to put her camp away right. She took off the cover and took down the poles of her tipi, and loaded them all just right on the big old yellow dog. "You can always tell what kind a woman is," her mother had told her, "by the way she puts her tipi away." Hummingbird Girl and Paint Girl were always careful to do things just exactly as they should.

They were glad to get back with their load to the main camp and their mother's big fire. Their mother was roasting a buffalo tongue on sticks over the coals, and their uncle, who had brought the tongue, was waiting for it to be ready to eat. His wife had a rule in her family about never eating roasted tongues, so whenever he wanted one, he brought it to his sister to be cooked. She didn't think it would hurt the wife to cook it, but she didn't say so out loud. "Rules like that are just for the men in a family," she told Hummingbird Girl when they were alone. "They don't apply to the women."

Hummingbird Girl sat down near where her uncle was stretched out on the ground, and got warm while she waited for the cooking to be over.

"Time for White Bear's raiding party to be coming in," said her uncle.

"Where did they go?" asked his sister.

The uncle jerked his chin to the southeast.

"Down on Red Water River," he said. "They were looking for white men coming up from Texas."

"White Bear usually finds them," Hummingbird Girl's mother said calmly.

"That's right," said her brother.

"It seems that there is more fighting, more fighting, all the time," his sister went on. "It used to be just the Utes and the Navajos and the Pawnees. They were all right, they'd fight our way. Fight a battle and win it or lose it, and then go on home and stay there. But these white men are different. They want to be all the time fighting. They don't stop for Sun Dances or initiation dances or anything."

"That's right," said her brother. "There sure are a lot of them, too. Every year we whip them, and they all run away; but the next year they come right back again, more of them than ever."

"I get tired of all this fighting," the woman went on. "Two years ago my husband got killed. Last year it was my nephew. Who's it going to be this year? Always when a war party comes in, somebody in camp has lost loved ones. It isn't like the old days, when you could fight all day and nobody get killed. Nobody used to want to kill anybody. It's these white people that want to be killing and killing."

She was getting ready to weep and mourn, the way the women did when they thought of their loved ones who were gone, Hummingbird Girl could feel her own throat being tied in a knot inside. If her mother mourned, she would want to mourn, too. She was a woman.

"Hush and be quiet," said her uncle. "Your husband was killed by the Pawnees, and you know it. Some Indians have always killed each other. It just seems worse since the white men came because the fighting goes on more steadily. Turn that tongue over or you'll burn it so that it won't be fit to eat."

"Well, all the same," said Hummingbird Girl's mother, "I'm glad we're camping this way out on this peninsula. I feel a lot safer here than anywhere else. It's hard for an enemy to get at a camp like this one, with water around it on three sides."

Hummingbird Girl thought about the deep ditch the boys had dug and the fort they had built, and started to tell her mother that she was protected on four sides. Then she remembered that girls shouldn't speak when grownups were talking, and sat back and was quiet. All the time through their supper her mother and uncle went on talking and talking about White Bear's raiding party and when it should be coming back.

After supper her uncle went back to his own camp, and in their camp they began to get ready to go to bed. It didn't take them very long to get things picked up and put away and settled down, and they were asleep as soon as everybody else.

It was late in the night, when the moon had gone down, that the trouble started. Hummingbird Girl didn't hear the sound the first time, but her mother did. Her mother jumped straight up in bed, and said,

"What's that?"

Hummingbird Girl waked and listened in one thinking. The next time the sound came, she heard it, too. Away and away there was a brassy sound. She had heard it one time before, and she knew what it was.

"It's the white soldiers' bugle," she called to her mother.

But her mother had known first. She had her moccasins on and was shaking Paint Girl awake.

"We can't take anything but food," she said to Hummingbird Girl. "Get the two big cases of dried meat. Later we can come back for everything else if there's anything left."

Paint Girl waked, and Hummingbird Girl told her to put on her moccasins. In cold weather they always slept in their dresses, but getting on the high, winter moccasins was as hard as putting on all your clothes in summer.

Their mother ran outside and began getting ready to roll the tipi up, because there was no time to take it down. Hummingbird Girl came to help her pull the stakes. They rolled the cover as high up the sides as their arms could reach, and then the mother took a forked stick and piled the cover into the crotch of the poles. That was to make it hard for an enemy to burn. All around them other women were doing the same thing; they were working hard and were quiet, but there was a lot of noise still in the camp.

It wasn't until they had the tipi up out of the way that Hummingbird Girl understood what the other noise was and where it was coming from. It was coming from the neck of the peninsula where the children had had the play camp, and it was men shouting and boys calling and horses screaming. All of a sudden Hummingbird Girl remembered. The ditch, their fine ditch—it was deep enough to trip the horses, and the wall made it too high for the horses or the men to climb back. That was what all the yelling was about. She should have felt safe remembering the ditch, but she knew she didn't. She was thinking that maybe a ditch was a dangerous kind of thing.

There was confusion all night. They didn't dare light fires, for fear the enemy would see them. The horses were worked up and excited, and when they got out of the ditch and stopped screaming, they started running back and forth. The men were trying to save the horses and still be ready to fight if the enemy came, and the women didn't know what to do. They were afraid to go where the men were, because they didn't want to get trampled; they had no fires, and with their tipis rolled up, they had no shelter, and all of the babies and little children were crying. It was a bad night, all right. The one good thing about it was that they didn't hear the frightening bugle any more.

The Ten Grandmothers

Day came reluctantly, as if it knew what a mess it was going to uncover and didn't want to look. The camp was all torn to pieces, but somehow nobody had been hurt. The horses were all right and the people were all right, though some of the boys were scratched and bruised from scrambling around in the ditch. They had taken some food out of their packs and were sitting around eating it and wondering what to do next, when White Bear's party rode in. Around White Bear's neck was hanging and shining a big brass bugle, a white soldier's bugle. When White Bear rode into camp, he stopped in the middle of the mess, put the bugle up to his mouth, and blew on it. He didn't blow the kind of strange tunes the soldiers blew, but he did make a big blow and a big noise. Now they knew what they had heard in the night.

It was too bad White Bear hadn't waited until he reached camp to blow his bugle the first time. Now everybody was scared and tired and worn out and disgusted, and just then they didn't care whether White Bear had a bugle to blow or not. Later on maybe they would, but now they didn't. They just sat and looked at White Bear, and his young men and said, "Get down, friends."

White Bear and the young men got down and looked around. Nobody told them what had happened, but they seemed to understand without being told. They went home to their families and began helping them get things straightened out. Nobody coming in with a war party had ever got that kind of welcome before.

It was noonday's middle when everything was right again. After all the work was done, and the earth wall had been used to fill in the ditch, and the holes that the gunshot dust had been taken from had been filled, too, Hummingbird Girl's uncle had the caller get everybody together in front of his tipi. He stood and looked at them, and it seemed to Hummingbird Girl that he wasn't seeing anybody but her and the girls her age.

"This is what I have to say," said her uncle. "This is a rule I am going to make. It is for everybody. Every family will hear it, and every family will make its own members obey. Nobody must dig ditches around play camps any more. Play camps are all right without ditches, and ditches are all right if men dig them and know where they are and can keep the horses out of them, but they don't go together. Nobody is to mix them up ever again."

That was all. Hummingbird Girl and Paint Girl went home and helped their mother get food ready. Then they sat down by the fire with some pieces of sinew string. It was really too early in the year to make string figures, but it seemed the safest thing there was to do.

Favorite Son

The Year Sitting Bear Brought His Son Home (1870–71)

I

YOUNG SITTING BEAR WAS HIS FATHER'S FAVORITE SON. EVERYBODY knew it. Lots of big, important families had a favorite child, and did things for him. Usually it was a son, because a son might be taken away from them in war, but sometimes, when there were no sons, it was a daughter.

Sitting Bear had been especially fond of this son ever since he had been born. When the boy was just a year old, he had taken him to Little Bluff to be named. Little Bluff knew that Sitting Bear was a proud man, so he named the child for his father. There wasn't any better name. Sitting Bear was a strong name, as strong as a bear, sitting and waiting for enemies. The first Sitting Bear was a strong man. He was strong in fighting and strong in power. Naming his son for him was good.

Sitting Bear gave Little Bluff four horses, four buffalo hides, four yellow buckskins, and four bags of paint for naming his son. Because Little Bluff was a big man, too, he kept the paints and gave the other presents away to old people who needed them, in the name of Young Sitting Bear. From that time on, he made nearly as much fuss about Young Sitting Bear as Sitting Bear did.

While Young Sitting Bear was growing up, his mother and Sitting Bear's other wives were nearly as proud of him as his father. His brothers and sisters were proud of him, too. They were always showing off his good things and the deeds people did because of him, to make themselves important.

When he was six years old and was taken into the little boys' Rabbit Society, Sitting Bear gave a feast for the members of that society that was like the feast he would give for grown men, for his own Crazy Dog Society. Everybody came to look on. All the little boys in the whole Sun Dance camp danced, with their little sisters dancing behind them; and the grown people stood around and laughed at them hopping up and down. Then the society and their sisters sat down to eat. There were all sorts of good things, and plenty of them; and when they had finished, they picked up the food that was left and threw it at each other until they were plastered with it.

It was the same way when Young Sitting Bear joined the Herders Society. There was a big dance, and a big feast for all the young men who were his age and belonged to the society, and Sitting Bear gave away, in his son's honor, horses and buffalo robes and the red and blue blankets that he got from the traders.

Sitting Bear was generous with Eagle Plume, too. He gave a feast for him when he joined the Gourd Dancers Society. But it was the kind of feast anybody might give; there wasn't anything special the way there was about the feast he gave for Young Sitting Bear.

Eagle Plume didn't mind. It was an honor to a family to have a favorite son in it. He was fond of his brother, and admired him. Young Sitting Bear looked like his mother: he was big and strong and handsome, but he had his father's little hands, as Eagle Plume had, too. They were both as vain of those little hands as their father was.

Young Sitting Bear had his own tipi from the time he joined the Herders Society on. It was a big one, and his father had given him the design for painting it. It was red on one side and yellow on the other. There was plenty of room in it for the whole society to sit and smoke and talk. Most of the time you could find the Herders Society in Young Sitting Bear's tipi. Every now and then his mother would come in with something for them to eat. It was like a feast going on all the time.

Both Eagle Plume and Young Sitting Bear had gone with their father on raids. Most men would have sent their sons with somebody else, but Sitting Bear was a big, important man. If he wanted to take his own sons with him, and train them himself, he could. Nobody would say anything.

Sometimes Eagle Plume sat with his brother in Young Sitting Bear's tipi when the Herders Society wasn't around. Because he belonged to another society, it wouldn't look right for him to be there at the same time they were.

One morning when they were sitting there, Young Sitting Bear was restless. He seemed to be thinking, but his thoughts didn't make him easy. He was fighting them for a while, and then he gave up to them. He looked at Eagle Plume for a minute and said, "I've been thinking a lot."

"What about?" asked Eagle Plume.

"I've been thinking about raids."

"That's the best way to get horses."

"Best way to see the country, too."

"It's a good way to get some clothes and women, too."

"There's a lot of country I want to see. Every raid I've been on, we went west. I want to go south. There's lots of country to the south."

Eagle Plume laughed. "That's what Bird Rising used to say. He went south."

"Do you believe that story?"

"Lots of men went with him. They all came back. All told the same story."

"They went south and south and south. The weather got hot and then it got wet."

Eagle Plume joined in. Bird Rising used to tell them the story of that raid when they were children, over and over the same way, and it was like a song in their minds that they both could sing.

"The trees got higher and vines hung down from them. Some of the vines reached the ground and turned around and grew up again. Some of the trees had long bags hanging from them. Birds lived in those things as in nests."

It was Young Sitting Bear's turn now. "They went south and south and south through the heat and the trees and the vines. Sometimes there were houses and they went around them. Sometimes there were towns and they went around those. All the time going south."

Eagle Plume's turn now. "They went south until they came to a river and that was where they camped that night. There were big fish splashing in the water. They thought they saw a water monster on the bank, but he dived. He must have been drowned because he never came up. That's where they built a fire and camped."

Young Sitting Bear was laughing so he could hardly tell his part of the story.

"Then they were sitting around the fire. Everything was dark. Then they heard people talking. They looked around for those people. All around everywhere." He shaded his eyes with his hand and peered intently in a circle around the ground.

Eagle Plume resumed the story. "Then something hit them on the head. Hard. They looked up." Both leaped to their feet, peering up at the tipi ears. "Then they saw. Those people were sitting in the trees up above them. They must have been wonderful people. They were throwing down leaves and branches on those poor Kiowas. They must have been wonderful things. They all had long tails."

They both sat down suddenly. Eagle Plume added in a sad voice, the way Bird Rising always did, "Then those poor Kiowas were scared of the wonderful things. They turned around and came home."

Young Sitting Bear laughed some more and shook his head. "I

don't want to go that far south. But I want to go part-way south. I want to go far enough to see what some of the people down there look like. Some of the people that don't have tails."

"Who's going? I didn't hear anybody talking about starting out."

"I'm going. I'm starting out. I'll call my society to go."

"You're going to lead your own party."

"Yes, I'm going to lead it. Our father has been teaching me. I know how."

That was all. When a man said he knew how, he must know or he wouldn't dare to say it. You had to leave it up to him, then. It generally meant that he had some kind of power that showed him how. Eagle Plume wondered about his brother's power. Nobody would risk leading a raid if he didn't have power.

"Those old men," said Young Sitting Bear, "—they were pretty good in their time. That was when they hunted everything with bows and arrows. Fought everybody with bows and arrows. But that was in the old times. Now we have guns to hunt and fight with. Now you have to plan things differently. It's time the young men began to do the planning."

There was truth in that, all right. Hunting and fighting were as different as living from the old days. You often heard the old people telling how hard it used to be, when there were no horses and you had to pack what you had around with dogs, and when you had to shoot your game and your enemies with bows and arrows. Horses and guns were better, Eagle Plume thought. He didn't remember when they had not had them, and neither did their father; but Taime Man could remember, and he sometimes talked about the old days when they didn't even have flint and steel and had to make their fires with drills.

"Are you going with me?" Young Sitting Bear asked.

Eagle Plume thought about that for a long time, sitting there in his brother's special tipi. It took power to lead a raid, and he didn't know for sure whether his brother had power. If he had it, everybody would know as soon as he spoke. It was dangerous, trying to do something if you didn't have the power. Eagle Plume made up his mind.

"I guess I won't go," he said. "I guess I'll stay here. When I go on a raid I'd rather go west. And anyway you're going to call up your society. I guess I'd better not go with them. Better go with my own society."

They left it at that. Eagle Plume went back to his mother's tipi and lay on his bed at the back of it and thought. There were many settlers in the country south of them. They were getting tired of having Indians kill their cattle or drive off their horses. Many of these raids had been carried on. The settlers were getting angry about it. They might really fight sometime. It was the Comanches who did those things, but how was a white man going to tell one kind of Indian from another? White men were so stupid, you knew they couldn't. It would be dangerous, all right, going on his brother's raid.

It was four days before Young Sitting Bear called his society together. In that time he had got everything ready. His gun was cleaned and polished, and he had made some bullets and even had his bow and arrows ready to fall back on. Then he painted himself, put on his war bonnet, and started through the camp. He was beating on a piece of hide with his bow, as if they were a drum and a drumstick.

All the other young men had been getting ready, too. They had their things all laid out, waiting for the drumming. When they heard it, they all gathered their things up, put them on, and ran out of their tipis to follow Young Sitting Bear.

He went all around the camp four times, with the whole society following him. They were painted and dressed up, but Young Sitting Bear was the only one with the right to wear the war bonnet. Grey-Eyed Woman had made it and put it on him two years before. He had worn it in a battle and had fought without retreating, and when he came home, Sitting Bear gave Grey-Eyed Woman four horses. Grey-Eyed Woman ran out and war-whooped now, so that Young Sitting Bear would know he had to give her another horse if he came back successful.

Everybody sang and danced until late that night. The full moon was right over their heads and had bleached out until it looked like a silver hair-plate before they sang the last song, the *Going on a Journey Song*.

> *Going away on a journey,*
> *That is the only thing.*
> *That's the only way for a young man*
> *To get himself rich and famous.*

Then, just before the young men started out and the other people went back to their tipis, Sitting Bear stood up and sang his Crazy Dog song for his son.

> *I live, but I will not live forever.*
> *Mysterious moon, you only remain,*
> *Powerful sun, you alone remain,*
> *Wonderful earth, you remain forever.*

That was a hard song. You had to fight a long time and be brave and famous to have the right to sing it. Eagle Plume wondered whether his brother would earn the right to sing it on this raid. He stood and watched his brother, with Wolf Lying Down, another favorite son, beside him, riding out of the camp in the moonlight.

II

The waiting time always seemed long. No matter what you did, there was nothing that would quite fill it in. You always found that you had pieces of days left over, with nothing to do with them. Other times you could use up all there was of a day and wonder what had become of it, but not when you were waiting. Then there was always some of the day that you didn't know how to use.

Eagle Plume thought that his father must be understanding that about the waiting time now, for the first time. Usually Sitting Bear had gone on raids himself, and other people had had to do the waiting. This time Sitting Bear was waiting at home, and someone else had gone on the raid. It was hard for him.

It was hard for Lone Wolf, too, with his favorite son gone. The two older men had always been good friends. Now they sat and talked to each other a great deal. They talked about the old days and the things they used to do and how they felt about them, but they never said anything about their sons. Sometimes they discussed the white men, and the soldiers at the fort, and the Indian Agent who had come to Fort Sill, but they were always nibbling around the edges of what they really were thinking about. Both of them knew their sons were gone, and they knew their sons were good friends, as good friends as they were, and that was all. They didn't have to mention it with their mouths. Their minds talked about nothing else.

The waiting time lasted and lasted. The moon had shrunk and flattened itself, like the melting and hammering of silver, five times, before they had any word. Then most of the Herders Society rode back into the camp with their faces painted black. Those two favorite sons were not with them.

Sitting Bear didn't say anything. He went over to his tipi, lay down on his bed at the back, and covered his head. After while Lone Wolf came in and sat down beside him. All over the camp was spread the wailing and mourning of the women.

Eagle Plume knew there were some things the women had to do— cut their legs and arms and cut off their finger tips and hair; paint their faces black and pile ashes on their heads. They had to do those things; they showed respect for the dead. Most times it would have been right to tear down the tipi and kill all the horses and tear up his brother's things.

This time it seemed wrong. He felt that his father would want to decide about that. When the women got torches from the fires and started to burn things, he went out and stopped them before they could set fire to his brother's tipi. They all stopped wailing and mourning and began to yell at him for not showing respect for the dead. Eagle Plume stood there and let them yell and would not let them burn the tipi.

Sitting Bear and Lone Wolf heard the wailing change to yelling. They pulled their blankets over their heads and came out to see what was the matter. Sitting Bear said, "My son is right. Leave that tipi alone. I have a use for it," and went back to his tipi. The women quit their yelling, then, and went on wailing. Eagle Plume wondered if they weren't wailing as much because they were bewildered as for any other reason.

Four days and four nights Sitting Bear and Lone Wolf sat in the tipi without eating or drinking. It was as if they had gone for power, except that they stayed right there in camp. Then they got up and came out. They looked like old, old men, with their faces fallen in to the bones and their eyes pushed in to the backs of their heads.

Sitting Bear got his war bonnet, his good clothes, his paint, and his gun and began to get ready to go on a journey. Lone Wolf went away to his own tipi. He did not get ready to go with Sitting Bear, but he called all the members of the Herders Society together, and told them they should prepare to go.

When Sitting Bear was all ready, he went over to Lone Wolf's tipi, where the young men were waiting for him with their horses. They looked as if they were all ready to follow him and fight. Sitting Bear spoke to them. Eagle Plume was ready to go, too. It wasn't his society, but his brother and his father were concerned, and he thought he'd better be ready to go along.

"This looks like going away for revenge," Sitting Bear said, "but it isn't that. I don't want revenge. Lone Wolf doesn't want revenge. Having revenge won't bring our sons back. So none of you must shoot at anybody we see, or make any trouble while we're gone.

"But I want my son with me. What is left of my son, I want with me. It has always been our custom, when a young man died on a raid, to bury him and leave him there. That is our old way. That is the way Lone Wolf still wants to do things.

"But I want to bring my son back. He should be here. This is where he belongs. He has a nice tipi, good clothes, all the things that a young man enjoys. I gave him those things so he could be happy. I want him to be here so that he can enjoy them."

Sitting Bear took a big, new, red and blue strouding blanket from behind his saddle and spread it out for them all to see. "This is a good blanket. I got it to give to my son when he came back from his raid. Now I am going to take it to him, and bring him home wrapped in his good, new blanket."

He folded the blanket carefully and laid it across the horse in front of the saddle. He swung himself up, and all the young men followed him. It was broad daylight, and they rode out of the camp without singing.

Some of the Herders Society guided them south on their journey. They went down through the Wichitas and past the fort and came to the Red River and crossed it. Then the country flattened out all around them, and you could hardly remember what it looked like with a river and mountains and trees to break it up.

They traveled all the way by daylight. At night they camped. They made fires and let them show, and they cooked their meat before they ate it. There was no hurrying. The society was guiding them, but Sitting Bear was leading them, and he wanted everything done just right.

Once they saw a white man, riding along with his gun over his arm. The young men forgot what Sitting Bear had told them before they started and wanted to kill the white man. Sitting Bear stopped them from doing it. "This isn't a journey for revenge," he told them. "I am making this journey to honor my son."

Eagle Plume never forgot how the place where his brother was buried looked. There was a high mesa rising straight up out of the flat prairie. On the east face of it was a fall of rocks. None of them looked as if they had been moved until you got close enough to see that some of them didn't have grass coming up around them. That was the place where Young Sitting Bear and Lone Wolf's son were buried. The young members showed them which pile of rocks covered Sitting Bear's son.

When Sitting Bear got down off his horse, the members of the society sat around as if they were wondering what to do. It seemed to Eagle Plume that he knew what his father wanted him to do. He went to help his father move the rocks.

He had never touched a dead body before. That was the duty of old people, mostly, who hadn't long to live anyway. Usually the Kiowas buried people as soon as they had died, and burned and gave away everything they owned and tried to forget them the way they forgot their names. Remembering the dead did not bring them back. It just made the people who remembered feel sorrowful.

They moved all the rocks and found a pile of clothes, and Sitting Bear spoke to his son for the first time that day. "You leave this to me," he said. "This is my part. Bring me the red and blue blanket." Eagle Plume went to his father's horse and got the blanket. When he came back, he saw that there was no body there any more, nothing but bones.

He spread the blanket out on the ground, and his father began to put the bones on it. As he took up each one, he cried over it and talked to it. Before he laid it on the blanket, he painted it yellow. That was the color of the Herders Society. All the time he kept singing a lullaby to the bones when he wasn't talking to them.

When he had finished, he and Eagle Plume set fire to the clothes that were left on the ground and took the rocks and added them to the pile over Lone Wolf's son. "We'll take your brother home and get him some new clothes," was all Sitting Bear said.

The journey home was strange. All the young men were afraid of the bones, and Sitting Bear rode alone, with just Eagle Plume beside him. Eagle Plume was afraid of the bones, too, but his father looked older than the earth and he was more afraid than ever to leave him alone. It was bad, when you began to be afraid that Sitting Bear might fall off his horse.

When they camped at night, Sitting Bear made a bed of buffalo robes for the bones to lie on, still wrapped in the good blanket. He sat beside them and sang lullabies to them, while the young men lay away from him, off to one side. Eagle Plume wondered if his father ever slept at all. He knew that he never lay down. If he slept he did it in snatches, sitting up beside the bones.

They saw more white men on this trip, but the young men were so afraid of Sitting Bear that they followed him in a straight line and never even looked as if they wanted to charge.

"That's good," Sitting Bear told them. "I am responsible for all of you. I want to get you back to your families safely. There has been enough mourning."

One day before they reached their own camp, they met soldiers coming from the fort. The officer rode up, stopped them, and asked where they were going. Wood Fire, who could speak English, told them. "Did you see any white men while you were gone?" the officer asked him, and Wood Fire said, "Yes. They didn't see us. We hid and let them go by. He wouldn't let us hurt them."

Sitting Bear was getting tired of the talking. He wanted to get home with his son. He raised his hand to the officer and they all rode on, leaving the white soldiers just sitting there staring after them.

Sitting Bear sent scouts ahead into the camp as if they were returning from a victorious raid. All the people were dressed and painted up when they rode in. A few women made the war-whoop, and Sitting Bear nodded to them and promised them horses, as he would have done after a great victory. Then he rode on to his own tipi. Eagle Plume followed him.

They left their horses for the women to unsaddle, but Sitting Bear carried the blanket with the bones himself. His son's good red and yellow tipi was pitched right next to his own, and he carried the bones in and laid them on the bed at the west end. He unfolded the blanket and laid all the bones out right, the way they ought to go. Then he called to his wife, his dead son's mother, "Get a big feast ready," he told her. "My son wants to give a feast for the members of his society."

Eagle Plume went to his own mother's tipi. She had gone to help the other wives with the feast. He sat there alone, watching the camp. People were very still. Most of them were staying in their own tipis. They were afraid to come out. They were afraid of what Sitting Bear had done.

After while Lone Wolf came out of his tipi and went all around the camps, calling the members of the society together. "Sitting Bear and his son are giving a feast for his son's society," he called. "All of the Herders are to go to the tipi that belongs to Sitting Bear's son for a feast."

Usually when something like that was called, the young men came right away. This time it took a long time for them all to get together. It wasn't as bad for them as it was for the other people, because they had ridden all that way behind Sitting Bear and the bones, but they didn't like it. Lone Wolf came over to Eagle Plume's tipi.

"Your father wants you to come to this feast," he said, and Eagle Plume got up and began to get ready.

It was a big feast, but they all sat as near the door as they could and ate quickly. Only Sitting Bear sat alone, on the bed next to his son's, and ate slowly. When they had finished eating, he spoke to them. "This is my son entertaining his friends in his tipi," he said. "He hopes you have all had a good meal."

They all thanked him for the food, but he shook his head. "The thanks go to my son," he told them. "He's giving this feast. He wants to give you all presents, too. He hopes you will all come and feast with him again."

His dead son's mother brought in the presents. You could tell she

didn't like it any more than the young men did, but she went over
and laid the things on the ground by the bed with the bones on it.
Sitting Bear gave each member of the society a new red blanket and
a bag of yellow paint.

"These are presents from my son," he said, and they all said "Thank
you for presents" to the bones.

"My son will keep on living with us just the way he always has,"
Sitting Bear went on. "He will keep on traveling with us on his own
horse. His tipi will be moved around like all the other tipis. If we
tried to leave him behind, he would get lonesome, so we won't do that.
Any time his society has a dance, he will want to be there. You must
be sure to let him know, so that he can get ready."

The society members all went away after that. Eagle Plume wondered if the Herders Society would do much dancing as long as his
father lived. It didn't seem likely. Sitting Bear began to talk to him,
then.

"This is my favorite son," he said. "This is my son that I love better
than daylight. But I have another son. He is brave, too. He doesn't lead
raids, but there are other ways of being brave. I want to do something
for my brave son."

At first Eagle Plume thought his father was making fun of him,
but then he understood that Sitting Bear meant what he said. "This
is what I want to do for my brave son," the old man went on. "I have
a lot of power. Some of my war power I thought I gave to my favorite
son. Other power I tried to give, but it didn't want to leave me. A man
has to think about what he's going to do with his power when he dies.

"The oldest power I have is that Grandmother bundle. It was my
father's and his father's and his father's. It is like a person, like an old
person. Somebody has to take care of it. Sometimes it is hard, having
to take care of that bundle.

"That is the power I am going to give to my brave son. Then, no
matter what happens, he will be safe. Nothing can ever hurt him.
He will live to be so old that his ribs fall in, and when he dies, everybody will have respect for him. That is what I am going to do for my
brave son, to make him live a long time.

"Tomorrow I will start teaching him how to take care of that
bundle. But tonight I want to be left alone. I want to sit here quietly
and talk to my favorite son."

He reached for his pipe and began to fill it as Eagle Plume left
the tipi.

War Song

The Year the Three Chiefs Were Captured (1871)

AFTER HIS SON WHO WAS NAMED FOR HIM DIED, SITTING BEAR seemed to turn into an old, old man. At the same time he appeared to stop caring about what happened to him. He made new friends, too. He never before had had much to do with White Bear or Big Tree, but now he went hunting with them and spent a good deal of time talking to them in his tipi.

Sometimes they talked about hunting, because it was getting harder to find buffalo, and you really had to hunt these days. Sometimes they sat and looked at the fire and let their minds go loose. Sometimes they spoke of ceremonies and songs and dancing, but most of the time they talked about the white men and whether they could do anything to get the strangers out of the country.

White Bear was a great talker. He was proud of the way he could talk. When he stood up to speak, words came pouring out of him like songs, but he didn't sing them. He spoke them, and they worked on the people who heard him as songs did. The people listening had to get up and act when White Bear spoke his songs.

White Bear was a fine-looking man. He was tall and had good features, and his hair was long and black. He liked to show off his hair, and usually he didn't braid it, but let it hang loose in the old way. When he dressed up, he braided his hair and wrapped otter fur around the braids, but he always let enough of the hair show that you knew how good-looking it was.

Big Tree was not much of a talker. He was a fighter, and as long as he could fight, talking or dressing up didn't count. He had the right to wear the war bonnet, and he was proud of it, but wearing it was the only dressing up you could ever get him to do. When it came to talking, he said just one word at a time, and sometimes it was hard for him to get even one word out.

Sitting Bear was different from either of them. He could talk if he wanted to, but most of the time he didn't want to. All he had to do was let people know he was planning to do certain things, and they came with him to do them. He didn't dress up much, because fancy clothes got in his way, but if it were a time for dressing up, he could do it. He was not a handsome man, because he was short and skinny and had a little mustache and squinted-up eyes; but you never forgot his face or the look in it. He was a man to be afraid of and to follow.

Sitting Bear grew to hate the white men. That was because they had killed his son down in Texas. When the white men first came into the country, Sitting Bear was like an old buffalo switching his tail to brush the flies off his sides, but since his son had been killed, he was like the same buffalo when he got angry enough to charge right into a bunch of flies and try to butt them to pieces with his head. The trouble was that flies just spread out ahead of the buffalo and didn't pay any attention to him. The white men seemed to be acting the same way.

Eagle Plume watched his father and the other two old men, and sometimes sat in the tipi and listened to them talk. White Bear wanted to go down to the fort and talk to the officers. He said the officers were smarter than the men, just the way chiefs were smarter than other people, and he thought that if he went down to the fort and made a long speech to the officers, they might go away.

Big Tree didn't think that would do much good. He said that White Bear was a good talker all right and could work on other Indians, but what was the use of making a speech to men who didn't talk like people. They wouldn't know what he was saying. It would do more good to go down to the fort some night and burn it down. Then they could kill everybody who ran out, and it would all be over.

Sitting Bear waited until they had both finished before he said anything. Then he said that talking came at the end of fighting, not at the beginning. When it was all over, you could talk it over and tell about it to other people. If you were going to fight, the thing to do was to go ahead and fight. But he didn't think fighting at the fort would do much good. If you burned the fort down and got rid of everybody there, the power that the white men called Washington would just send out more people to build it up and live in it. The thing to do was to go to work on the white men who were fencing in grass and running cattle on it and building little houses in the open country. If you got rid of them, then the troops would all stay in one place at the fort and wouldn't make so much trouble.

Eagle Plume went away and thought about it all. It was his own father who wanted to kill off the white men, and Eagle Plume knew he ought to want to join his father in fighting. But he didn't. It seemed to him that fighting was the wrong way to go about getting rid of the white men, and that his father would have greater success if he used his power and tried to get rid of them that way.

Sitting Bear, White Bear, and Big Tree talked the situation over with each other and with the young men, and the young men thought Sitting Bear had the best idea. They were willing to do what he wanted, but they asked him to use his power to help them. The night before they were going out to tear down the first fences, Sitting Bear called all the men together in his tipi.

Sitting Bear belonged to a society called the Eagle Shields. It was like the Crazy Dogs, which was for leading fighters and to which he also belonged, but the Eagle Shields was for power. Every member had a yellow shield with a blue eagle and two blue guns painted on it. All painted themselves yellow, with their chins and foreheads black. And each one of them had a magic knife.

Sitting Bear used his knife this time. All the men were sitting around the tipi, and the eleven other Eagle Shields were there to help him. He laid the knife on the ground west of the fire and spread a black silk handkerchief over it. When he had sung and prayed, he picked the handkerchief up again, and the knife had turned into a feather—a crow's wing-feather.

Eagle Plume watched his father pick up the feather. Sitting Bear held his head back and his mouth open, with the feather over it. When he had sung another song, he swallowed the feather, tip first, and sat down. The other Eagle Shields began to sing and drum, and when they had finished Sitting Bear stood up and coughed, and they saw the tip of the feather sticking out of his throat. He coughed three times, and each time a little more showed. He coughed the fourth time and pulled the feather out. It was his knife again.

That was strong power, Eagle Plume thought. His father was teaching him the power and the rules that went with the Grandmother bundle, and there was a lot to learn about it, but he wanted the other power, too. Watching his father go through that ceremony, it seemed to him that the other power must be stronger than the Grandmother power.

After the young men had started out[1] and everybody had had some sleep and something to eat, he went across to his father's tipi. His brother's mother gave him dried meat, and he sat and ate and watched the fire until Sitting Bear spoke to him.

[1] The story that follows the raid and the arrest of Sitting Bear, White Bear, and Big Tree differs in certain details from the more official versions, but it is nonetheless important, for it is the Indian informant's version of the affair, as he remembered it. For other accounts, see Carl Coke Rister, *Border Command* (Norman, 1944) and Colonel W. S. Nye, *Carbine and Lance* (Norman, 1942).

"There are still things to learn about that Grandmother."

"I want to learn them when you're ready to teach."

"That's strong power, that Grandmother. You have to learn how to take care of it right, or it can hurt you. Doing the wrong thing with power, that's what is dangerous."

"There is other power stronger than the Grandmother, I think."

"There's other power that's stronger than one of the Grandmothers, but no power that is stronger than all ten of the Grandmothers. Every time a new power comes into the tribe, it has to call on the Grandmothers to help. Even the Taime had to do that when it was new. Then those Grandmothers came and helped. That's what made the Taime strong. That's what makes any power strong."

Eagle Plume wondered if he had better go on talking. He hadn't talked much to his father about these things since his brother had died. But he wanted to know, and he wanted the Eagle Shield power if his father would give it to him.

"There's other power I'd like to have to go with that Grandmother and help me take care of it."

"What other power is that?"

"It's that Eagle Shield power."

Sitting Bear sat and looked for a long time at his moccasins and at his little hands holding his pipe. Then he said, "There is some power that is good for living at home, and some power that is good for going on the raids. That Eagle Shield power is for raiding. When you have it, you will always be successful in fighting. But it's hard power to take. You can't be around anybody that's wearing feathers. You can't eat tongues. When a knife drops point-down into a fire, you can't eat anything that's cooked over that fire. Whatever you do, you have to be careful. That shield mustn't get wet. It mustn't have fire near it. It has to lie out on a rack behind the tipi except when it's raining, and then the first thing that happens you have to bring it indoors. It's hard, taking care of that shield."

"It's hard taking care of any power. Some of those rules are the same for the Grandmothers—like the fire and the water."

"It's different with the Grandmothers. They've always been. Even a long time ago when we lived in the north, the Kiowas had the Grandmothers. But this Eagle Shield power, that's new. Just not long ago a man dreamed it. When he was living, he gave it to other men to carry on, and now that he's dead, they're carrying it on. It works for them."

"Maybe it could be handed on like the Grandmothers."

"Some kinds of power can be handed on. The Grandmothers get

stronger as they go on. But this power is different. I think it will end when the men that have it now die. I don't think it's for handing on. I think the men will end and it will end with them. Maybe it will help kill them; I don't know. That kind of power can turn and hurt a man sometimes."

Eagle Plume sat still and looked at his own hands holding the little, straight, old, deer leg-bone pipe. They were almost as small as his father's hands. Then he said, "Thank you for telling, father," and got up and left. If his father didn't want him to have the power, that was all right. Sitting Bear had reasons.

Two days later the young men came in. They hadn't had far to go. They had found the first fenced place and let out the cattle and torn down the fence and burned the house. When the man tried to fight them, they had to kill him. His wife and one little girl escaped, but they brought two more little girls back with them.

White Bear was very angry, and Big Tree backed him up. They said that if you were going to kill one in a family, you'd better kill everybody, because the others could get away and tell on you. Besides, there wasn't much use taking prisoners when they had a hard time getting enough to eat for themselves.

Sitting Bear was angry, too. He said there was no sense in staying right at home to fight people. You might as well let them come up and fight you. When you went raiding you ought to go far enough away that the enemy couldn't just walk into your camp and help himself to you. He told the young men they were stupid and that the next time they went raiding, they ought to go down into Texas so that the soldiers would have a hard time following them and might think that the Comanches or the Apaches had done the killing. He wouldn't let them hold a victory dance, for fear people would know they had made the raid.

He was right, too. Only three days later the soldiers rode up, and the officer got off his horse and walked over to Sitting Bear's tipi. The three chiefs were all there waiting for him. They knew who he was and he knew who they were. He had a young man with him to interpret. It was Wood Fire, who had been living at the fort and taking care of the horses because he didn't have any family to hold him back. The soldiers had taken him in and had taught him their language so that he could help them by interpreting.

The officer didn't get excited the way most white men would have done. He sat down and smoked and looked at the fire and waited. Wood Fire must have been telling him about good manners, because he was the first white man of any kind they had seen who knew how to act.

When they had all smoked, the officer began to talk.

He said, "There have been some young men raiding."

White Bear answered him, "We have heard about that. Those young Comanches and Cheyennes are hard to hold down. Their older men don't know how to control them."

The officer said, "I heard they were young men from this camp."

White Bear told him, "There has been no victory dance here. Some of our young men have been out hunting, that's all."

The officer sat still and looked at the fire. Then all of a sudden he looked straight at White Bear and said, "I think the young men from here have been raiding. You say not. I think this is too big for me to handle. The general had better handle it. You three men had better come to the fort and talk to the general. You three chiefs. He will kill a beef for you."

Sitting Bear stood up. "He needn't kill a beef. We don't like beef. It's tough and coarse. What we want is buffalo."

The young officer said, "Maybe we can get a buffalo. But I think you'd better go and talk to the general."

Sitting Bear looked him all the way up and down. "I think we better talk to the general, all right. Chiefs don't make peace with little, young men. When big men talk, they talk to big men. Go and tell the general we're coming, young man."

The young officer knew he'd been insulted, but he didn't let it make him angry. You had to respect him for what he did then. He got up and put on his riding gloves, fitting them on his hands just right. Then he brought his hand up to his forehead the way white men did when they wanted to show respect, and he said, "I'll tell the general you're coming, old man," and went out of the tipi, got on his horse, and rode off with his back as straight as a tipi-pole.

The women went right off and started taking the tipis down and packing up and getting ready to scatter out, but Sitting Bear stopped them. He made them do everything just right, the way they always did. They took the tipis down and packed things away, loaded the horses, and got ready to start just as they always had.

Eagle Plume's mother packed everything. Something made Eagle Plume take a long time getting ready himself. He painted his face and put on his best clothes, and when he was on his horse, he saw Sitting Bear come out of his tipi, and then he was glad he had dressed up.

Sitting Bear's face was painted black and yellow for the Eagle Shields. He had on a yellow buckskin suit with fringe so long it dragged off his leggings on the ground. He had on silver rings and bracelets, and silver chains in the holes all around the outsides of his ears. He wore his war bonnet, and he was carrying the crooked spear that went with it. He had his wildcat-skin quiver on his back, with the long bois d'arc bow sticking out of it, and his eagle shield on his arm. Eagle Plume had never seen his father look like that before.

It took longer to get Sitting Bear's camp ready than anybody else's, because there was the extra tipi with his son's bones in it. But they got it down, with the bones wrapped in their red and blue blanket, and tied it on the son's horse. Then they all started off.

As they were camped at Rainy Mountain, it wasn't very far to the fort. Sitting Bear wouldn't let them hurry. He made them take four days for the trip, as if they were going to the Sun Dance. Every night they stopped before it was clear dark and made a big camp. There was no dancing in those night camps, but some of the men got out their drums and sang. They didn't seem to be able to sing happy songs, only sorrowful ones.

On the fifth day they came to the fort. It was spread out. There was a square where the soldiers marched back and forth, and there were stone buildings all around it. Down away to the east of the square was a stone horse corral. It was so far away there had to be special guards around it at night. That wasn't the Indian way. If you kept your horses up near camp at night, then you only needed one set of guards. But white people were careless about fighting, anyway.

Off to the south of the square there were some more stone buildings. One of them had iron bars going up the windows, like gun barrels built into the stone. It was stupid to build the stone around the barrels like that, Eagle Plume thought. It plugged them all up. They never would be good for shooting again.

The general's house was on the west side of the square where the place of honor ought to be. It had a long porch in front of it, with four steps going up from the ground. The chiefs went over and sat on the steps, while all the people filled the square and crowded the soldiers out to the edges. The general sat in a chair on the porch. Even for a chair, it was peculiar. It had curved ribs at the bottoms of the legs, and it went back and forth, back and forth. It made you sick to watch it, but the general didn't seem to mind. He must have had strong power to get used to that thing so that he could sit in it.

The talking went on for a long time. Everything had to be interpreted, and that made it take longer. Wood Fire did the interpreting. He seemed to do fairly well. They could all understand each other, but it was slow business.

War Song

The general said just one thing, over and over. He said that he knew it was their young men who had raided the white man. He knew they had taken some of the children away. He wanted the children given back to their mother, and he wanted them to give the woman presents to make up for the house and the cattle she had lost, and he wanted them to give up their young men to make up for her husband, who was killed. He kept saying those things over and over.

Big Tree and Sitting Bear answered him at first. That was what they had planned. They said their young men had gone hunting, that was all. They had no victory dance in their camp after the white man was killed. Maybe the general should talk to the Comanches or the Cheyennes. They were bad people for making trouble, especially the Comanches.

The general tried a new way of talking. He said the white men wanted to be friends with the Indians. He said they knew that the Indians had more land than they needed, and the Indians didn't want to farm it anyway. The white men knew about farming, and they needed land. They would pay the Indians for the lands that they farmed. There was enough for everybody. They could all live peacefully together. If the white men killed the Indians, they would be punished. If the Indians killed the white men, they ought to be punished, too.

That was when White Bear became angry. He got up, with his hair hanging in beaver-fur wrappings and his red and blue blanket around him, and looked at the general. The young officer who had come to their camp was standing behind the general, and White Bear looked at him, too. Then he looked all around at the soldiers, and at last he began to make a speech.

"This is our country," he told the general. "We always lived in it. We had plenty to eat, because we had the buffalo. We were happy. We got along all right with each other. When we needed horses, we raided the Utes or the Navajos; when they needed horses, they raided us. It all went back and forth. It was fair. We didn't farm the land. We left that for the women, Caddo and Wichita women. We don't need to farm. Men need to hunt.

"Then you came. First the traders. That's all right. We need blankets and kettles. Then the soldiers. That's all right. We're soldiers ourselves. We understand about fighting, just the way you do. Now these other men come. They are farmers. You saw they want to work the land.

"That's all wrong. Land doesn't work. Land doesn't want to be worked. Land gives you what you need if you're smart enough to take it. This is good land. This is our land. We know how to take what it gives us. It takes care of us.

"We don't want these people working this land. That's the way to kill it, if you try to take things out of it. When they work the land, they drive the buffalo off it. The buffalo go away. Then we haven't anything to eat. We live off the buffalo. Buffalo are smart. They know you can't work the land.

"We have to protect ourselves. We have to save our country. We have to kill off those men who are killing our land and driving the buffalo away. We don't hate them. We just have to get rid of them. That's why we have to kill them off, to save things so that we can go on living.

"Now you want to know who killed those men. Now I'll tell you. I did it! I was the one. I killed that farmer and took his children. It was all me. I did it alone!"

That was just like White Bear, thought Eagle Plume. He would get so excited listening to himself talk, he'd forget what his words meant. He said things he hadn't started out to say. It was bad this time. Now the soldiers would take him away.

Sitting Bear got up, then. He didn't want to leave any more of the talking to anybody else. White Bear sat down, looking pleased with himself; and the soldiers might have grabbed hold of him, but Sitting Bear began to talk.

"Some of what White Bear says is true," he said to the general. "Some of it is wong. We have to have our land for the buffalo. We have to have buffalo to eat, and the buffalo have to have grass to eat. We don't want white men coming in and spoiling our grass and running off our buffalo. That way makes it hard for us to live. But White Bear didn't do all that killing by himself. That's not true. Maybe he did some killing a long time ago when he was a young man. But look at him now. He's old. He couldn't do all that killing alone." You could tell that he was trying to help White Bear out, but White Bear looked as if he wished he'd do it some other way.

The general frowned down at the porch floor and asked, "Who helped him then?"

That was a hard question for Sitting Bear. He didn't want to give the young men away, because they were depending on him to save them. Too, he had just finished saying that White Bear had help and didn't do the killing alone, so White Bear was depending on him, too. It was all difficult. He just looked at the porch and shook his head. "Maybe you helped him," suggested the general.

Sitting Bear looked out and around. He looked at the soldiers around the edge of the marching-space and at the people in the middle. Then he looked especially at the horse with his son's bones tied on it. Something went out of him towards the horse, and he just shook his head as if it puzzled him. "Maybe I did help him," he said and sat down.

The general looked relieved. This was easier than it usually was to straighten things out. It would be easier to handle two old men than a dozen young ones, too. That was when Big Tree began to understand how things were going. He stood up and looked at the general, and he began to make a speech. It was a bad speech because Big Tree wasn't used to talking.

"Those two say that they're the ones that did it," he said, "that they did it all by themselves. That's not the way it was. Whatever they did, I did, too."

Well, there it was. Their three greatest men, and the three that they needed most to tell them what to do with the white men, had given themselves up for killing a white farmer and running off his cattle. It was hard to have the whole tribe suffer for just one white farmer. White men were worth a whole lot when it took three chiefs to pay for killing one of them.

Eagle Plume knew what his father wanted him to do. There was one thing his father wanted, and it was up to him to do it. He was standing near the east edge of the crowd and the soldiers were moving up to the west, getting ready to grab the three chiefs. Eagle Plume got hold of the bridles of two horses. One of them was the one with the Grandmother bundle on it, and the other was the one with his brother's bones. He knew that his father would want those two things taken care of. He wanted to look back and see that his father saw him, but he knew he didn't need to, for his father would know. So he went on. He drew the horses out and away, and they went quietly with him, down to the east towards the horse corral. He walked ahead of the horses, leading them, so that they would hide him from the soldiers and that they would think they saw nothing but two horses going off.

Everybody was looking the other way, anyhow, looking at Sitting Bear. He stood up and threw his arms out wide, like White Bear, and began to sing. He was singing his Crazy Dog song, the one he sang before his son was killed.

I live, but I will not live forever.
Mysterious moon, you only remain,
Powerful sun, you alone remain,
Wonderful earth, you remain forever.

The Ten Grandmothers

It sounded wild there on that porch in front of the general, and it scared the general and the soldiers. The general lifted his hand, and the soldiers came out of the windows of the house and grabbed hold of Sitting Bear and hung on to him. Others came up and grabbed White Bear and Big Tree. The soldiers took all their weapons away from them, and they took even their war bonnets. They were left with just one feather to the three of them, and it was the crow's wing-feather, that went with the Eagle Shield medicine, which Sitting Bear had braided into his scalp lock.

Eagle Plume camped alone on Medicine Creek that night. He didn't want to go clear away, even to take care of his brother's bones and the Grandmother, but he didn't dare stay too close. All the other people had scattered when the three chiefs were taken, but some of them had been slow, and they had been rounded up and kept in the marching-place. He could see their campfires shining down there. The people who had got away didn't dare light campfires. If they did, the soldiers would find them, or the rain that was beginning to fall would put them out. The fires wouldn't do them much good.

Eagle Plume sat between the two horses and wondered what was going to happen. Everything had been quiet after the three chiefs were taken. Just the women crying and mourning—that was all you could hear. That carried a long way. But there weren't any other sounds.

Towards morning Wood Fire found him. Wood Fire had bread and Eagle Plume had dried meat, and they sat with their blankets around them and ate together.

Wood Fire said, "You must have been in a hurry."

"I was," Eagle Plume said.

"You left a trail a white man could follow," said Wood Fire.

"I was in a hurry," Eagle Plume told him. "There are lots of trails, anyway. They'll have to follow all of them, before they get through."

Wood Fire sat doubled up in his blanket and let the rain hit him.

"Things are bad down there at the fort," he said. "Nobody hurt yet. The general wants to keep everybody together, but they're trying to get out. They want to get away to the Staked Plains and hide out. That's the way they're going to get hurt, running away from the soldiers. The soldiers are going to hurt somebody, chasing after them."

"That's bad, all right," said Eagle Plume.

"They won't shoot those three chiefs," Wood Fire went on. "They don't want to do that here. They want to take them down to Texas to kill them. That's where most of the raiding was done. They want to hang them, when they get them down there."

War Song

Eagle Plume watched the horses. "They oughtn't to do that. They have no right to hang them. A man ought to be shot, if he's going to be killed."

"That's what your father thinks. He thinks a man ought to be shot. He ought to die fighting. If they don't hang them, they're going to lock them up. Keep them in a house until they die."

"They won't have to keep them long. They'll die quick in a house."

"They had them in a house last night. In that house with the guns on the windows, down under the floor in little rooms. White Bear was talking all night. Making his boast about what he was going to do to the soldiers when he got out. Your father didn't say anything."

"My father would be thinking."

"That's what he was doing. Along towards morning he called me. He told me to find you, to tell you they were taking him away. He wasn't going to go. He said, 'Tell my brave son I won't go with them. I won't go further than the pecan tree by the road south of the fort. Tell him to take care of those sacred things for me.'"

Eagle Plume still sat still. "Did my brother's mother get away?"

"She's with the group headed west. She'll get out on the Staked Plains all right."

"I have some of those sacred things here."

"She took some of them with her. Those Eagle Shield things, she took those."

Eagle Plume stood up, "My father was wearing the feather that went with those things. She must have the other things."

"After your father sent me to find you, he swallowed that feather. If he uses his power right, that'll make it turn into a knife."

Eagle Plume looked at Wood Fire's horse. "That's a good horse you have there."

"I have another tied down by the creek in the willows."

"You can get away on that horse that's tied."

"Yes."

"You give me this horse. You go on that horse that's tied. Take these two horses and the things on them to my brother's mother. Tell her I'll come along as soon as I can. I want to say good-bye to my father."

Wood Fire gave him the lines of the saddled horse and took the other two. He led them away towards the willows, but Eagle Plume didn't wait to see what he did. He got on the saddled horse and started out towards the fort.

The ground was broken and rocky, with plenty of cover. He worked his way to the ridge that ran east of the fort, and then followed it along south, keeping just under the edge of the ridge out of sight. He didn't see anybody, but he could hear the Kiowas even through the noise of the rain. Worried sounds, they were making, like mourning when they didn't dare to wail and cry. Hurried sounds, like trying to break camp and get away and not let anybody know, but in too much rush to cover all the noise up. Bad sounds, all of them. They pressed against his heart as if they would go clear through.

When he was about level with the fort, the ground began to flatten out. He tied his horse among some rocks. The soldiers might look for it in the trees by the creek bank, but they wouldn't think to look here. Then he went forward on foot. There was a rise behind the one big pecan tree, and he lay flat there, waiting.

Wagons were coming along the road from the fort, now. He could hear the iron shoes of the horses strike the road, and the creaking of the harness made out of stiff leather. The canvas sides of the wagons were down, because he could hear the cloth slapping the wooden frames. The soldiers were talking and smoking. None of them seemed to be in a big hurry. The rain was easing, and soon it would stop.

When the wagons were even with him, he could see them. There were guards on horseback around them, and the men sitting on the drivers' seats had guns. There were more guards in the backs of the wagons. Two wagons and twelve soldiers to take three old men to prison. It looked as if they were afraid of those old men, or wanted to do them honor.

When the wagons were almost past him, Eagle Plume saw his father in the back of the first wagon. He saw his father raise his hand towards his mouth and cough. There were chains holding his hands together, but when he coughed, Sitting Bear managed to get the chains off. His hands were too small to be held by chains that would hold other men's hands. When he coughed the fourth time, there was a knife in his hand. It must have been that Eagle Shield knife.

Sitting Bear began to sing. His voice was loud and clear and happy, like a young man's, just starting out.

"Get ready, my son," he sang, "Fill your pipe for we shall smoke together today. Make room for me. I am coming."

> *I live, but I will not live forever.*
> *Mysterious moon, you only remain,*
> *Powerful sun, you alone remain,*
> *Wonderful earth, you remain forever.*

Then he stabbed the guard beside him. The man went backwards over the tail-board of the wagon, and as he fell, his gun went off.

War Song

White Bear and Big Tree, in the second wagon, had heard the song start, and now they started singing it too, as if they had the right. Only singing the song didn't do them much good, because they didn't belong to the Eagle Shields and didn't have any magic knives.

The wagons had stopped and the soldiers were piling up around the one with Sitting Bear in it. They took him out and laid him on the ground under the pecan tree. The bullet from the soldier's gun had hit him, and he was going to die, but he was still singing his song; still talking to his dead son.

Eagle Plume got away without anybody seeing him. He got Wood Fire's horse and started out. There was no use trying to follow any one trail. He'd just have to find his brother's mother when he got out on the Staked Plains. Then he could tell her about it, and they could do what Sitting Bear would want them to.

Things That Die

*The Year the Three Chiefs Were
Captured (1871)*

THEY WENT OUT ON THE STAKED PLAINS LIKE COTTONWOOD leaves running ahead of a high wind. There was no time to choose what to take or what to leave behind, and as a result some of them took funny things, things that they didn't need. Afterwards everybody laughed at Bow Woman because she had taken three brass cooking-buckets and had forgotten to bring anything to cook.

Many of them did things like that, though, because there just wasn't time to go back to the camps and get the packs of food, and they had to leave things lying around on the ground behind them. It was bad, because the Staked Plains were a poor place for hunting at any time. Once or twice a year you might get buffalo there, and sometimes there were antelope, but that was about all.

Summer ended on the day Sitting Bear died. It was raining then and it kept on raining. It was a cold rain, and everybody was wet and cold and starving. It was a bad time for the whole tribe, and it was made worse by families' getting split up and separated, and even men who had been good hunters for years never did find their children. Some families were broken up for good.

Eagle Plume had ridden for two days on the ragged, loose trail that the people had left before he found Wood Fire. Then he found him with what remained of Sitting Bear's family, with his brother's mother cooking food for him. Wood Fire looked comfortable and easy.

"Get down, brother," he said.

Eagle Plume got down and came and lay on the ground in the rain. There was no tipi, just a cover spread over some brushes. His own mother was in the shelter, and when she saw him, came out with a bowl of wild plums in her hand. That was all she had to give him. His brother's mother took some of the meat away from Wood Fire and gave it to him. Nobody said anything.

When he had eaten, he told them, "My father is dead," and waited for the women to start wailing. But too much had happened to them. One more grief, even as big as this grief was, couldn't get near enough to hurt them.

126

Things That Die

Wood Fire said, "Tell," and Eagle Plume told.

"They took him back to the fort to bury, I guess," said Wood Fire when he had heard, and Eagle Plume said, "That's what they must have done."

His brother's mother said, "There is the end of the old life and the old ways," and Eagle Plume's mother said, "There is the end of the Kiowa tribe."

Wood Fire just sat and looked at the little smoky flame under the arbor, and said nothing. Eagle Plume turned his head and looked out of the door. In the slow, long dusk that came through the rain he could see his brother's horse grazing out there, with his brother's bones on its back.

"I think it is just the end of my father and his ways of doing," he said. "The tribe is still going on and living is still going on. Those things don't end because one man ends, even a big man. But that one man's ways end with him."

When it is dark, the owls fly, and they can twist a man's face and mark him for life. This time Eagle Plume wasn't thinking about owls. He got up, went out, and took the bridle of his brother's horse. His brother's mother came behind him.

"What are you doing?" she said. "What are you going to do?"

"This is the ending of my father and his ways," said Eagle Plume. "He was a good man, most ways. But there was this one thing that he did that everybody was afraid of. There was this one thing that nobody liked. My brother has been dead a long time. He was buried once. Now I'm going to bury him again."

Wood Fire came behind him, and stood beside his brother's mother. "There is something else you ought to bury," he said, "your father's shield."

Eagle Plume had the bridle in his hand and the horse was following as if it knew he was doing the right thing. "You have been calling me brother," Eagle Plume said to Wood Fire. "If you are really my brother, now is the time to help me. You can bring that shield."

The shield and the war bonnet and the things that went with them were all on another horse. Nothing had been unloaded and Eagle Plume wondered why.

"We were afraid to take things off the horses," his mother explained. "It's not right, just two women and a stranger taking those things off the horses."

Wood Fire brought the other horses up, and they started walking east through the rain, leading the horses. Neither of them said much. They just went along putting one foot out and then the other foot out, until they found they were going up a rise. When they reached the top of it, Eagle Plume stopped.

"This is a good place," he said.

Wood Fire held the horses, and Eagle Plume began to dig a hole. He made it good and deep, and there were plenty of rocks around so that there was no danger of the coyotes' digging up what they buried. First they laid his brother's bones tied up in the red and blue blanket in the grave. Then Eagle Plume filled the hole with dirt and piled rocks on it.

After that he dug another hole, to bury the shield, the shield and all the things that went with it—red paint and yellow paint and black paint and white paint. The yellow buckskin dancing suit and the long spear with feathers and fur tied on it had been left at the fort or he would have buried them, too. The war bonnet with its painted buckskin case was there also. All those things Eagle Plume should have put into that hole.

"It's like burying a man," he said, "when the man isn't here to bury."

After he had filled both holes and piled rocks on them, he took the bridle of his brother's horse. It was dark, now, and he couldn't see to shoot, but he led the horse by the grave, so that it stood over it. The horse was very quiet, as if it still thought he was doing the right thing, not panicky and frightened the way horses usually were when they knew they were going to die. This horse just stood still when he cut its throat and kind of folded together when the blood ran.

He went over to the other horse. Wood Fire was still holding it. "That's wrong, brother," he said. "You'd better not kill this horse. Your mother or someone else may need it. It's a good horse."

If things had been different Eagle Plume would have been angry, but his life had no room for anger left in it. "That was my father's saddle horse," he said. "It ought to be killed where he was buried. The things that mattered most about him are buried here. I've got to kill that horse."

"This is a good horse," said Wood Fire stubbornly. "People will need good horses."

"This is what my father would want," said Eagle Plume, and he reached out and gashed the horse's throat. It died as silently as the other one. The men turned and started back to the camp of the two women. There was fire waiting for them there.

When they sat by the fire again, Wood Fire spoke. "That is the end of one kind of living," he said. "I think all the old things will be dead soon."

Things That Die

Eagle Plume had found two sticks and was holding them out towards the fire, one in each hand, to dry them. "I think the old things won't die so easy," he answered. "I think there are still some people left who love them and think they are right."

Wood Fire said, "There are always some people who hang on to the things that should be buried, just because they can't stand to give them up. That's the way some people are."

"There are some people who know they have to keep things alive for the other people," Eagle Plume told him. "Some people have the right to keep the old things going."

"Well," said Wood Fire, "some people have the right to get new things started."

Eagle Plume wondered how many years he had lived. He felt as if he were older than the earth and still had only begun breathing. All ahead of him he felt years coming when he would try to keep old things alive and try to tell other people why he did it. Now it was beginning.

"You have to have new things," he said. "You have to have new springs to make the grass grow. But grass grows out of the old earth. You have to have old things for new things to have roots in. That's why some people have to keep old things going and some people have to push new things along. It's right for both of them. It's what they have to do."

"I think I'll go back to the fort in the morning," Wood Fire said.

Sitting Bear's first wife spoke from the dark back of the arbor. "Don't go," she begged him. "We need you. We two women would have starved to death without you to hunt for us these past days."

Wood Fire shook his head. "I think I'll go back," he told her. "My brother is here to hunt for you."

"That's all right," said Eagle Plume, "If there's anything to hunt, I'll hunt it."

"Why does he want to go back?" asked Sitting Bear's first wife. He's a good young man. He's smart. He's a good hunter. We need young men like that now. The whole tribe needs them."

"He's too smart to stay," said Eagle Plume. "He's got to go because he's so smart. He's the only man we have that can speak white man's language. After a while, when they get tired of chasing, they'll have to send someone to make peace. That's when they'll need a man with two tongues. We'll need him, too."

"That's right," said Wood Fire. "That's what I was thinking."

Wood Fire rode off the next morning. They gave him what little food they had to take with him, dried plums and some meat. The meat wouldn't keep in that wet weather, but it might last him through the day. Then they went on in the rain that kept slanting down like the grey stone knives that the Grandmothers' keepers had.

They went on for a long time. Eagle Plume cut a hole in a stick for each day after he had caught up with his mothers, and there were seven sevens of them before he stopped. After that he let time run on into years and the years beat down on his head like the rain. He had been in the Staked Plains before, but never when it was raining and cold, and he had thought that it must always be sunshiny there, with heat that pulled the juices right out of you.

Now he saw it differently. The grey-white clay packed on their moccasins and made hard balls around the horses' hooves, so that they had to stop to cut it off. When they had been going four days, they had to throw their moccasins away because they were stiff and dried out with the grey-white clay and no good. They found no place to stay in all that time. The rain came down and down, and the only good thing about it was that one family and then another family drifted together until they were all in one herd in the rain just like buffalo.

Eagle Plume tried to keep them with their noses turned down wind, like buffalo, too, but that was harder, and it was all anyone could do to keep them together. There were two Crazy Dogs with them and they worked like buffalo-hunt police, keeping the people all herded together and going one way. Most of the time they went west, but then they turned and went south. The hardest task was to keep from going east, back to their old homes.

It was when they had come to feel as if they lived in this bad country that they saw people coming—soldiers, riding with an Indian. They rode up with a white flag tied to the end of a stick, and the two Crazy Dogs rode out to meet them.

They talked for a long time. The soldiers wanted them to come in. They could come back and live in their old homes, and the white people would pay them money to let them live there, too. The white people would teach them how to farm and get a living out of the ground when the buffalo were all gone. They would all live together in the old country.

The Crazy Dogs and the soldiers talked a long time. Then the Crazy Dogs came back and reported. "Wood Fire was interpreting," one of them said. "He talks good. Both languages. I think he told us what they said, all right."

The people thought it all over and talked it all over. There was no food left for them in the Staked Plains. All the flats were flooded and the high ground hidden. Winter was there and was getting strong. They were all whipped out. They thought they would go back. The soldiers said they would take care of the people until the herds were built up and they could look out for themselves.

It took them a long time to go back. They didn't try to make the journey shorter. They wanted to see their home, but they were afraid to look at it. Eagle Plume wondered why. Rocks and trees and creeks didn't change. None of those things could grow different; they weren't like people's hearts.

Then he knew. The people's hearts had changed, and that would change their eyes, not the objects the eyes saw, but the way they looked at those things. All the eyes would look with grey, now, and without color. It was strange, but it was true, as his own eyes showed when they came to End of the Mountains. All the rocks that had stood so red, like blood that had poured from the top of the earth and run down, were grey-bare now. They were turning brown under his eyes.

Arrowhead River was the same way. There used to be breaks in it and ripples that shone back the sun. Now it was running bankfull, and there was just a flat, even, grey-brown scum over its whole surface.

Wood Fire rode with Eagle Plume. He would have talked if he could have reached Eagle Plume's mind, but that was so far away he couldn't come near it. Eagle Plume had not sent his mind away out of reach, but it had gone, and he hadn't tried to hold it. He didn't want even its edges touched by another man's mind until he knew what he was going to do himself.

It was late in the evening when they came into the fort. There were lights in the windows up on the hill. They could see them from where they stopped at the horse corral. The lights looked warm and good. It would be good to have a real fire again.

A soldier was opening the gate of the stone corral, and Eagle Plume sat quietly on his horse, waiting for the pack animals to be driven in. But they were not going. An officer called to Wood Fire and said something to him. Then Wood Fire spoke to the people in Kiowa.

"This is where you're going to stay," he said. "All of you are to go in here. Let the soldiers take your horses. They'll take care of them."

There was a murmuring and a crying among the people. They didn't understand. Wood Fire's words were Kiowa, but his voice had changed. His whole way of speaking was different. Eagle Plume rode up to him.

"Do they want us to go in there?" he asked.

"That's it," said Wood Fire. "You speak to them. You tell them what they have to do."

Eagle Plume turned and spoke to them. The Crazy Dogs should have been giving the orders but they didn't seem to understand either.

"This is where we get down," Eagle Plume told them. "This is where we are stopping. We are going into this horse corral. This is the end of our trail."

The people were too tired to be angry. They got down off the horses and went into the corral. The soldiers let them carry in their little things that they had left, and then led all the horses away. After a while the soldiers opened the door of the corral and drove in two beeves. "Those are for you to slaughter," the officer said through Wood Fire.

Everybody got a little meat when the Crazy Dogs had killed the cattle and divided them. There was a little wood and some straw, and they made fires and cooked the meat on live coals. Then they lay in their blankets and slept.

Eagle Plume wasn't sleeping. His mind was awake even though his body was still. Wood Fire opened the corral gate and came and sat beside him.

"What will they do with us?" Eagle Plume asked.

"Keep you here through the winter; then in the spring let you go out and start to work. They are going to send farmers, then, to teach you."

"They think we will learn farming and will live quietly like Caddoes."

"I think we can learn farming," Wood Fire said. His Kiowa was funny-thick. "I think if we want to, we can learn a lot of things from the white men."

"Those who want to can," said Eagle Plume. "Not everybody wants to."

"Those who don't learn will starve."

"I think they won't starve. I think there will be other ways of living than farming. If the white men pay for using the land, we can live off that. But I think starving is better than those two ways of living."

"I have a farm started," said Wood Fire. "I'm going to take your brother's mother there in the spring."

"That's good," said Eagle Plume.

"What are you going to do?"

Then he knew the answers to all the questions. He knew what he was going to do. He let his mind come back where it could touch

Wood Fire's. "My father left me that Grandmother bundle," he said. "That's what I've got to do. I've got to take care of it. That bundle has power. As long as I take care of it, it's going to take care of me. I'll keep on living and taking care of it until my ribs fall in from old age. That's what my father told me to do."

When he looked around, Wood Fire had gone away as if he were afraid.

Shut Inside

Horse Corral Winter (1874–75)

THEY WENT TO TEXAS FAST, AND CAME BACK SLOWLY. THERE was nothing to come for, and the soldiers were driving them. Things made them hold back and be afraid to come.

Going, they had noticed nothing of the country. Rain and mist had shut it from them most of the time; they had traveled much at night, and it was country they knew too well to need to see. Coming back was different. Now every bit of it was important, and they looked at it all and remembered shapes they could not be sure they had seen before.

All of the trees were bare, and you could see the shapes cutting across the shapes of the earth. With the leaves gone, you might have thought the trees would be all one color, but they weren't. The bark of the willows was green and that of the cottonwoods grey; and that of the scrub oaks had a red-brown look. It all seemed important now, as important as the blue of the sky and the red of the earth and the greeny-brown of the grass they trod.

When they came to Fort Sill, they expected that the soldiers would let them camp along Medicine Creek. That was not the way it was planned, though. Kicking Bird and his band had been there all the time, and they were camping; but as the rest had run away, the soldiers had to make sure of them. They shut those people up in a horse corral and counted them every day.

The corral was made of rough stone, not shaped or trimmed, but just picked up on the sides of the hills and along the creeks. It was rough and yellow-looking. It was square, and all around the walls inside there went a sort of roof that stuck out from the walls and left an open space in the center. The roof had been built to take care of sick horses and foaling mares, and now it could take care of the women and children. There was no room to put up shelters of any kind in the center.

That was a long winter and a hard winter. The Kiowas could see the sky and the sun above them, and there were square holes cut in the corral walls where you could look out if you were tall enough, but that was all there was of the outside. When they had been counted, cattle were driven in to them. Since there was only the open place in the center of the corral for butchering, and no place to dry the meat or even to build real cooking fires, most of the time they ate what they had raw. The beef was tough and stringy and tasteless, and they grew tired of it. The children would sit and cry sometimes for good buffalo meat.

With nobody going hunting and bringing in new hides to be worked, their clothes became shabby. Their moccasins wore out and just dropped off their feet. They could go down to the well, one family at a time, and bring back water for drinking, but they never seemed to have enough for washing. What with the dirt and the butchering right there where they were living and the smell of the beef getting into their systems, everybody in the corral smelled strong before very long.

That was the winter that Spear Woman felt that she really got to know Hunting Horse. They had been married eight years, and he and Bow Woman had been married seven, and they had all been happy together; but it had been a young kind of happiness. It seemed to go on and on around them; they felt while it was happening that it always would. Now it had gone clear to pieces, with no happiness left in the world anywhere. Shut up inside the corral walls, Spear Woman began to find out that Hunting Horse wasn't just a young man out hunting for his horses. He had wisdom and power, like an old horse that had been on many hunts and knew what to do which-ever way the buffalo turned. She began to know that, whatever happened, she could lean on him if she had to.

There wasn't much for anybody to do. There was nothing to work with, and without work, the people hardly knew how to fill the time. Spear Woman got hold of some of the cow-skins, when the beeves were butchered, and went to work to tan them. They all needed clothes, and tanning was something to do. She had no brains, and there was just a little tallow on those lean beeves, so tanning was hard work. Some of the other women tried it, too, but it was so hard most of them gave up. Finally just Spear Woman kept on.

She needed hides, a lot of hides, because Bow Woman was going to have a baby soon, and they needed a way to take care of it. It was up to Spear Woman to get things done, because the traveling to the Staked Plains and the coming back had worn Bow Woman down until sometimes they wondered if she could live through having the baby. They all watched over her and took the best care of her they could. That was where Hunting Horse was so good. He cooked every bit of meat for her, even when he had to sneak logs out of the uprights holding the shed roof to get fuel for a fire.

Spear Woman left that part up to him. She was busy herself with other things. Babies had to have soft hides to be dressed and wrapped in, so as soon as she got enough cow-skins tanned to make dresses, she and Bow Woman took off their buckskin clothes and saved them to make things for the baby. Their cow-skin dresses looked funny and felt worse, and they smelled stronger than any other clothes, but they were covering and could be got used to.

With the next cowhide Spear Woman got, she started making the baby's cradle. She had had to leave her own cradle, that her mother had made, behind when they ran away. Making the new cradle caused her to think of her mother. That made her cry, because she thought that her mother must be out with the band that hadn't come in yet. She hoped her mother was with that band and was alive.

If she could have got hold of what she wanted, she would have had a bois d'arc frame for the cradle. Bois d'arc was the hardest wood, and it never cracked or splintered. You could shave it down to thin boards with a knife, and then point one end of the boards and round off the other end. In that way, if the cradle with the baby in it slipped and fell, the points at his head would stick into the ground, or the rounded ends at his feet would roll, and the baby would not be hurt.

It was the same way with the hood over the baby's face. It was deep and rounded on top, so that no matter what position the baby was in, he would be safe. The cradle should be big enough to stick out all around him and hold him, so that whether his mother were riding or walking, or laid him down or hung him up, nothing could get to him to hurt him.

That was the way a cradle should be, safe and solid. But it took a long time to get all the right things together to make one like that, and you had to have the right things. Nobody ever tried to make a cradle without them.

Spear Woman was so worried about making the cradle that she talked it over with Hunting Horse. Most men wouldn't have been interested, but right then he was glad of anything to talk about.

"Why don't you make just a rawhide tube, like the Comanches put their babies in at night?" he asked.

That didn't seem right to Spear Woman. "That's Comanche way, not Kiowa," she said. "This is a Kiowa baby, and I want him to have a Kiowa cradle. It has to look right."

Hunting Horse went over where her three cow-skin rawhides

were stacked and looked at them. "These sure are stiff and hard," he said. "That part down the center of the back is just like a board."

"I couldn't help it," said Spear Woman. She thought he was making fun of her tanning. "I didn't have any tools to scrape them down with, just my knife. I got the meat off and the hair off, and that's all. They aren't even all over, the way they ought to be."

"Well," said Hunting Horse, "looks to me like that's a good thing. Why don't you cut out the middle part down the backs and use it like boards?"

That was something that Spear Woman never would have thought of, but it was the right thing to do. She took the biggest hide, and went to work cutting. Her knife had become dull with being used for everything she did, and the cutting was slow work. When she began to give out, Hunting Horse got his knife and began to help her.

"I don't know why I give out this way," said Spear Woman. "I never used to."

"You aren't getting enough to eat," Hunting Horse answered. "None of us are, but you've been giving most of yours to Bow Woman." He didn't say that he'd been giving most of his to Bow Woman, too. He just went on cutting.

They worked together on the cradle from that time on. Making it was slow, because they had to do everything with their knives, and the knives kept getting duller and duller. But they cut out the cradle boards and the hood and the cover, and they even cut rawhide strings to tie everything together. That was when Spear Woman began to worry about what to use for lining the cradle. The baby had to have something soft to lie on.

Wood Smoke was outside all the time that they were in the corral. He wasn't even staying in Kicking Bird's camp, but was up on top of the hill with the soldiers. When the soldiers came down to do the counting, he came with them, as interpreter. It didn't seem right, having him live with soldiers when most of the tribe were shut up; but it wasn't as if he had any close family to be shut up with, and it didn't matter if he felt different about the situation. Nobody was angry with him for it, but all thought he was lucky to be outside and going around all the time.

It was Hunting Horse who thought about getting Wood Smoke to help them. The next time the officers came for the counting, Hunting Horse waited until it was over, and then he spoke to Wood Smoke. He told him what they needed, and Wood Smoke promised to go to Kicking Bird's camp to see if anybody there would help them out.

Four days later he came back with some little rabbit hides. They had been tanned soft and were all fluffy. They were the best things a baby could have to lie on, better than Spear Woman had had for her own first baby. Thinking about her first baby made her cry again, because wherever her mother was, the boy was with her. In a way Spear Woman was glad he was not here. She hated to think about his being shut inside walls without enough to eat. Many children had died here already. It would be better for him to die outdoors if he weren't going to live.

She put the thought of her own child away from her and kept on thinking and planning for Bow Woman's. That was the baby who was coming soon and that was the baby who was important right now. She wasn't sure just when the baby would come, but it would be soon, and she wanted to be ready for it.

When she and Hunting Horse finished the cradle, they sat and looked at it, and it leaned against the wall and looked back at them. It was so funny, like a solid, solemn, little old man, that they both began to laugh at it. They laughed and laughed, and the cradle just stood there and looked back at them and shamed them for laughing at it.

"He needs earrings," said Hunting Horse, and he took off his long, silver, crawdad earrings and tied them, one on each side of the cradle face.

"Ornaments ought to go on top," said Spear Woman, when she could get her breath back.

"That's just on ordinary cradles," said Hunting Horse. "This cradle is different. This is an old-man cradle, and he needs old-man earrings."

When they showed the cradle to Bow Woman, she was happy because they had made it for her baby, but she didn't seem to think it was funny. When she saw Hunting Horse's earrings tied on to ornament it, she began to cry. She cried and cried and couldn't stop, and when she was crying, they knew that the baby was coming. They had finished just in time.

Most times men would have gone away and stayed away when a baby was getting born, and that was what Hunting Horse had done when Spear Woman's babies had come. This time there was no place for him to go. There were plenty of women who had come in and were shut up with them, but everybody was so crowded that it was hard for many people to get around to help Bow Woman. Spear Woman had to do most of it herself. She kept Hunting Horse busy all night, borrowing wood and heating water and carrying things for her.

Shut Inside

That baby was slow getting itself born. There wasn't much they could do to help. They took rocks from the floor of the shed, heated them, and put them in Bow Woman's lap and behind her back, to make the pain easier. They gave her hot water and weak soup to drink, to make it easier for her inside. Most of the time they kept her lying down on her side, but sometimes when the pains were getting harder, Spear Woman would let her get up and walk around. The only place for walking was around their campfire, and finally Bow Woman got so dizzy she nearly fell in. Then they made her stretch out on her side again, and kept her that way until the baby began to show. Then Spear Woman let her kneel up, and knelt behind her, to catch the baby. Even after it was there, lying on a piece of rawhide near the fire, they were too busy waiting for the after-birth to know more about the baby than that it was alive.

Getting rid of the after-birth was hard. You had to bury it deep, where coyotes wouldn't get it, and you ought to bury it away from people, so that there would be no danger that anybody would dig it up. Things were safe from coyotes, inside these walls, but there was no place for anything to be away from people. Spear Woman left Hunting Horse with Bow Woman and went away herself and buried the after-birth by the gate. That was one place where the Indians weren't likely to be walking on it, and it didn't matter about the white soldiers. She didn't care if bad luck hit them.

When she returned, she bathed and dressed the baby and put it in its cradle, with the long, old-man earrings hanging down on each side of its face. Then she called Hunting Horse away from Bow Woman.

"Come here!" she said. "Come here and look at your daughter with her fine silver earrings." And when Hunting Horse looked at the baby's little, solemn face, as serious as the face of the cradle, they both began to laugh all over again. That was one good thing, they always did have a lot of things to laugh at together, just the two of them.

From that time on, they had plenty to do. Bow Woman stayed lying down for eight days, and then she got up and helped take care of the baby. Other women in camp were having babies, and Spear Woman had done so well in taking care of Bow Woman that the others began to send for her to help them.

Some of the men teased Hunting Horse and wanted him to show them how to make cradles, but he didn't seem to mind. He just told them he'd like to see the first cradle one of them made, if he had to make it all alone, and went on helping to keep up the fire and get the meat cooked. Some of the other men had managed to get some bones and had carved and polished them, and made a hand-game set. They sat around most of the time, gambling for what little meat they had, but Hunting Horse never joined them in that.

They all felt better and more like doing things. Partly that was the spring coming. There were no trees close to the corral, but on the east side, when you looked through the holes in the wall, you could see down to Cache Creek. First there was the littlest haze of green along the branches, as if the morning mist had risen and changed its color. Then in the bends of the creek there you saw a little purply mist on some branches and the beginning of white on others. It went on for a long time, with the green and the white getting clearer and the purple getting pinker every day, and then you could know the colors and see that the redbud and the wild plum were flowering beside each other. It made everyone feel livelier just to get little peeks at the trees, and one day the people heard a sliver of sound and knew it was a meadow lark. They knew then that no matter what happened to them, they would live.

The last band came in four days after they had heard the meadow lark, and when all the people were there and could be rounded up and counted, the soldiers changed their plan of treatment, and let them all go out and camp along the creek in a place away from Kicking Bird's camp. Partly the soldiers didn't want any fighting with the people in Kicking Bird's camp, and partly they wanted the others where they could get at them and count them whenever they thought it necessary.

Spear Woman had hated being counted all winter. It was the worst part of all, the feeling that you were somebody's property and could be counted like a cow. But now she forgot all about it and didn't mind. She even forgot about all the old people who had died during the winter. That was because her mother was one of the old people who had lived. She had come through that winter, and she had brought Spear Woman's children with her. It had been hard, and the children hadn't grown much, but they were alive and that was what counted.

When she had her own babies back, Spear Woman turned Bow Woman and the girl baby over to her mother. She sat down alone in a patch of sunshine, and Hunting Horse came to sit beside her. They just sat there, and took turns holding their littlest baby.

Hunting Horse looked at this son and felt proud. It was a good thing having sons.

"Now that he has a little sister," he said, "we got to think about naming him. He hasn't even had his ears pierced yet. Those are two things we've got to do right away."

Shut Inside

"Just as soon as we get out," said Spear Woman.

"I've been thinking about getting him a name," Hunting Horse went on. "I always wanted to give away four horses when my son was named. But now we haven't any horses."

"You can give people sticks," Spear Woman reminded him. "That shows they're going to get horses."

"That's what we'll have to do," said Hunting Horse. "And another thing, I always wanted Sitting Bear to name my son so that he could give him a strong war name. But Sitting Bear is dead now, and all the names he could give are dead too."

"Maybe our son won't need a war name," said Spear Woman. "It looks to me as if the wars are as dead as the war names. I guess you'd better pick out a peace name for him."

"That's right," said Hunting Horse. "If we get out of here, I'll pick out a peace name and get Kicking Bird to give it to him. He's a peace man."

"Lots of people are blaming him for being shut up here," Spear Woman reminded him. "They aren't going to like it much if you ask him to give the baby a peace name."

"They don't have to like it," was all Hunting Horse said. "If that's the sort of name my son needs to live with from now on, that's the sort of name I think he'd better have. That's the way it's going to be. People won't have much time for hating when we get out, anyway. They've got to get to work making themselves some kind of a life."

Hanging the Red Blanket

The Year of the Power Contest
(1881–82)

I

IT WASN'T SO MUCH HAVING THE SOLDIERS COME THAT changed things, Spear Woman thought, as having the buffalo go. They went all at once, as if a norther had swept them from the prairies, and the story of the Comanche woman who said she saw them going into a hole on the north slope of Mount Scott almost seemed as if it might be true.

When the buffalo were gone, life seemed to have gone with them. It was hard to get anything to eat, for the deer had been killed and driven off long ago. There were no hides to make tipis, and the old ones got smoke-stained and ragged. Even the grass was changing, for the east winds were blowing in new, different seed that made stronger roots than the old grass had. This new grass was short and coarse and had an all-over dull color, like a dun horse. There was no sheen to it anywhere.

People still camped together along the streams and near the springs, but water was harder to get than it used to be. Instead of going dry for just a little while in the very hottest weather, springs and creeks dried up in early summer and stayed that way until the fall rains. Then the rains came with such a rush that the new short grass couldn't hold the water back, and the run-off began to cut slits in the downhill slopes, like knives gashing into meat.

Whatever you started to think about, though, you always came back to one thing—food. Water and grass and color were important for happy living, but food was important for any kind of living at all. You couldn't keep the children well and happy with just scraps of deer meat or beef that the men had gone down into Texas to kill. It was hard on Spear Woman's mother, too. Old people missed the things they were used to. It seemed as if there never would be any way to get them what they wanted and needed.

Spear Woman stopped trying to work for a moment, to listen to her mother, telling stories to the children under the brush arbor. Old, old stories. Spear Woman had heard them all her life. She knew them

142

the way she knew her own name. But it was strange telling, just the same. Even when she had been growing up, nobody would ever have told Trickster stories in the daytime. But that was what her mother was doing; she was telling the story of how Trickster stole the buffalo from White Crow and brought them up out of the earth to be food for the people.

The children were taking it all in. They loved the story. Next to eating food, little ones liked hearing about it. When the story ended, Spear Woman looked over at her mother and laughed. "Na-na-na-na! Trickster will come and cut your nose off, telling stories about him in the daytime!"

Her mother answered, "There's not much old life left. Trickster would want the children to hear about it while there's still somebody to tell."

She came across to watch what her daughter was doing, and when she saw, her face changed and went hard all over. "You are drying meat, daughter?"

"Yes, mother, I am drying meat."

"What kind of meat is it, daughter?"

Her mother knew already what kind of meat it was. She could see. It was mean to make Spear Woman say, but she said it, "Jack-rabbit meat, mother."

"That isn't fit for people to eat, daughter. Nobody but coyotes and Comanches would eat jackrabbit meat."

"When it is winter and you and my children are hungry, then I will be glad to feed you as if you were all Comanches."

Her mother's face stayed hard, but tears came out of her eyes and ran down over it and made shiny spots at the corners of her mouth. "You are a good daughter. Where is your sister?"

"She has gone with our husband, to fix any meat he kills."

"I hope they both work hard!"

Eagle Plume was coming across the camp towards them. He sat down and watched Spear Woman working with the jackrabbit meat. He knew what it was, too, but he didn't say. Things were hard for Eagle Plume these days, too. His father and his brother were both dead, and his wife had gone blind just after her baby was born. Then he had the Grandmother to look after, now that he was the only man left at home in his family, and that made a great deal of work. Having the Grandmother bundle and a blind wife kept him close. It wasn't often that he could even walk across the camp to another tipi to visit.

"It's a hot day, cousin," he said.

"Yes," said Spear Woman. She was ashamed of the jackrabbit

meat, but she didn't try to hide it. After all, there was no disgrace in trying to feed your family something, whatever it was.

"This time of year, we should be getting ready for the Sun Dance."

Spear Woman stopped, with the knife in her hand. She had forgotten about the Sun Dance. That used to be the one thing that they built the year around, and she had forgotten all about it. "Three years, cousin, since we had a Sun Dance," she said.

"That's right," said Eagle Plume, "three years."

"Where is the Taime, now?"

"Over at Elk Creek. I don't suppose we'll have any more Sun Dance. It's hard for the people to get together."

"What will we do?" Spear Woman was frightened. Without the Sun Dance, even if she hadn't thought of it for a long time, things would be worse than without the buffalo. Those were the two things that were always there. Things changed around them, but the buffalo and the Sun Dance stayed the same. Now they were both gone, together.

Eagle Plume seemed less frightened. He sat looking at the ground, tapping on it with a little short stick. "There will be a new dance. There will be a new belief, something that the people have never heard of, for them to believe in. I don't know what it will be. Something that is new. I have dreamed that. The dance will come with it. Then there will be belief without dancing. Not the same kind of belief. A new one, again, I think."

Two new beliefs. A new dance and two new beliefs. It was strange. But Eagle Plume had dreamed it, and he had inherited power and power dreams from his father. Most things he dreamed came true, all right.

He got up to leave now, and Spear Woman watched him. He was a short man, like his father, with bowlegs that showed how much he had ridden in his younger days. His hair was scanty, and there was a little stray beard on his upper lip. His hands were like his father's, too, smaller than a woman's. The men in that family all had small hands and were vain of them. They used sign language a great deal whenever they talked, so as to show off their hands. But for all he was funny-looking, crooked, short, and bearded, and for all he was vain of his hands, she found that she trusted Eagle Plume. She believed what he said. She pushed the hair back from her forehead with the crook of her forearm, and watched him from beneath it.

"I think you are right, cousin!" she said. "I think that those things you have dreamed will happen."

"They will happen," said Eagle Plume slowly. "My power says so.

It says that you will take part in the dancing and I will take part in the not-dancing belief." He went off to his tipi then, and Spear Woman sat and watched him go.

Hunting Horse and Bow Woman got in late, after black dark had come. They had killed a doe, and Hunting Horse was ashamed. He didn't want to ride into camp in daylight with a doe on his saddle for people to see. Spear Woman cooked the tongue quickly, over the coals, and Hunting Horse and Bow Woman divided it. Spear Woman knew that they could have eaten a tongue apiece, but nobody said anything about that.

When they had eaten, Hunting Horse stretched on his back, with one leg pulled up to keep the firelight out of his eyes, and began to talk.

"We went a long way today," he said, "over the single butte."

"Did you see anybody?" asked Spear Woman.

"Not very many people. Just Having a Long Name."

"Was he hunting?"

"He had hunted."

Hunting Horse's voice was strange when he said that, and Spear Woman looked up quickly.

"What did he get?"

"Not meat. He had a vision."

Something in that odd voice of his and in what Eagle Plume had said that afternoon—something that was part of the children not having enough to eat and her mother telling Trickster stories in the daytime—something that was all this and more came up in Spear Woman's throat. It seemed as if all those things were going to choke her.

Hunting Horse went on, with his voice seeming to get deeper and deeper.

"This is what Having a Long Name said to tell you. He had a vision. His vision told him to have a ceremony, and to call people to help him. Seven men and seven women, to help him. It told him what to do and whom to call. If he does those things right, and the right people come to help him, he will bring the buffalo back."

The fire fell all to pieces in a pile of coals before Spear Woman could talk at all. Her husband and her sister had come back to tell her this. They had brought back one doe, and they told her that there was a man who thought he could bring the buffalo back. She had been all day fixing jackrabbit meat for the winter, and he thought he could bring the buffalo back. She made patterns on the floor with her finger and rubbed them out with the heel of her hand for a long time, and thought. All the patterns looked like buffalo horns.

"Why did he tell you to tell me?"

The Ten Grandmothers

"He said that you were one of the women to help him."

Bow Woman spoke for the first time, "Having a Long Name is a good man. He comes from a good family. His father was Woman's Heart."

Hunting Horse had gone back to his own voice now he had given his message.

"Having a Long Name never had power before."

"That's true," Spear Woman said. "He is a grown man, and this is the first time he has had power. How are we going to know his power is true?"

Hunting Horse shook his head. "We have no way of knowing. Only the man knows if his power is true. If it is true, then he won't be afraid. He won't be afraid of the power, or anything else. Nothing ever can frighten him."

Spear Woman drew more buffalo horns on the floor and rubbed them out until her hand and wrist were dark with the dust. Then she said, "I think I am afraid of this power. I think this power won't work. The buffalo are gone, and I think the old life is meant to go with them. When seven men and seven women are needed to help work the power, I think maybe the power itself is afraid."

Hunting Horse took that message to Having a Long Name the next morning. He was gone a long time, and when he came back, it was late afternoon. He drank water and sat down in the shade, and Spear Woman stopped scraping the doe skin and sat beside him.

"That man," said Hunting Horse, "has changed his name. He calls himself Buffalo Coming Out. He believes. He must believe, or he wouldn't dare take that name."

Spear Woman sat quite still, not even trying to draw with her finger. "That is the name his power gave him to make him more powerful," said Hunting Horse.

"If the buffalo came back," said Spear Woman, "what would they eat? What would they drink? Would the good grass come back? Would there be water all through the summer? Would the gullies close up again? Would the soldiers go away?"

"Buffalo Coming Out says that everything would be the way it was before. The grass would grow, the water would stay all summer, and all the white people would be gone."

Spear Woman just told him, "I'm afraid. I'm afraid of that power. You better tell him I don't want any part in it."

Hunting Horse went away to tell Buffalo Coming Out. When he came back, Buffalo Coming Out came with him. Buffalo Coming Out was a tall man to begin with. Now he had a red strouding blanket wrapped around him, up over his head hiding his face, and he looked as tall as a tree. It was the biggest red blanket Spear Woman had ever seen, and it looked like sunset on red, muddy water. It seemed to shine the light back.

Buffalo Coming Out didn't sit down when she asked him to. He stood in front of her, straight and stiff and seeming to get taller all the time, and spoke to her.

"My power is good and strong. I am not afraid of it. It will bring back the buffalo and the good grass and the fresh water. It will push back the soldiers and the white farmers and all the people who make trouble for us. It will make the whole world the way it was before."

"That is all good," said Hunting Horse. "It is a great honor that that power has chosen my wife." Spear Woman didn't speak. The words wouldn't have come if she had tried to make them.

Buffalo Coming Out went on. "My power has told me to take some helpers, seven men and seven women. The power wants help from everybody. All the people will have to come together the way they do for the Sun Dance. The Grandmother bundles will have to come, too. All the power in the whole tribe will have to help. There are dances and songs that go with this. I have learned them and I will teach them to my helpers. That is what my power says that everybody must do. Everybody must help, because this power is too big for any one man. That is why you have been given your part."

It didn't seem so lonely as it had before, and Spear Woman felt a little better about everything. "All right," she told him. "I'll help your power any way I can. Who are the others who will help?"

He told her and started to go away. Then he turned back, looking so tall that he seemed to touch the low, stormy sky, and said, "My power says for everybody to move from here. Down to the two hills where Packing Rocks is camped. There will be water there, and a flat place to put the sweat-lodges."

II

Moving was harder than it used to be. They hadn't so many horses, because two had starved to death the winter before, and there were the children and her mother, who was getting fussy and scolded them all for everything they did. Sometimes she forgot about the respect she owed her son-in-law and even scolded Hunting Horse as if he were her own son. But he was good. He didn't mind. He just went on working and pretended not to hear.

The hardest part was packing all the things they had got from the traders. The iron and brass kettles were heavy and took up a lot of room. And it was strange, but beaded clothes were heavier and harder to pack than old-time painted ones. They seemed to be getting a lot of things they didn't need, right when they really hadn't enough to eat.

When they came over the fold of the earth and looked down into the little draw where Packing Rocks always made his summer camp, something turned over inside Spear Woman. The draw was long and narrow, running north and south between two little low hills. The tipis were set in a circle like the Sun Dance circle, all over the hills, and down along the creek in the draw the brush had been cleared and men were working to build the sweat-lodges. Spear Woman stood beside her roan mare, holding the children on its back, and looked along the draw and counted. Five rows of five sweat-lodges, and seven rows of seven sweat-lodges. That made a lot. But all the keepers' tipis were pitched together in one bunch, right behind the lodges, so that meant that all the Grandmother bundles were there, and all the keepers were working. Everybody must be ready to help Buffalo Coming Out with all the power he had.

Up on the top of the west hill, facing east, was a great, big, clean, new white tipi. A buffalo-hide tipi. Where had that come from? There was only one woman in the whole tribe who would have a new tipi all put away like that, and that was Comanche Woman. She cut tipis for the other women, and they gave her so many hides that she always had an extra tipi.

When they had made the camp, near Eagle Plume's, and had put the children to sleep, Hunting Horse came back from the big tipi up on the hill. "That's where Buffalo Coming Out is," he said. "He wants you to get ready and go up there. This is the first night. This is the night they're going to dance all night."

Eagle Plume was waiting outside when Spear Woman came out of the tipi. "That is right, cousin, to put on your best clothes. You should show respect for anybody's power. This is showing respect for my power, too. My power said that you would take part in the dancing belief."

All the way across the camp and up the hill to that tipi that stood there by itself, the choking thing was stronger in Spear Woman's throat, and her hands were holding themselves in tight fists at her sides. She was afraid, but her feet were moving her forward where she didn't want to go, and she thought that what her feet were doing was right even if her heart wasn't.

When she came to the tipi, she stooped and looked in. Seven men sat on the south side. Their faces were painted red, and they held wolfskins in their hands. Six women sat on the north side. Their faces were painted red, too, and they had blue beads and a strip of beaver fur tied to the backs of their heads. Between the fireplace and the west side there was a buffalo hide propped up on sticks, to look like a real buffalo. Between the fireplace and the door, there was a big rock like the one in the story about Trickster's bringing the buffalo. Buffalo Coming Out was not there.

Spear Woman sat down on the north side near the door. Her throat had a tight knot in it, and her heart was beating against her ribs as if it wanted to make a hole in them and come out. The woman next to her handed her a blue-bead-and-beaver hair ornament and helped her tie it on. The men were working over Buffalo Coming Out's red blanket. They were tying things on it.

"Where is he?" whispered Spear Woman.

The other woman whispered, too. "He's eating. That's part of his power. He has to eat alone, now. That's what the power told him. Nobody must come near when he's eating. He's coming pretty soon now."

The tipi wall didn't move when Buffalo Coming Out came in. He was just there, without anything to tell them he was coming. He sat on the west side and waited until they were all as still as he was. There were crow feathers tied in a bunch behind his head, like the ones on the Taime, and he was painted yellow and green, like the Taime, too. He looked like the Taime, only very tall and walking around. He began to talk.

"We have all been fasting, when we didn't want to. I thought that if I wanted to fast, it would be good. I went out on a hill alone. I was naked, and I took just my pipe with me. I prayed and cried and begged for mercy for four days and nights. Then something happened. A wildcat came to me. It was walking between two wolves. The three told me what I must do. Eat alone, like the wildcat. If anybody came near me when I was eating, snap at him, like the wildcat. Sing like the wolf, the way the wolf sings at a full moon. Teach others to follow me, like wolves. Teach them to sing the same way. Get everything ready. Then hang up the red blanket, with the right things tied on it. Let the people come and give presents to the red blanket. Then the rock will move, and the red blanket will move, and the buffalo hide will turn into a buffalo, and the buffalo will come back."

Everything was still again when he had finished talking. He took a drumstick and began to beat on the ground in front of him. It sounded far away, like buffalo running over the earth. The other men began to drum on the earth, too. When they all sounded together like a herd of buffalo, he began to sing.

All the people joined in and helped him. There were a great many songs, and they sang each four times. They sang all that night.

Afterwards, Spear Woman wondered why she could remember only scraps of what went on in that tipi for the four nights. Sometimes she thought it was because she was afraid and tired from singing all night. Sometimes she thought it was because the power didn't want her to remember. But only little bits of thoughts ever came to her about those four days and nights at Packing Rocks' summer camp.

She remembered the singing and the drumming on the ground. She remembered going each morning, when dawn was beginning to crawl along the edges of the sky, to take sweat baths, and that the keepers of the Grandmother bundles and their wives came for that and went from one sweat-lodge to another, carrying the Grandmothers in and out. She always remembered Buffalo Coming Out, like a tall, walking Taime, but the thing that she remembered most strongly was watching the rock and wondering if she would have time to roll under the wall of the tipi and get away if the buffalo came pouring out from under it as smoke came from a smothered fire.

On the morning after the fourth night, when they were all thin from singing so hard, and they had taken sweat-baths and the keepers of the Grandmothers had taken the bundles back to their own places, Buffalo Coming Out called them into his tipi. Not the one where they held the ceremonies, but the one where he lived. He talked to them again.

"My power says that this place is no good for this ceremony, that we will have to move. It says that everybody in the whole tribe must help, or the buffalo won't come back. Not just you people here, but everybody must help. We will have to hold a Sun Dance to make everybody feel right for helping. We'll move, over to the Big Bend, and we'll set the tipi up on the north hill there, and we'll hold a Sun Dance. Then the buffalo will come. You go and tell everybody."

People were already packing and getting ready to move when Spear Woman got back to her own tipi. She moved around stiffly, like an old, tired horse, helping with the packing and keeping the children still. Two thoughts were going over and over in her mind. One was that it was a good thing they were moving, because the grass was gone and the water was almost gone here. The other was that you couldn't have a Sun Dance without a buffalo hide, and there was no place to kill a buffalo any more.

The moving went on. It took them two days to get to the Big Bend.

Hanging the Red Blanket

They used to make it in one. When they reached there, the grass was all dry, and soon it was trampled down and dusty like the grass they had left. There was water in the river, but it was muddy and tasted dusty, and the children went thirsty a long stretch at a time before they would drink it.

Crow's Eye had the right to kill the buffalo for the Sun Dance. He talked a long time with the men in his society and rode off to the southwest.

"Where will he go?" Spear Woman asked Hunting Horse, and he answered, "There's a white man named Goodnight. He has a big place down in Texas. He keeps buffalo there, fenced up like cattle. Crow's Eye will have to go there. It's a long trip."

While Crow's Eye was gone, the people kept coming in, more and more of them. All the people had heard there was going to be a Sun Dance, and they were coming to it. Taime Man was too old to come himself, but his daughter came with the Taime tied to her saddle. She was taking good care of it, you could tell that. She picked out an old man to help her. He had made many Sun Dances, and he knew how. You might say he had the right to help with the Sun Dance. Everything was getting ready.

But still it was wrong. All the people were there, and they were camping in the old place, where they had held lots of good Sun Dances, some of the best they had ever had. The societies danced in the evenings, and the people went out and brought back branches, and built the Lodge. But they had to let a Kiowa woman cut the center pole, because the captive woman, who always had cut it, was dead, and Taime Man's daughter was bossing things that had always been bossed by men, even if the old man who was helping her was doing the ceremony.

Buffalo Coming Out had the big, white tipi set up on the north hill, looking over the Big Bend and the river and the whole camp. Nobody but his helpers went near it, and nobody talked much to them when they weren't there. Everybody was getting ready, and everybody was afraid of the thing they were getting ready for.

When Crow's Eye came back, he had a buffalo hide. A yearling bull, too. But the trip had been so long that the hide had begun to spoil, and it smelled strong. Everybody was tired with the heat, and the hide was rotting, and all the good had gone out of the Sun Dance. They danced just one day.

That night Buffalo Coming Out called his followers together and gave them their instructions. When they all knew what they were going to do, he let them go home. There was no dancing or singing that night.

The next morning they went up to his tipi early. He was dressed and waiting for them, like a tall Taime. Then Spear Woman knew what was wrong. The old power had gone out of the Taime, and Buffalo Coming Out was imitating something that was dead already. It didn't make much difference who believed or who didn't believe, because dead things couldn't come back.

The men gathered up the red blanket and laid it over Buffalo Coming Out's shoulders. He led his followers out of the tipi, and stood in front of it, facing east. The women took the blanket away from him, and hung it on a frame, like a hide-scraping frame, there in front of the tipi.

People were coming up the hill with presents in their arms, all the things they had left after they had given things to the Sun Dance. They came and touched Buffalo Coming Out and talked to him and tied the presents on the red blanket as if it were the Taime or one of the Grandmothers. Then they went away down the hill. Buffalo Coming Out's followers stood behind him and sang.

Why did the people keep coming, Spear Woman wondered. They must see that this thing was dead, too. As dead as the Taime. As dead as the buffalo hide hanging in the empty lodge below and making the whole valley smell. It was all dead, all of the old life.

The red blanket hung in front of the tipi for four days and nights. All that time Buffalo Coming Out and his followers stayed in the tipi and sang. He taught them dances, and sometimes they got up and danced inside the hot tipi that seemed to be coming down on top of them. When they danced, Frizzlehead was holding the rock down, so that the buffalo couldn't come out of it too soon. Sometimes Spear Woman thought that the rock moved of itself, but most of the time she thought that if it ever moved at all, it would be because Frizzlehead pushed it.

The last night they were all tired out. They had sung and danced and prayed and cried for mercy. Buffalo Coming Out stood up and took off his Taime headdress and stood facing them, with just his long breechclout on.

"Now it's up to me," he said. "This is the last chance. If I can make the buffalo hide stand up and be a buffalo again, the buffalo will all come back."

He crawled under the hide and kneeled there. The men began to drum and sing, and it sounded the way it had that first night, like buffalo running, a long way off. Frizzlehead held on to the rock, hard, and Buffalo Coming Out began to shake and roar and paw with his feet like a buffalo bull. They sang four songs and waited. The hide was a hide, and the rock was a rock lying on the floor.

Buffalo Coming Out came from beneath the hide. The sweat had cut slits in his paint, like flood water slitting the earth, and his face had stopped being a face and was like a piece of painted hide. He stood for a long time in front of them, with his arms held straight up over his head, and then he began to talk to his power very quietly.

"This is the way it is ending," he said. "My power was good, but it wasn't strong enough. I have failed. All the time I knew I might fail. I believed, but not hard, like the men in the old times. They never knew they could fail. All of these people have worked hard, helping me. They have given just as hard as their flesh could give. But it was my power, not theirs. If I couldn't make it work, they couldn't help me. Whatever is going to happen to anybody because of the power failing, I want to happen to me. I want to take the whole thing on myself. Nothing should happen to these people who helped me. They had no visions. They did not do anything but obey my power. I want them to be spared."

When Spear Woman went home after that, the knot was untied in her throat for the first time in all those days. She was not sitting on her legs and being carried along; she was moving her legs herself. Eagle Plume stood at the foot of the hill watching her. He turned when she got to the bottom and walked along beside her.

"His power has failed," said Eagle Plume.

"There was not enough strength. He prayed to take all the failure on himself, that nobody who helped him was to be punished."

"That is right. A man ought to do that. He owes it to the people who helped him."

"I think it is my fault that the power failed. All the time, I was thinking, 'What am I going to do if the buffalo come? I'll be afraid. How can I get out of the tipi?'".

Eagle Plume stood very still. "Not believing in power can keep it from working, but I don't think just one person's not believing is enough if the power is as big as he thought it was. I think it will be big enough to kill him, now it has failed, but not big enough to hurt anybody else."

Spear Woman started walking again. "I hope that is true. I wouldn't want anybody near me hurt because I had come near power."

Eagle Plume still walked beside her. "My wife can see again."

"Did this power do that?"

"No. I prayed. I told you there is a not-dancing power coming, and

I will have some of it. I think a little is here now. I prayed, and she can see again."

"That's good. Where will you go to look for your new power?"

They were in front of the tipi now, and Eagle Plume reached out and touched it without feeling it.

"I won't go and look for this power. This power is coming to me. When it comes, I will know. All I have to do is wait for it to come and get stronger. I think it will be a quiet power. I think it will have songs, but no dancing."

Spear Woman shook her head. "That's still like the old-time power. That's all dead. The buffalo took it away when they went. Your power will come. It may be good for me. But I think there is a new kind of life starting now. I thing we will need a new kind of power to live in it. Not dancing and not singing power. I think what we need now is thinking power, inside ourselves, to make us plan how to live and keep our children living.

She stood and watched Eagle Plume walk away. He was singing a little song to himself under his breath, and he was beginning to beat time to it with his little hands.

Going Away

*Nez Percés Visit the Sun Dance
(1883)*

SPEAR WOMAN COULD NEVER HAVE TOLD WHICH OF HER children she loved the best. Some mothers could, but having a preference always sounded silly to her. Her children and Bow Woman's were all mixed up in her mind, so that sometimes she wasn't sure of which ones she was the mother. They all lived and grew and played together, and she loved them all.

Hunting Horse felt a little bit different. Two of the children he would always remember by their mothers. He would remember his youngest son, who was Spear Woman's child, and he would remember the daughter who had been born during the horse corral winter. Those two he could never be mistaken about.

If they had been rich, it was likely that Hunting Horse would have made a favorite son of this youngest. He would have gotten him the best of everything. That boy would have had the finest clothes, the very best horse there was, if his father could have had his way.

As it was, they had no way of making a favorite son of him. Fewer and fewer families could have favorites and those who had enough horses and other things to have one didn't always take the trouble. Things weren't the way they had been, when to have a favorite was to give honor and credit to the whole family. Now it was different. People used to say they made a big fuss over their favorites because the young men might go off on a raid and get killed. Now there was no more raiding, and no more danger on that account.

Hunting Horse was a man who could surprise you with what he would say. Even when you knew him as well as Spear Woman did, he could be surprising. She was surprised now, because Hunting Horse had taken a streak of not talking. He was a man who liked to talk and who talked a lot. Then, a while back, he had just stopped. He was not gloomy or unhappy, and he always answered when you spoke to him, but he just didn't start saying things for himself.

Spear Woman let him alone for seven days, and then she became tired of the way he was acting and spoke to him about it.

"What's the matter with you, going around here with your mouth shut tight like an old terrapin?"

"I've been thinking," answered Hunting Horse. "I've been thinking a lot."

"You've been thinking off and on all your life," Spear Woman told him. "I don't see why you have to act as if it hurt you now."

"I never thought things before that did hurt me," he said. "It all seems hard. I guess you better get Bow Woman. Maybe, if we all talk it over, it will help."

Bow Woman was in her own tipi, sewing moccasins. It was late summer, and she was trying to get enough ahead to take the children through the winter. She brought the moccasins and her awl and sinew with her and came and sat in Spear Woman's tipi.

"I've been thinking," said Hunting Horse again. "I've been thinking a whole lot. Some of the things I've been thinking about you know. You know how the buffalo have gone. Buffalo Coming Out tried to bring them back, and it killed him. He died, and his mother died within a year."

"That's true," said Spear Woman. "They just died. The power was too strong for him to live with after it failed. So it killed them."

Hunting Horse didn't seem to pay much attention to her. "That's not what I'm thinking about," he went on. "It's more than that. Buffalo were what we had to live on, and they're gone. Now we live any way we can. Deer meat, jackrabbit meat, rations, just about anything we can get."

"I don't know that anybody ever thinks about anything but food any more," put in Bow Woman. "That's not such new, important thinking."

"I'm coming to the new thinking," said Hunting Horse. "You be quiet. I have to explain what made me think it. Well! All this means that old thinking and old ways have got to change. People are going to have to live differently. They're living differently right now, but they won't give up and admit it. They keep on saying they're living the old life, when anybody can see the way they're living is nothing like it."

"That's true," said Spear Woman. She hated it, but ever since the buffalo-coming-out ceremony had failed, she had felt more strongly how different everything was always going to be from what they had known.

"It means living in a new world—new things and new rules for doing them by," Hunting Horse was going on. "That's going to be hard for us older ones. Some of those things we won't be able to learn.

Going Away

Other things we can pick up easy. But some of our children are young enough. They can learn everything, all about the new living."

Spear Woman spoke before she knew. "But that means our children will think differently and live differently from us."

Hunting Horse nodded his head. "That's what it means, all right."

Bow Woman spoke up. "I don't like that. I don't like that way of doing things. I want my children to live like me and think like me."

"Listen," said Hunting Horse. "This is what I've been thinking. I think this is the way it is. If our children stay here and live with us and don't see anybody else, then they'll grow up living and thinking like us all right. But that will make it harder for them. Sooner or later they'll have to get away from us and be around other people. The more they're like those other people, the easier it'll be for them to get along."

"That's true," said Spear Woman. "It's the men like Eagle Plume, that just look like everybody else and don't show much in crowds, that live the longest and seem to get along the best."

"That's it," said Hunting Horse. "I don't think our children are just like everybody else. I think they would show up in crowds. But I want to give them a chance to learn how other people are thinking and doing, and then they can be leaders and show other people what to do."

"That's a good plan," said Bow Woman. "How are you going to work it?"

"This way," Hunting Horse told her. "I'm going to take my youngest son and send him to Fort Sill. The officers have a school for Indian children there. They'll teach him what he ought to know."

It seemed to Spear Woman that things were turning over and over inside her. She would never have thought that Hunting Horse could think these things. It was as if he had picked up a big stick of firewood and hit her on the head with it. She put her hand over her heart, that was jumping up and down, and tried to hold it steady. "When do you want him to go?" she asked.

"Right away," said Hunting Horse, "as soon as you can get him ready. I've thought and thought about this, and it seems that it's what we'll have to do."

Spear Woman looked through the tipi flaps and watched the children tumbling in the sun like puppies. They were rolling over and over.

"He's such a little boy," she said. "Let him stay home another year. He's learning by playing. Children learn a lot from each other. That's the way we learned all we know."

"He's got to go while he's still little," Hunting Horse told her, "or he won't have time to learn all the things he needs. He's got to learn English and reading and writing. The way he is now, he isn't learning about anything but living."

Spear Woman stopped pleading then. She knew what that son meant to Hunting Horse. If he was hitting her with a stick she couldn't see, he was hitting himself, too. After that they didn't talk about it at all. She and Bow Woman just started to get things ready. They did the best they could, because they wanted their boy to look right beside the other children.

It took them four days. They cleaned all his clothes. Bow Woman finished the moccasins for him. They dressed him in the best they had, with paint on his face and along the parting of his hair. Hunting Horse got the old, rawhide cradle they had made in the horse corral and took his own old, long, crawdad earrings from it. He fastened them in the boy's ears. "These are kind of family earrings," he said. "It looks like your turn to inherit."

The little boy was pleased with himself, you could tell. When they had him all dressed, he went around, stepping carefully like a wild turkey so as to show off his good clothes without getting his new moccasins dirty. While he was parading, Spear Woman got a pony for him and Hunting Horse's blue roan, and brought them up.

"Now," she said, "you two men are ready. You can ride." She was surprised at the easy way her own voice came out of her mouth.

Hunting Horse had got down and was fussing with his headstall. It reminded her of the time he asked her to ride in the Sun Dance parade with him. "You get your horse, too," he told her. "We'll all three ride out on this raid."

Spear Woman pulled in a deep breath for the first time in the four days. She would get to go along. That way she would be with her boy a little while longer. It meant that Hunting Horse wouldn't have to ride back alone, either. She'd been dreading that for him.

When she was ready, they started. They went down past Cutthroat Gap and along the creek, going south and east, to get to the fort. The fall coolness was all around them, turning to heat at midday. They stopped and rested until the noon had cooled off and then went on again. Their stopping-place was beside a little, clear spring, coming out on the east side of the hill below the gap. There was water cress in the pool it made, and they pulled up handfuls and ate it with their dried meat for lunch.

It was mid-afternoon when they reached the school. Children were playing in front of the square, stone building. They surprised Spear

Woman, because they all looked alike. She could not understand how twenty children, each with his own face and his own voice, could manage to look all like one child. It was a good thing her boy was coming. He would be one that would stand out and look different.

The man who was in charge of the school came over and shook hands. He called one of the bigger boys, and sent him off somewhere. When the boy came back, he had Wood Fire with him, as interpreter.

"Do you want this boy to go to school here?" he asked. Wood Fire's Kiowa seemed to get worse every time you saw him. It was all getting mixed up with the way he talked English.

"That's what we brought him for," was what Hunting Horse said in his good, clear Kiowa. You knew when he talked that he used all the right parts of his throat, the way he ought to.

"What's his name?" asked Wood Fire. That surprised Spear Woman. You didn't usually come right out and ask what somebody's name was. If you didn't know it already, you hinted around until somebody else told you.

"Grass Stem," she said. Hunting Horse just stood there. He was the one who had made the plan, and they were working it out, but he seemed to be more surprised by what was happening than she was.

"The boy's name is Grass Stem, and the father's name is Hunting Horse," said Wood Fire in English to the school teacher. He had known what the next question would be.

"Grass Stem Hunting Horse," said the school teacher. "That's a long name. We'll have to shorten it. Bring the boy along."

Wood Fire held out his hand, and the little boy took it. He looked littler that moment than he had in his cradle. Spear Woman kept her face stiff and rigid so that her tears wouldn't melt it. "Can we stay a few minutes with him?" she asked. "Do we have to leave him right now?"

Wood Fire shook his head. "You can stay awhile," he told her. "You can stay until he gets on his school clothes and comes out. That way you'll know everything is all right for him; and you can take home those things he has on."

"Can't he keep on those clothes?" asked Spear Woman. "Those are his good clothes. It makes him happy to have them on. He's going to be lonesome when we're gone. He's just a little boy."

The child stood next to Wood Fire and watched the other boys play. His long braids hung down his back, and the silver earrings swung beside his face. He shook his head, and they swung hard.

"None of the other boys has on clothes like these," he said. "They all look alike, and I look different. If I stay here, I want to look like them." He took Wood Fire's hand and went off with him towards the school building.

Now it was beginning. Spear Woman sat down on the grass beside Hunting Horse and thought. All of these changes she had felt were coming, all of these changes they had all known were coming, began here in her own child. It had hurt her when the child pulled itself out of her body, but nothing like the way it hurt her now he was pulling himself out of her heart. He wouldn't want to hurt her or to leave her, and already she was hurt clear through and he had gone farther than he could ever go again. So she sat and pulled up grass stems one at a time and saw them in her hand and threw them away.

Hunting Horse was still. He was being hurt, but not in the same way, and he could keep it from showing better. He had wanted this hurt and had looked for it, and pain that you expected was not so bad as that which came to you unaware. His hands were still, and he watched the schoolhouse door.

It was only because Wood Fire was walking beside him that they knew Grass Stem when he came out. He looked taller, as if the stiff blue trousers and stiff white shirt had grown him up into a man. He was picking his feet up and putting them down carefully. This time it was so he wouldn't spoil the big new shoes that went all around his feet. But the thing that surprised Spear Woman was that they had cut off his hair and had taken off the long, silver earrings. He came beside Wood Fire towards them, not holding to the man's hand any more, but walking alone. He was holding a little bundle under his arm.

He stood in front of them, a long, little way off. His face was steady, without any jerking like getting ready to cry. In some ways, he seemed to understand what was happening better than they did. He held out the bundle to Spear Woman.

"You'd better take these back," he said. "I'm not going to need them."

Hunting Horse took the bundle and stood there over his child. "Are you going to be all right, son?" he asked.

The little boy looked back at him for a moment. "Yes, father."

"Can he come home sometime?" Hunting Horse asked Wood Fire. "He might get homesick."

"He can come home at Christmas," Wood Fire answered. "That's in the middle of winter. And then he can come home again for all next summer. That way you can see him."

"Not in between times?" asked Spear Woman. "Just those two times and not in between?"

Going Away

"Schoolmaster likes it better if he doesn't," Wood Fire answered. "It makes it easier for the child. But you can send him things, and if you can get the trader to help you, you can write him letters. All those things you'll have to send to him by his school name."

"He gets a new name now?"

"He gets a new name, like when a young man kills an enemy in battle and they change his name to do him honor. This is the same thing." He turned to the child. "Tell your mother your new name."

"Stanley Hunt," said the child in his strong little voice.

"That's a good name," said Wood Fire. "Stanley is the name of one of the officers, and *Hunt* is for his father. It's like *Hunting Horse,* only shorter. That's the name he'll go by here. Can you remember it?"

They practiced it a few times, and then they must leave. Even if it meant riding all night when the owls were flying, they had to go back. It hurt them too much to stay here.

Hunting Horse shook hands with his son. "Good-bye, Stanley Hunt," was all he said. Spear Woman didn't say even that much. She just gathered the little boy to her and held him close for a minute, and then she turned and got on her horse. They rode off together, while Stanley went across the yard to play with the other boys.

PART III : *The Time When Buffalo Were Gone*

New Power

House-building Winter (1884–85)

THEY HAD GONE TO TEXAS, AND THEY HAD BEEN BROUGHT BACK BY the soldiers. They had been shut up in the horse corral at Fort Sill all one winter, and gone free again when the horses of the troops had eaten all the grass down to the bare roots. They had lost their young men in the fighting and the chasing, and they had lost their food when the buffalo disappeared. Then they had hung the red blanket, and the buffalo had not come back. It was a bad time for everybody.

Quanah and the Quohada Comanches had gone further into Texas than anybody else, and had stayed there longer. But at last the time came when even Comanches, who could live on what the coyotes would leave, were starved out, and they came back from the Panhandle and the Staked Plains and sat down around Fort Sill and waited for the soldiers to feed them.

Quanah was their chief, but he left it up to the soldiers to feed them, too. It was really up to him to get food for his people, but he didn't even seem to try. He left it up to the soldiers and went off to visit the Mescalero Apaches, who were having a pretty bad time of it themselves.

Those were the years when it didn't matter where you went or what you did. You left bad things at home and found worse ones waiting for you. All the people were starving together, starving and waiting. Something was coming, everybody knew that. The only thing they wondered about was whether it could be much worse than what they had already.

Then Quanah came back from the Mescaleros and seemed to bring hope with him. The Comanches felt it first, because they were his people, and whatever he brought went to them first. Even if his mother had been a white woman who gave him grey eyes, they believed in him and had respect for him.

Eagle Plume began to feel that something had happened to the Comanches when two of them rode by his tipi early one morning, singing. They were practicing the song over and over, and he could hear them a long way off, before they got there and after they had gone by. It was a song about the morning star, and it ended, "Father, have mercy on us." It was a good song.

Eagle Plume thought it over and hummed it over for the next four days. Part of it he could get, but there was one word he couldn't. He knew he had it wrong, but it didn't worry him much. The fourth day, he got on his horse and rode over to see Quanah, down south of Mount Scott.

The government had had Quanah's house built by that time. It had a big porch around it, with steps going up, and Quanah sat on the floor at the top of the steps, and looked along east to Medicine Creek. The road to the post went by his door, and he could see anybody traveling either way. He saw Eagle Plume coming and was ready for him. Eagle Plume could speak a little Comanche, so Quanah could talk to him all right, even without sign language.

"Get down, friend."

"Here I am, friend."

It was cool there on the porch, with the afternoon sun on the other side of the house and a big puddle of shadow to sit in. Eagle Plume sat still for a long time and watched Medicine Creek and the road with nobody riding along it.

"This is a fine house, friend."

Quanah snorted like a horse that didn't want to be saddled. "It's a house. I don't like houses."

"There are still tipis. You could live in a tipi."

"I have eight wives. They all get along well together, but they can't live all in one tipi. That's no good. I have to have eight tipis for them. Where can you get eight tipis? They'd have to be canvas tipis, and then they'd wear right out. That's no good. Buy more tipis every time you went to town. But the government wanted to build a house for me. The men picked out the land and did everything. I said all right. This is a good place to put a house. Water, shade, pasture—got everything. Build me eight rooms and I'll live in the house, I said. So they built eight rooms, one for each wife. Now it's all right."

"That's all right."

They watched the shadow go down towards the creek, as if it were thirsty and wanted a drink before it became part of the night, and Eagle Plume felt power coming to him from Quanah. He had come to the right place, he thought. Quanah had something to give him.

"Two of your young men rode by my tipi the other night. They were singing."

"Young men sing a lot when they ride."

"This was a new kind of song. I never heard it before."

"They have been learning new songs lately."

"It sounds good to hear people sing again. Nobody's wanted to sing much, these past years."

"It's hard to sing much when you aren't happy."

"I think you are happy."

"That's right. I'm happier than I have been for a long time."

"It must be strong power that can make a man happy."

"It is strong power."

They watched the shadow again. It had reached the creek now and was drinking it up. One of Quanah's wives began to sing in the house behind him.

"Even the women are singing again."

"This power I have, it came from the Mescaleros. They've had it a long time. They got it from the Mexican tribes. Now they've given it to me."

"Tell me about your power, if it will let you."

"My power wants you to know. It knew that you were coming. But this isn't the place to tell you. You'll have to come back, in seven nights, and then I can show."

"Your power will want presents before it can begin to work."

"This power is not like that. You won't need to bring presents this time. Later you will want to give something, I think."

Eagle Plume rode home. The moon came up on his right and made the earth as orange as the sun had made it red. His horse knew the way, and he let the lines drop on its neck and watched the earth and the moon and thought. Then he was singing the song the young men sang when they rode by, but he still had not got it all right, just the way they sang it.

When he rode back to Quanah, there was a big tipi pitched on the east side of the house, facing east, with a big woodpile beside it. Men were coming and going, and somewhere women were cooking. They were all moving round and getting ready, like getting ready for a dance. Nobody wore dancing clothes, and they had painted just their faces, so this power wouldn't need dancing. This was the new kind of not-dancing power, the kind that he had dreamed of. Now that he saw them all dressed up, he was glad he had worn his good clothes.

He sat on the porch with the Comanche men until Quanah came out of the house. Quanah was a tall man, and his up-and-down red and blue strouding blanket made him look taller. He had his braids wrapped in otter and white buckskin moccasins with long fringes on his feet. The other men stood up and wrapped their blankets around them and followed him into the tipi.

Inside the tipi there was a fire burning to the west of the center. West of the fire was a moon made of earth. The logs of the fire were crossed. Quanah sat behind the moon, and the other men made a circle around the tipi. They sat on a deep bed made of sage brush.

When Quanah had prayed, he took something out of a little sack he wore around his neck, and put it on the moon, right in the center. Then he sat down behind it, and began to speak.

"This is a power that has been given to the Indians," he said. "It is for all the Indians, to keep them Indians. The Mescaleros got it from the Mexican tribes. They gave it to the Comanches. Now we have our Kiowa friend here. We're going to give it to him. He's the one that was sent to learn it and teach it to the other Kiowas."

He stopped and waited, and Eagle Plume said, "Thank you for teaching."

Quanah went on. "This is strong power. It is old. A long time ago, before the white men came, there was a woman down in Mexico. She was captured by an enemy tribe. They took her away from her people, but after a long time she managed to escape and started back.

"She was lost and starving. She didn't know where she was. She couldn't get anything to eat, couldn't find her own people. She began crying for mercy.

"Then something spoke to her. It said, 'Eat the thing you see at your feet.' She looked down, and there was this thing."

He held up the thing he had laid on the moon in front of him. It was round and green, and had a kind of white fuzz all over it. "This is the thing she saw. It was green and fresh, not dried up like this, and she could eat it easily. That's what she did. Then she felt good again. She felt refreshed all over. She went to sleep, and then she saw that thing standing in front of her. It was like a man, with the new moon over his head. He had a star in each hand. He told her, 'Tomorrow you'll find your own tribe. Tell your brother all about this. He'll know what to do.'"

Quanah stopped and looked down at the thing on the altar. His voice deepened. "The next day she found her tribe. Then she told her brother. He had seen the man, too. He knew what to do. They went to the place where she had found that thing growing. They found lots of it. They had to hunt, because it hides itself. They dug the roots up and took them home, and her brother made a ceremony. All that was a long time ago. These people belonged to a Mexican tribe."

Quanah stopped again and looked around at all of them. "That's the ceremony the Mescaleros learned from the Mexican Indians and taught us. That's the ceremony we're going to have now. That's the ceremony we're going to teach the Kiowas."

He had a kettle drum and rattle and a bunch of feathers and a carved wooden staff in front of him. He laid them all out, and then he took a bag of tobacco and some corn shucks from a bag.

"First, everybody has to smoke," he said.

The man who was sitting on the north side of the door came and took the tobacco and corn shucks from him and passed them around to everybody. He started on the south side of the door and went all the way around the tipi.

They all smoked. The door man threw cedar incense on the fire, and they all perfumed themselves. Quanah gave the drum to the man on his left, and took the rattle. Quanah began to sing. He sang the song four times. It was a song to the thing on the moon. Quanah talked to it, and called it "Father Peyote." It was the name of the father Eagle Plume had missed in the song the first time. Now the word was clear.

When Quanah had sung the song four times, he stopped and gave another sack to the door man. The door man passed it around. Eagle Plume could see now. The things were round, green-grey buttons, thin and curled up at the edges, dry and hard and with white fuzz all over them. "You have to take four," said the man next to him, and Eagle Plume took them and held them in his right hand, waiting.

When everybody had some, Quanah held his first one out to the fire. They all did the same thing after him. Then he scraped off the fuzz with his thumbnail and put the button in his mouth and began to chew. They all did the same thing.

Even in a ceremony, when you should just be thinking about sacred things, Eagle Plume felt himself being surprised. The thing was harder even than he had expected it to be, and it was bitter. There was another taste down under the bitterness, a taste like the way cactus smelled when you stepped on it. The two together were pretty bad. As he chewed, his mouth puckered, and the thing he was chewing swelled until it seemed to fill not just his mouth, but his nose and eyes, too. He had to fight to keep on chewing, and then he had to fight even harder to get it down.

But that was what he was supposed to do, he could tell. Quanah was talking again. "This isn't an easy thing to take," he said. "It's made hard on purpose. It's made hard so just anybody won't be able to take it. People won't want to take it for fun, or just to see what it's like. You've got to really want to take it to swallow it."

He took the rattle and the other man took the drum, and Quanah began the singing again. Then when the song ended the fourth time, they traded, and the other man sang. Then they began to pass the drum and rattle around the circle so that everybody could take part in the drumming and singing. People sat quietly around the tipi and listened and ate some more peyote. "You got to eat them all four up before the water-bringing song," said the man next to Eagle Plume. "That's the midnight song."

The next one wasn't so hard to swallow. When the drum reached Eagle Plume, he had the third one down. He thought he could sing. He drummed when the other man sang, and then he took the rattle and began to sing himself. He didn't know any of the Comanches' songs, but a song made itself in his heart and that song he sang.

When they knew it was midnight by the shape of the stars through the tipi-ears, Quanah went outside. He had an eagle wing-bone whistle with him, like a Sun Dance whistle but without any feathers on it, and he whistled four times. Eagle Plume thought it must be once to each of the four corners of the world. Then Quanah came back into the tipi and sat down in his old place.

The door man got up and held the flap of the tipi open, and a young woman came in carrying a brass bucket of water. She was one of Quanah's daughters. She had on her best buckskin clothes, and she had her face painted. She put the bucket down just inside the door and stood behind it with her head bent while Quanah prayed for her long life and good health.

Quanah poured water across the moon to the edge of the fire, and then he drank himself, and then the door man passed the bucket around to everybody and they all drank, four swallows each. It was surprising to Eagle Plume how thirsty he was, but the man beside him warned him, and he was careful not to drink too much.

They passed the peyote around again after midnight, and then the drum and the rattle and the singing started again. Once in a while people got up and went out of the tipi for a few minutes and came back again, but something seemed to be holding Eagle Plume right where he was. There was a pressure against him that wouldn't let him go, and at the same time he didn't want to be let go. The fire held his eyes and the songs held his heart until sound and flames were the same thing, and he couldn't tell what he saw from what he heard.

He was watching and listening, and his body was one big eye and one big ear when he saw the flames change. Colors started at the coals and ran up to the smoke, waves of color running up and out like waves of water when you throw a stone in a puddle. The fire went up, but it seemed to spread out, too, towards him. But instead of being afraid of getting burned, he wanted it to come up around him and take him in, because he felt that there was something in that fire for him.

The waves of color came around his moccasins and split down the middle, like laying a branch across water waves. He looked down the split, and saw the fire and something moving right in the heart of it. He looked and saw that it was his own old power, the mountain boomer that had come to him first when he went out to look for power when he was a young man.

The mountain boomer stood up in the fire and talked to him. Its words were in the song, so that he heard them with his ears, but they were inside him, too, so that he heard them with his heart.

"This is the new power that has come to the Indians," the mountain boomer said. "This is the power for all Indians because they are Indians. It is bigger than a tribe just the way it is bigger than a man. It is to make tribes part of being Indians.

"Quanah is a teacher, and you can learn from him. But you are not all a learner. You are a teacher, too. When you have learned, you must go home and teach other people. Teach them all the things you know, so that they can start teaching, too.

"You have that Grandmother bundle. That was good power for your father. In his day he needed it. It is still good power. Anything that teaches people to live right is good power. But this time has come. The old power needs to be helped. It needs helping from outside, from all the people.

"This is what you must do. You must keep that Grandmother bundle and take care of it the right way. This power will help you do that. You must have them both together and use them right, with your other power from the Sun Dance. You must use power to help people and heal people and teach people. Then it will all work together."

The greyness of the ashes came up suddenly and covered the mountain boomer and the color and it seemed for a minute as if it would cover Eagle Plume, too. Then it all went away, and he sat in Quanah's tipi listening to Quanah sing a song about the morning star, the same song the young men had sung when they rode by his tipi.

The young woman came back and other women came with her. They brought corn and fruit and pounded meat and water, and everybody ate and drank. Then they smoked, and Quanah poured water from the drum on the fire to put it out, and they all left the tipi. The women moved the tipi and set it up in a new place, to show that it was just a tipi now, and not a place for worshiping.

The men sat or lay in the tipi all the rest of the day. Some of them slept and some of them talked; but Eagle Plume took his mind inside himself and just thought. Along in the afternoon the women had all the things ready, and they went over to the house for the feast.

When everybody had had enough to eat and had wrapped up what was left to take home, Eagle Plume went to find Quanah. Quanah was sitting by himself on the porch at the head of the steps, tapping on the ground with a stick, as if the whole floor were his drum.

"You had a vision," he said.

"My old power came to me in color waves. It told me what I must do."

"I think you will keep this power I have given you."

"That's one thing. My power says I can teach it to others."

"That's why you were sent here. It has to be taught to the other tribes."

"I think there are other things to learn about it, things I don't know yet."

"That's right. There are lots of other things about it that you'll have to learn, but you'll learn them. That just takes time for a while."

"Thank you for teaching, friend. I'm going home, now."

"Yes, you better go now."

Riding away, Eagle Plume thought of Hunting Horse and Spear Woman. Spear Woman was his cousin and a good woman. She ought to learn about his new power. They would be able to help him to use it a lot.

Dangerous Man

*The Year There Was No Sun
Dance (1888)*

PRICKLY PEAR RODE SINGING BECAUSE THE MORNING FELT GOOD, cool but warm underneath. It would feel good on the bare skin all over your body, but a Christian couldn't ride naked. A Christian couldn't ride singing peyote songs, either. He stopped, looked around for his wife, who was at home, and began to sing again, a mission song.

"Heaven is like a garden, and all the people I loved are there walking around . . . ." It wasn't so different. Except why a garden? Caddoes and Wichitas had gardens and raised corn and beans, and why a Kiowa should go walking around in a garden except maybe to borrow some watermelons—he shook his head. But it wasn't so different—all the people you loved were up there walking around. That was good. That was good in the old days, before the mission came, when you thought about Heaven as a plain, like this one, only with buffalo instead of beef cattle.

"There you are, brother," Big Tree's voice sounded almost in his ear. Big Tree was his wife's older brother, and since his wife was older than Prickly Pear, that made Big Tree an old man—at least fifty-five, old enough to have respect for.

"There you are, brother," Prickly Pear came out of his own saddle and held the other's horse while he dismounted. Big Tree had been a great war chief a few years ago, and a young man showed him respect and waited on him.

They sat in the little tilt of the prairie which might later in the day give them shadow, and Big Tree rolled a cigarette. Even being a Christian didn't keep him from smoking. Prickly Pear felt proud for a moment, because he had stopped smoking when he was converted.

The cigarette was rolled and lighted—lighted with a match. Big Tree always had matches. Prickly Pear himself sometimes ran out of them and sometimes forgot and got them wet so that they wouldn't light, and his wife made him carry flint and steel as in the old days

173

The Ten Grandmothers

Smoke made blue lines against the different blue sky. Big Tree spoke.

"I have seen Snapping Turtle."

"Where was that?"

"Over at End of the Mountains. He was riding hard this way. I think he was angry."

"He is an angry man."

"He is too easily angry."

"That is true, I know."

"He is dangerous, too, when he is angry."

"He is dangerous at any time, my older brother."

Big Tree crushed out the little end of the cigarette and put it in his pouch to smoke later in his pipe.

"He is very angry with you. He hates you now."

There was an ant crawling near Prickly Pear's hand on the grass, and even now he had to think for a moment about Trickster and the ant, and why she is nearly cut in two. He still watched her but not thinking, when he spoke.

"A time ago I was a young man in the Blackfoot Society. Snapping Turtle came to me. He had seen the white soldiers, and he knew they were coming. He told me he would take young men, young men who weren't afraid, out of the old societies, and he would make a new society."

Big Tree nodded. "That is true. That I saw."

"I saw the soldiers, too. I was afraid, but I didn't want to think I was afraid. I didn't want Snapping Turtle to think so, too. I joined him. All right. There were other young men, too. They joined him. Some of them weren't afraid. They weren't afraid even of Snapping Turtle. They said to him, 'Show us your power.'"

Big Tree began to roll another cigarette. "It is bad to say to any man 'Show me your power.' He may show too much."

The ant was gone, now, and Prickly Pear had nothing to think about but what he would say. "That is true, I know. Snapping Turtle said to us, 'Now I am going to die. When I am dead, carry me down to the big bend of the Washita and set me on the bottom. Go away then. Four times in the day you may come and see me, sitting there. When you come, sing this song, all the time you are coming. Then you must go away again.'"

Big Tree leaned forward and let the cigarette go out in his hand. "This I have never heard before, brother."

"He told us not to tell. Many young men were there. Seven fours and seven fours of young men were there. But we were not to tell. I am a Christian now, so I am telling."

"Christians should tell each other."

"Yes. Then he died. He was stiff all over, and hard to touch. His muscles were like touching dead wood. We had a hard time bending them so that he was sitting up. Then we carried him down and put him under water at the Big Bend of the Washita."

"It was dangerous, to go that way under water."

"His power came out of the things that were under the water. That was why he called himself Snapping Turtle. All those green weeds, all those water spiders, even those fish, his power came out of them. So he wore blue paint, like water."

"Hah! Then you had blue paint too?"

"I did then, but it was dangerous. I threw it away. When I go in the water, I choke."

"What happened then to Snapping Turtle?"

"All day he sat there under the water. Four times we went down, singing that song he gave us all the way. Each time he was sitting there on the bottom, with little ripples just going over his head. Then that night we wondered. He hadn't told us to get him out, just to leave him there. It was getting dark. We didn't know what to do. We lighted a fire and cooked meat and sat there wondering. Then we heard his song, and he was standing over the fire. He dripped so much, he put it out."

"No man could do that without power."

"It was strong power. He began to give it to us after that, but some of it I was afraid of. I wouldn't take it—power to get women, power to kill people with sun rays—those are dangerous things."

"Did you see him use them?"

"All these things I saw. Four times he said, 'I will shoot a certain man with sun rays,' and the man died. It had to be the first rays, just as the sun rose. They went through the tipi-lacings and struck those men as they lay on their pillows, and they died. I knew those men. So did you. One lived at Saddle Mountain who was your brother."

Big Tree sat very still. The ant had gone over to him and was crawling around on his tobacco pouch, but he didn't even see her. "That is how my brother died. We found him there in his bed, with the sun shining in his face. Did you know it then?"

"Not then. Four days afterwards Snapping Turtle called us together. He said, "I have killed this man. Now he is dead. I said that I would kill him, and he died.' Then I was afraid. I said, 'That man is my wife's brother. I think it is wrong to know who killed my wife's brother. I should kill you.' But I was afraid of his power. He said,

'I can kill you first. I like you best of all. But I will kill you first if you try to kill me.'"

"That was bad. You ought to kill the man who killed your wife's brother. You ought to use his own power against him."

"I hadn't taken that part of the power. That is bad. Every time you use power that way, some one who is near to you dies."

"That is true. Four months later Snapping Turtle's fourth wife died."

"Yes. She was taken from him because he killed my wife's brother. I was sorry when she died. She was a good woman. He used his power to take her away from Buffalo Hump, and she always went around not quite knowing, but she was a good woman."

"When she died, he was in a peyote meeting."

"I was in that meeting with him. We were singing. We are all singing peyote worship songs, we young men, but he was singing old-time power songs. That is bad in peyote meeting. That peyote is good stuff; it can heal you, make you well from many sicknesses. You can take it just any time, not in a meeting, and it will make you well. It does something to your blood that is good. When a thing is good like that, by itself, you have no right to use it to kill or take people's wives."

"Missionaries say peyote is no good."

"I think what they mean is peyote belief is no good. Peyote itself is not bad. Just to believe too strong in it is bad. But peyote is good like all other plants. The power put them all there."

"I think they mean belief is bad, not plant is bad."

"Yes. When Snapping Turtle sang those old-time power songs in peyote meeting, they came and told him his wife was dead. Something went wrong with his power right there. He started to choke and strangle. We pounded him hard on the back to make him stop. Then we threw water on him, and as that was his power, he did stop."

"I guess water was his power all right."

"It still is. He told us next time he died to put him under water and he would come back like before. But I was getting scared. I was unhappy. You wanted me to be Christian. My wife wanted me to be Christian. A man owes respect to his wife and her older brother. So I went Christian."

"I am pleased and my sister is pleased that you went Christian. And it is good because you are young and strong and can help clean up church house. The missionaries appreciate that. Even if they are both women, they are grateful to have a man clean up the church house."

Dangerous Man

"Every one is pleased. I am pleased, too. I like to sing and pray. I don't mind cleaning up church house if it helps them. It is pretty good, I think, that I get away from Snapping Turtle in time, before he made me use power to kill somebody."

"That is all right, but maybe he will use his power to kill you. He is a dangerous man."

"He has been talking against me, I know, but he will not try to kill me. He is not that angry. He has to be very angry to try to kill somebody."

Big Tree rose and stretched. "Bring the horses, younger brother, and ride with me. This afternoon I am going to butcher a beef and I need help. I was coming to get you. If you will help, I will give you a quarter."

"Good." Prickly Pear brought the horses and held the elder man's while he mounted. "I was riding to the church house. Last night was prayer-meeting. I thought I would clean up before Sunday. Tomorrow my wife and I are going to Fort Sill for ration issue, but we can use beef."

Big Tree nodded. He did not like having ration issue, but even he went to the fort twice a month for flour and sugar and coffee. "My wife and I go next week. That's why I'm butchering to-day."

The open plains were wide around them as they rode. Summer was not like this and spring was not like this, with the sun pouring like water out of a hot bucket and still the little wind that rattled the chinaberries cool—not a big wind that would come later with the big clouds, but a small wind that butted against you as you rode like a young calf.

Big Tree's wife was a kind woman. She boiled coffee in a big grey granite pot, and poured sugar right into the pot itself—lots of sugar, so you wouldn't feel greedy if you took more than one spoonful. She made fry-bread, and she had some beef dried and pounded with choke-cherries. It was the way they used to fix buffalo meat, but it didn't quite taste like buffalo meat. It was strong, and even if you knew it wasn't bad, it tasted strong. But it was good, and he ate plenty. Big Tree liked for you to eat a lot; it showed respect for his food.

When they had finished, Prickly Pear said, "You said grace before we ate, older brother. I will tell the Lord thanks again." He bowed his head and repeated in English the words the missionaries had taught him. "For this and every blessing we receive at Thy bountiful hand, oh, Lord, make us truly thankful. Amen." Maybe you didn't have to say grace twice for every meal, but his wife liked to, and that was a good meal. He felt thankful for it. It was a blessing to have relatives like Big Tree.

Big Tree smoked two cigarettes and waited until the shadows began to shape themselves away from the trunks of the trees. Then he rose, and walked out of the tipi. He still walked straight except for the bend in his legs. He was getting on, but he rode and walked like a young man. Hard to believe that he had been a war chief and killed people; he was so good and generous now, and everybody loved him. His little grandson had caught his hand and was running along beside him like a little colt, and when they came to where the horses were hitched, the old man lifted the child into the saddle in front of him and let him hold the reins.

The cattle were in the brush by the creek, and it took a little time to find them. Then Prickly Pear raised his gun and fired into the air above his head and shouted. The cattle broke out of the brushes and scattered, not the way buffalo would do, spreading out like a fan and all facing out so they could see what was coming, but just running around. It looked silly, as if they didn't have much sense. Well, anybody could tell that they didn't. There was no use trying to run them like buffalo. Big Tree must have thought so, too, because his gun fired once, and there was a big, young steer on the ground.

The little boy jumped down and began running towards it. "I want the liver, grandfather! I want the liver!"

"What would you do with all the liver? You'll get some of it, but you couldn't eat it all."

"Raw liver! Raw liver! I get some raw liver!" the little boy ran around and was happy because he would get some raw liver like any man who was butchering.

Big Tree made the first slit in the hide and took off the skin and the feet, and then he and Prickly Pear began to peel back the layers of flesh on the peeled-back hide. That way they would take the whole beef apart and have it all in one pile on the skin so that it wouldn't get dirty. White people were messy. They just hacked a beef open down its belly and let the insides spill out. But the Indians were clean, and they wanted the insides because they were the best part. They took the beef to pieces a layer at a time, and left the insides all together in a bunch in the center of the pile and then opened the bunch carefully and took things out one at a time, clean. That was the right way to do. Then you could eat every part.

When all the meat was peeled off, Big Tree stood up straight and stretched for a moment; then he said, "It's getting late. I'm about ready for some liver myself."

"It's your beef. You got the right to open it." Prickly Pear sat back on his haunches to watch. Big Tree went at it just right, and everything came out whole and clean. The little boy came running up.

"There's the liver! Grandfather, I want the liver!"

Big Tree separated it from the rest. He cut off a slice, squeezed gall over it, and handed it to the child. "There. Go eat that, big man!"

He cut two more slices and squeezed more gall on them. He gave one to Prickly Pear and began to eat one himself. He looked up along the little rise from the creek, to state, "Someone is coming. A man on horseback."

"You better cut him some liver."

"I bet that's what he's coming for. Whenever you butcher, somebody comes along just in time for the liver." But Big Tree was a good man. He would never say, "Go on away. We haven't got any liver, or, "We won't give you some." Instead, he cut off a piece and had it all ready, with the gall on it, when the man rode up. They saw it was Snapping Turtle.

"Get down, friend," said Prickly Pear, but Snapping Turtle just sat on his big blue mare and looked at them.

"These are my Christian friends," he said in his voice that was deep and thick and seemed to come through water. He even sang in that voice instead of lifting his songs as a man should. "When my Christian friends eat, they say grace. They have no food to give to a heathen."

Big Tree was patient. "I have food to give to any man who comes when I am eating or he is hungry. Get down, friend, and have some liver."

Snapping Turtle did not get down, though. He just sat on his big blue mare, looking at them. Then he said, "What my Christian friends say over their meat will spoil it for a heathen."

"It won't hurt your power," Prickly Pear said. "We didn't say grace over it. It is just the meat, the way that it was killed."

Snapping Turtle let the reins drop on the mare's neck and leaned forward over the saddle horn. "You didn't say grace over your meat?"

Big Tree was still patient. "Not out here in the pasture. When you eat in the house, at the table, then you say grace. You don't have to say it over every bite of food that you eat."

Snapping Turtle shook his head. "What I have heard, I have heard that good Christians say grace every time they eat. Some of them say it twice, every time that they eat. A man who doesn't say grace is not a Christian, I think."

Prickly Pear stood up. He was holding a piece of liver in his hand,

and it was all slippery, but he didn't mind that. He began to make signs while he talked, to show that he meant what he said.

"When I eat at a table, someone says grace before the meal. Then I say my grace when I finish. That is right. First you think the food is going to be good, so you say thanks for what you think is going to happen. Afterwards you know it was good, so you say thanks for what did happen. It is like that. But when you are butchering and just pick up a little scrap of meat and chew it—"

"What you have in your hand, my friend, is not a little scrap of meat. It looks like a whole flank!"

Prickly Pear stopped to stare. It was a pretty big piece, all right. It looked greedy, standing there talking with a big piece like that in his hand. He looked around, hoping that Big Tree didn't think he was greedy. Snapping Turtle went on talking.

"You came to me to join my society. I wanted to give you my whole power. Even then you were no good. You wanted to belong to the society, but you didn't want all the power. You didn't want all the duties that go with it. They're hard, those duties. You don't want anything hard."

"That's not true! I work hard. Any man has to work hard, to live in these times."

"You work hard. You plow like a Caddo woman. Work that was meant for any woman is hard for any man. It's trouble for you because you're not a whole man. You weren't a whole member of my society. You aren't a whole Christian."

"I was a whole member until I found out that belonging to your society meant killing people. That's bad. I won't do that."

"You were a whole Christian until you found out it meant saying grace every time you ate. You're just lazy. No wonder you work hard, doing women's work."

He picked up the reins, and the blue mare shifted her feet. "Now, listen, I am tired of you and of part-men like you—men who just want to belong, but don't want to earn the right to belong. This world is full of part-men now. There are too many of them. I will make one less. Then maybe the others will learn something. I am going to kill you. Tomorrow morning, when the sun shines through the tipi-lacings and strikes across your face where you lie on your pillow, you will die. I will make you dead the way I made this man's brother, Grey Wolf." He struck the mare with his quirt and the clods were still splattering around them from her hoofs when they couldn't see him. He was gone that quickly, leaving them too struck even to resent the insult of naming the dead.

Dangerous Man

Big Tree turned back to the pile of meat on the ground. His wife would be coming soon with the drag to take it in. He separated a quarter and held it out to Prickly Pear. "Here is the meat that I promised you."

Prickly Pear took it. Something was happening inside that made it hard for him to talk, and yet now that he knew what Snapping Turtle was going to do to him, he wasn't scared. It just seemed to him that he had a lot of things to attend to, and he'd better go ahead and do them.

"Thank you, brother. That is kind of you. My wife will need this."

"You will need it, too."

"You heard what he said. I don't need meat after tonight."

"That is not true. He cannot kill you."

"He killed your brother and my wife's brother. He can kill me."

"Power is strong. In the old days, no one could fight against power."

"Power of that kind doesn't get weaker." Prickly Pear tied the quarter of beef to his saddle, and mounted. "I will leave you now. I will ride up to the mission and tell them they had better get someone else to help clean up."

Big Tree came over and put his arms around him, reaching up to do it. It was like what they did to a young man when he went on the war raids, and they were sorry because they might never see him any more. "Good-bye, brother. Don't worry about my sister. I will find her another husband, the way I found you to take care of her when her second husband died."

"Thank you," said Prickly Pear, "Thank you for the beef, too." He went up the little slope, not quickly like Snapping Turtle, but slowly, so as not to scatter clods down on the rest of the beef. At the top he met Big Tree's wife, but he just waved and called to her and rode on. Big Tree could explain to her what had happened.

Now that it had happened, he felt very easy. It was just not feeling at all. He was light inside, and his arms and legs were light. But there was a feeling that he had to hurry. He seemed to be thinking of quite a lot of things that he ought to be doing between now and daylight tomorrow morning. It was almost dusk now, with the shadows melting into the shapes of the ground already. Winter was coming and shortening the days. Well, it would take longer getting to be morning, once it was dark. He stopped at the white frame mission.

The two missionaries were sisters. Neither of them had ever had a man, so they had no children, but they were good, as good as women who had been mothers. They were sitting in the kitchen, eating, and there was an oil lamp on the wall over their heads. It gave a good, steady light. It was even, not like firelight. They would like some beef. Prickly Pear knocked on the door. The older one came and held it open, and he brought in half the quarter and laid it on a little table by the stove.

"Get down, Prickly Pear," said the younger one. She thought she said it in Kiowa, and he knew what she meant, so it was all right, but it certainly sounded funny. When he was just starting to be a Christian, he had had to hold himself tight inside so as not to laugh when they started to talk Kiowa. They tried hard, and it wasn't their fault if their mouths were the wrong shape to make the words come right.

"Howdy," he said in English. He knew some English; he had learned it from the soldiers at Fort Sill. It wasn't hard, even the officers' little children could speak it well. "I bring you some meat. Big Tree butchering."

"Thank you. And thank Big Tree. Do you want the key to the mission so you can go in and clean up?"

"I guess not."

"Tomorrow, then?"

"Tomorrow you better get some one else clean up."

"What's the matter, Prickly Pear?" the older one sounded worried. Maybe she thought he was backsliding.

"I ain't quitting on you. I ain't backsliding. But tomorrow I'm going to be dead."

"Dead! What's the matter? Where are you sick?"

He shook his head patiently. That younger one surely did get excited easily. Just like an old quail with a bunch of little ones, trying to lead you off.

"I ain't sick. I feel good."

"Then what makes you think you're going to die?"

"Snapping Turtle told me."

"Told you what?"

The older one was hard-talking, that way. Even English sounded harder, the way she said it. But she was kind. It was just her voice.

"He said he was going to kill me with sun rays at sun-up tomorrow morning."

"Is that all?" the older one sat down beside the table and caught her breath and began to laugh. "I was frightened for a moment. I thought you meant what you said."

"I do mean it. He means it, so I guess I'm going dead tomorrow."

The younger one stood up and put her hand on the older one's shoulder. She wasn't silly any more. Suddenly she had power. "Be quiet, sister. It is true to Prickly Pear. This is what we were sent out to fight. This is the very power of wickedness, and you don't know it when you see it. Prickly Pear," she turned to him, "this is what the Christian God sent us out to fight. He has power. He has stronger power than Snapping Turtle. You can see. Now we will pray to the Christian God to use his power for you, and you will be safe."

Prickly Pear stood and thought. He thought a long time, "All right. You go ahead and use your power. No power ever did beat Snapping Turtle, but maybe yours is better. You try it."

"It won't work if you don't believe, Prickly Pear. You have to work, too. This power we all have to help, if it's going to work." Suddenly she dropped to her knees on the floor, and her sister dropped beside her. "Kneel down, Prickly Pear, and we'll all pray for the Christian God to save you."

It was a long prayer, and part of the time he was thinking that no power ever beat Snapping Turtle's yet, and part of the time he was thinking about the food getting cold on the missionaries' table and what his wife would say to him when he went in and their dinner was all spoiled, and part of the time his mind was just moving around the edges of the prayer and wondering if it were true that any power could work against Snapping Turtle's. Then the older missionary said, "Amen," as if she were saying "Good-bye" to her God, and they all got up off their knees. He went out and got on his horse and rode off. He didn't want to sing much, but the words of the song of the morning were going around in his mind, "Heaven is like a garden, and all the people I have loved are walking around up there . . . ."

His wife met him, and she was cross. She was not gentle like her brother. Maybe being older made her feel that she could boss Prickly Pear as his mother used to.

"Where have you been? What have you been doing? With everything to do to get ready to go to Fort Sill tomorrow, you ride off and spend the whole day away from home. Where were you?"

"I was at your brother's. He sent you this beef."

"That's better. Did you help him butcher, or did you waste all the day?"

"I helped him butcher. There was more beef, but I gave some of it to the missionaries. You couldn't have eaten all of it alone, anyway."

"Eaten it alone? When do I have a chance to eat anything alone? Have you stopped eating beef?"

"I'm going to stop tomorrow. I'm going to stop everything tomorrow."

"That's a silly way to talk." She gave him fry-bread and stew, and he started to eat. He had had nothing since noon except a little bit of liver. This tasted good. Too bad they were out of coffee and sugar.

"The only way you'll stop eating beef is to die."

"That's what I am going to do."

"You're going to die!" Her mouth hung open like a caught fish's, and she just stood and looked at him. Then she got her breath and started to talk again. "What makes you think so? Where are you sick? Have you got a pain? Maybe you'd better take a sweat-bath."

"I don't feel sick." Did all women think that just because you were going to die and knew it, you felt sick? "I have no pain. Snapping Turtle told me. He's going to sun-shoot me tomorrow at sunrise. You'd better get some one else to drive the wagon to Fort Sill."

"He's going to sun-shoot you." She sat down quietly beside him. "That's bad. Did you tell the missionaries?"

"Yes. They prayed. They asked their God to take care of me and save me."

"Did he say he would?"

"He didn't say anything. I guess he can't talk, that God. They say He just has power and uses it without talking."

"Did they say he would?"

"They said it was all right, but you better get some one else to drive tomorrow. You can bury me before noon, and still get down in time for issue."

"If they say He'll save you, He'll do it. I won't need anyone else to drive."

"I don't know if He heard them. Maybe He was eating, too." Prickly Pear put down his bowl and stood up. "Anyway, I want you to have them bury me. Don't bury all my things with me. Do it their way. Don't kill a horse over my grave. You'll need both the horses to get to Fort Sill. Give my good clothes to your brother, Big Tree. Just bury me in old things."

She stood up, too, facing him. She was a big woman, and standing there she looked the way he remembered his mother looked.

"If you die, I will do as you say; but you won't die. You will live, if that God says so."

He nodded. "That God just don't say anything. But maybe He'll do something. I'm going over to Packing Rocks and get him to drive for you tomorrow. He doesn't have to go down till next week, when Big Tree goes, but I guess he'll drive for you."

"You come back here! If I need Packing Rocks tomorrow, I can get him myself. I don't think I'll need him. Now we're going to bed."

Dangerous Man

He didn't want to go to bed. The sooner he went to bed and to sleep, the sooner morning would come and he would be dead. But she was a good woman. Some ways she was smart as a man. She could take care of things, and he had told her what he wanted done. He went to bed.

It was a long night or a short night. He slept and couldn't know. Then he was awake and staring up at the smoke-hole between the tipi-ears. There was light behind it, not full daylight, just light that was soft and pink. Without standing up, he rolled from his bed to the floor, and lying there saw the first sun-rays shoot through the holes of the tipi-lacings and fall across his pillow.

He crawled out of the tipi, and not until he was well away from it did he stand upright. Then he just stood there, and felt himself alive and growing up from the ground. He wasn't all light any more; there were roots in his feet that went down and took hold of the earth, and that was all right, because it let him know that he was alive.

His wife came out of the tipi and walked up and stood facing him, as she had stood last night. "There, you see. You didn't die."

"I didn't die." It was good; it was all good. The wind against his face and the coming warmth in the sun; the crackle of the fire, the smell of meat and fry-bread, the sound of singing—the sound of peyote singing from Snapping Turtle's tipi. The roots went away from his feet and left him standing there all light again.

"You'd better go see Packing Rocks."

"Why?" As far as she was concerned, it was all settled.

"He's there in his tipi using his power to kill me. He's using it hard."

"It's no good, that power. You're alive."

"He's working at it. I'll be dead."

"Eat your breakfast."

He ate it, still wishing for coffee and sugar. Well, they'd have them tonight. *She'd* have them tonight. He finished eating.

"I'm going to go get Packing Rocks."

"No you're not. I don't want him."

It was no way for a woman to speak to a man, but it was the way she always did speak. "You'd better let him drive. If I die before we get back, you'll have too much to do; with a wagonload of stuff and me dead on top of it."

"I can do it if I have to, but I won't have to. Go hitch up the wagon."

It was all wrong, somehow. She should do what he said, not the other way around. But he did as she told him, and she climbed over the wheel and got in, and he started the horses.

The Ten Grandmothers

The camp curving along the creek looked pretty when they reached the rise behind it. The rattling and singing were louder here, and there was a funny kind of choking break in the music from time to time. Snapping Turtle was eating peyote while he sang old medicine songs. Using all the power at once on him, then. It was bad. The peyote wouldn't like that. The choking break was louder. It sounded like strangling. And then the music stopped and the strangling went on, and then everything stopped. People ran towards Snapping Turtle's tipi, and a woman began to mourn and wail.

"Go on," said Prickly Pear's wife quickly. "Go on now. He's dead. The God has killed him. You can't use power to kill other people and not get killed sometime yourself."

Prickly Pear shook the reins over the horses' backs and drove on towards Fort Sill. He knew now. Power didn't have to speak right at you to work.

The elder missionary looked out of the window and stared. "There's a crowd of people coming up the hill, sister, carrying something. We'd better go out and meet them."

From below, the mission looked smaller than a tipi, but it was big enough for the people to stop. Four men carried a long, sheeted bundle, and they laid it on the ground before the missionaries. Packing Rocks, as the oldest, spoke.

"We have brought you Snapping Turtle. He looks like dead."

The older missionary turned back the sheet and looked. Then she looked at Packing Rocks. "I think he is dead, too."

Packing Rocks nodded. "He has died before and has come back."

"Only one man has ever done that, and He was a good man, not like this one."

"This man was a bad man, but he has done it."

"He could not. He was asleep or fainting."

Packing Rocks shook his head. "He was dead. He was stiff, like now. He told us to put him in water and leave him all day, and he would come back. We did that, and he came back. He was alive again. He told us whenever he died, we should do that."

"Are you going to do it now?"

"That's what we don't know. He was a bad man. He killed many people. He tried to kill Prickly Pear this morning. We think that is why his power killed him. He choked to death on peyote he was eating. Peyote power is good. It wouldn't want to be used to kill people."

"Does anyone want him alive again?" There was a dead silence.

No one moved or spoke, and at last Packing Rocks said, "I guess they don't want him alive again."

"Good," said the elder missionary briskly. "Some of you men go out in the yard in front of the church house and dig a grave. Dig it good and deep so that he can't get out of it if he tries. And then my sister and I will come and see to things."

The four men carried the body away to the graveyard, and the elder missionary turned to her sister. "It may not be exactly what we were sent out to do, my dear, but this time I think we would be well-advised to give a heathen a decent Christian burial."

Running Away

The Winter the Boys Froze to Death (1890–91)

I

STANLEY HUNT WENT TO SCHOOL BECAUSE HIS FATHER wanted him to, and he stayed there because he wanted to; but not all the boys and their parents were content with the school. Some of the boys were unhappy in school, and when they were, their parents seemed to know it. Mothers and fathers would come and camp along the creek behind the school and wait there. When you smelled campfire smoke in the morning, you knew there would be a boy missing before night.

Sometimes when the parents didn't come, boys would run away. They would become quieter and quieter, and then one morning they would not be there. Sometimes they managed to slip clear away and get home. Sometimes Wood Fire, who was sent after them, would catch up with them before they got very far, and would bring them back. The schoolmaster usually whipped them when they came in, but whipping didn't seem to stop the running away. It just made the next ones who ran away be more careful about getting caught.

Sometimes Stanley tried to find out what it was that made the boys leave. They had enough food at the school all the time, except when they were being punished by not getting anything but bread and water. The schoolhouse was always warm except very early in the morning when they first got up. They had to do chores, but if they had been at home, they would have been herding horses or helping their fathers with other things. They had to study books, but if they had been at home, they would have been learning from the old men. It was all just about the same.

Sometimes Stanley thought he was close to the thing that made the other boys run away. When he had been dreaming about his mother or about a warm fire in a tipi, then he would wake with tears on his cheeks and understand. But the feeling never lasted beyond daylight. With the new day there came always new things to do and think about, and he forgot about his emptiness in the night.

Running Away

It was spring that made the boys most restless and made the running away worst. In spring it seemed as if they couldn't stand walls and doors and floors; as if at any cost they must put distance between themselves and the fact of the school buildings. In summer they were all at home anyway, and in fall they had just come back and were settling down. Winter weather was bad enough to make them want to stay close, but spring was almost more than they could stand.

This was an open, easy winter. Stanley was having a good time. He knew enough English to be able to talk to the schoolmaster, and he and some of the older boys talked English all the time, to show off in front of the ones who were slower in learning it. They even made fun of Wood Fire, because they could tell now that his English was as funny as his Kiowa.

Some of the boys didn't seem able to learn English. Bear's Head was one of them. He had an English name, George Smith, but it was like him that the English name never seemed to belong to him and that nobody ever used any but his Indian one. He was a big, slow, stumbling boy, who was better at following than at leading, but once he had his feet set in a path, nothing ever would turn them aside. No matter what you said to him in English, he always answered, "Haw?" and kept on saying it until you spoke to him in Kiowa. Nobody knew whether or not he could understand any English at all.

He went around a lot with Walter Burns. Walter could speak good English when he wanted to, and he went by his English name; but most of the time he was with Bear's Head and spoke Kiowa. They were an odd team, because Walter was as quick as Bear's Head was slow. He was always thinking of things and getting them done in one motion. He was as restless and nervous as a Cheyenne. You kept expecting him to run away, because he was nervous, just as you would expect Bear's Head to stay where he was because he didn't care. But you knew if Walter went, Bear's Head would go, too, still because he didn't care.

They were older than Stanley and usually didn't pay much attention to him, but sometimes they did. There was the time when the cook baked all the apple pies and put them in the pantry to cool. Walter knew he would get all the pie he wanted at supper, but it would be cold then, and he wanted it hot. He and Bear's Head scouted around until they found Stanley. That was his first year, when he was still a little boy and could go through the small pantry window that the other two couldn't. They boosted him up, and he slid through and passed the pies down to them. He was leaning way out the window with a pie in each hand, when the cook walked in and caught him and held him there by the seat of his pants. The other boys got away, but they got no pie for supper that night, after all.

After that, Stanley knew they would try to get him into trouble, so he left them alone. He wanted to learn and find out about the other kind of world where the missionaries came from, and he studied hard. This year, because the weather was warm and good, the boys could be outdoors most of the day, and he played so hard that all he could do at night was go to sleep. Walter and Bear's Head didn't play much. They spent most of their time lying around on the ground watching the playing, with little Ned Hamilton, who admired them a lot, and lay there watching them more than he did the play. Then at night they were all three wide-awake, and they thought up things that got them into more trouble, while the others were sleeping. Once they turned the cows loose into the garden, and another time they painted the schoolmaster's horse green with house paint. Each time they got shut up in the cellar as punishment.

The weather kept on being like spring, moist and warm with just a little coolness in the air under the warmth, and in December the buds were shaping along the elm and mulberry boughs and the grass was green under the brown. Once in a while there was a little frost, but not enough to hurt anything, just enough to make the grass slippery underfoot for a while. By mid-morning the frost would be gone. The weather made you restless the way spring did.

One morning Stanley waked and felt something different in the air. The coolness under the warmth was cold, and there was a black misting along the horizon in the north. But the sun was shining, and the warmth covered up the cold until you had to feel for it with your skin to know that it was there.

The rising bell rang him out of bed and into the dining-room. Breakfast was on the table, and all stood until the schoolmaster said grace, and then they sat down and began to eat. There was oatmeal, with brown sugar to put on it. It was good. There was much sugar. You could have all you wanted. The schoolmaster went around between the tables and called the roll for the morning and told each boy what he was to do. When he finished, there were three boys missing: Walter, Bear's Head, and Ned.

The schoolmaster and the school farmer looked for the boys. Their beds were empty, and they were not anywhere near the schoolhouse. Then the cook came to tell them that somebody had got through the pantry window and had taken two pies, a hunk of cold beef, and a loaf of bread. It was just like those boys. They must have run away and taken Ned with them. The schoolmaster sent for Wood Fire and told him to saddle his horse and go after the boys.

Wood Fire looked at the north horizon, where the blackness was shaping from a line into a cloud, and then he smelled the air.

"Coming storm," he said.

The schoolmaster looked around. "Nonsense," he said briskly. "There's no storm coming. The weather's just the way it has been for days. Get busy now. Get started."

Wood Fire shook his head. "Coming storm," was all he said, but he went off and saddled his pinto. As he rode out of the school gate, he met Stanley, just going towards the building.

"Where's your father camped?" the man asked, and the little boy jerked his chin and lip to the south and west, and said, "Over there." A long time afterwards he wondered why Wood Fire asked him that at all, and he wondered, too, how he knew, so surely, just where they were.

Wood Fire rode off, thinking about it, too. That boy had come to school young. He was getting so he'd as soon speak English as Kiowa, and he really looked comfortable in his school jeans. But if you asked him where his father was camped, he knew, and he told you, without any question at all, even though nobody from his father's camp had been near the school since he had been brought back in the fall.

There had been no frost in the night, and there was little enough on the ground to show the trace of light boys going quickly, even if there were three of them. The chances were that they would go south and west, too, and even if they missed camps of their close relatives, they would come on Hunting Horse's camp. If they got there, they would be fed and sent on their way, Wood Fire knew. So he started south and west.

Behind him the blackness shaped into a real cloud, and from it came a strange, crazy, cold little wind that ran along the ground and tripped his horse. Then it grew into a bigger wind, and the black smoked up into the sky and covered the blue to the north and east, and Wood Fire bent forward and began forcing the pony, so that he could come up with the boys before the real cold did. It was bad to be out in this kind of weather, even if you knew what to do about it; and he wasn't sure the boys knew. They wouldn't have sense enough to stop. They would want to keep on going so as to get in out of the storm.

It was a real storm now, and the cold wind was pushing little bits of sleet along the ground and making the going slippery for the horse. The sleet didn't seem to come out of the air; you could hardly feel it on your face until it had coated the ground thinly, and then it began to strike at your eyes. Wood Fire kept on going, still looking out and ahead, thankful that his back was to the worst of the storm.

Before he came to Hunting Horse's camp, both he and his pony were fairly well done in. The pony had slipped on a downhill slope and had wrenched a shoulder, and all afternoon Wood Fire had been more out of the saddle than in, going off the main trail to look for the boys. He wondered if they had anything to make a fire with. They'd been at school long enough to forget about using flint and steel and think you had to make a fire with matches.

Hunting Horse and Spear Woman were surprised to see him. "Get down," they said, and Hunting Horse led the pony away and tied it with his own, while Spear Woman heated up a kettle of meat and broth and put the coffeepot on the fire. They got Wood Fire warm and fed, and then they waited while he smoked until he was ready to tell them what had brought him.

"Some boys ran away from the school," he said.

"When did they go?" asked Hunting Horse.

"This morning before daylight."

"Which way were they going?"

"I think this way. This is the nearest camp where they would be fed before they could be sent back."

"We would send them back," said Hunting Horse. "We would feed them, but we would send them back. We think they ought to go to school."

"They might get away again before you could start them back," said Wood Fire. "That's what they'd be planning."

"What made them run away?" asked Spear Woman. "What was the trouble?"

"There was no trouble," Wood Fire answered. "They got restless, and they didn't want to stay."

"Maybe they were homesick," said Spear Woman.

"Maybe," said Wood Fire. "Some boys do get homesick. These boys never seemed homesick before, though. I think they were going for mischief."

But the first words stuck in Spear Woman's mind as she got ready for bed and after she was stretched pretending to be sleeping. Some boys do get homesick. They got homesick enough to go into danger to get home. Other boys didn't get homesick. She had a boy at school, and he never seemed to get homesick. He just stayed there where he was all the time.

She waked to a world that was white, white all around the tipi.

Running Away

Sleet on top of the ground and snow on top of the sleet and still falling. Hunting Horse and Wood Fire looked out and shook their heads.

"Bad going," said Hunting Horse.

Still, when they had eaten and made up bundles of food to take with them, they tried to lead the horses out into the storm. The pinto didn't want to go. He was favoring the shoulder he'd wrenched the day before, and he would put the point of that hoof to the ground, like a dancer that is showing how delicate one toe is. Hunting Horse's big roan was better, but he didn't like that weather either. Both horses and men slipped and slid back and forth, and before they were out of sight of the tipi-smoke they knew it was no use. They turned and headed back.

They were holed-up in the tipi for four days and nights, with snow and sleet taking turns piling deeper and thicker and firmer around them. They had wood and enough to eat, so it was all right for them, as far as their bodies went. Their minds were different. Their minds went running out into the storm and trying to pull the bodies along after them, nagging and fussing and scolding like cross old women that they must get up and get started; they must go and find out what had become of those boys. Then another part of the mind would answer that it was no use to go; even if they could get away from the tipi, they couldn't find the boys in all that sudden whiteness that was changing the shape of the whole earth. Still another part of the mind would answer that the boys were Indian and would know what to do and how to take care of themselves. Then the first part of the mind came into the struggle again, restless and tossing and worried, to say that the boys had been at school a long time and had partly forgotten how to be Indians and wouldn't know how to take care of themselves. And the whole thing would start all over again.

It was Spear Woman who gave up first. On the fourth morning the snow had stopped and the stars were out when she waked, and she fairly pushed the men out of bed and almost wouldn't feed them before she pushed them out of the tipi. But it was no good. They were gone all day, and it was late night when they came in. They had been over to Cache Creek and back, to where Bear's Head's parents were camped, but they had found no trace of the boys.

"Maybe some stockman picked them up," said Wood Fire, but it didn't comfort Spear Woman. She knew now that the boys were dead.

II

The snow melted and the sleet melted finally, and green came through the mud and covered it up. The buds on the trees swelled and swelled, and down in the draws the redbud was purple and the wild plum was white. It was spring and time to go after Stanley. Hunting Horse and Spear Woman saddled their horses, leading one for the boy, and started for the school. Since that first trip to start Stanley in school, Spear Woman had always gone with Hunting Horse to bring her son home or to take him back to school.

They rode north and east quickly, hardly stopping to eat, hardly noticing the place where the red bluffs came up out of the ground, their rounded tops like a promise that the mountains were beginning here where the red soil ended and the black began. They were at the school by mid-afternoon, and camped on the creek before they went to tell Stanley that they were there. The schoolmaster let him go back to camp with them, and they ate and talked and at last slept.

The next morning was pure delight. Stanley liked school, but he liked to be with his parents, too, and to be with them and out in the spring morning was good. They ate quickly, saddled the horses, and started. Hunting Horse was so happy that he even let his horse buck and run, as if he were a young man just starting out, without sense enough to save his strength and the roan's for the trip ahead.

It was noon when they reached the red bluffs. There was a spring on the south side, and they stopped there to rest and eat and talk again before they went on. Hunting Horse and Spear Woman were ready to be still a time, now, but Stanley was getting more excited as they got closer to home, and he left them to run up to the top of the bluffs. He was with them, and then he was gone, and they heard his voice calling. There was something in its tone that took them up the slope quickly.

He was standing a little way off from a pile of rags, looking frightened and brave and young when they came over the rim to the top of the bluff. At first that was all Spear Woman thought—that it was a pile of rags. Then she saw the bones sticking out and covered her face. Hunting Horse went closer and looked.

"It's those boys!" he said.

Stanley gave a sharp, little cry, like a sigh too big for his throat, and ran to his mother. She held him against her, hard, with his face pressed into her dress, and over his head she looked at her husband.

"How did they get here?"

"Lost in the snow."

"They wouldn't go on top of a hill. Good shelter down the slope, but the top's dangerous. That's where it's coldest."

"They came here, lost."

It all filled up inside Spear Woman then. This was what sending boys to school did. It made them so restless they ran away, and it took away the knowledge of how to care for themselves, so that they froze to death on top of a hill. This could happen to any boy. It could happen to her boy. She tried to hold him closer, but he was already pressed against her as tight as he could get.

"What are you going to do?" she asked.

"Can't do much of anything," Hunting Horse said. "Cover them with rocks and tell their folks."

"They know already," Spear Woman was sure of that.

"I guess they know, all right. But we'll have to tell them. You help me get rocks."

She wanted to, but Stanley was still clinging to her and she couldn't get free of him. If she let him go, she thought, he might be like those boys, too—just a little pile of rags, with bones sticking out. Even if he wanted to be free, she couldn't have let him go at that moment. They held to each other while Hunting Horse slowly brought rocks and piled them over the rags.

When he had finished, he said, "Freezing to death doesn't hurt. It's just like going to sleep," and she answered, "Being alone and afraid is what hurts."

They went down the hill and got on their horses and rode away from the lonely red hill. They turned east instead of south. Before they went to their own home, they had to find those boys' parents and tell them their sons were dead.

Searching to Know

*The Ghost Dance Winter
(1890–91)*

KIOWAS HAD ALWAYS MADE THEIR OWN PLANS AND DONE things in their own way. Then they knew whether a scheme would work out or not. If it would work, it was all right, and they would use it; but if they thought a plan would not be successful, they left it alone and did not worry about it.

That was why they did not get excited at first when the Cheyennes and Arapahoes did. There was restlessness running along under men's minds all through that country, and it came down across the edges and into the Kiowa country, and soon all the tribes were thinking and saying the same things.

The Man from the North, the Man from the North had seen Jesus. He had seen all the dead people. He had seen the buffalo. He had seen the country where the dead people lived with Jesus and the buffalo. There were rivers and good grass there, and plenty to eat for everybody. It was the country the white people called the Happy Hunting Ground. It was the country everybody would want to go to.

The Man from the North said that they could go. That was the country which was promised to the Indians at the beginning of time and which they were living in when the white people came and spoiled everything. That was the country the Indians were meant to have. All they had to do was to run the white people off. Then everything would belong to them again. They wouldn't have to have fences and roads and cows unless they wanted to. The buffalo would come back, their dead friends and relatives would come back, and everything would be just the way it was before.

Wooden Lance was a careful man and a thinking man. When they had made the buffalo coming out ceremony, he was there watching. He wasn't one of those who were helping, but he was one of those who watched and hoped and helped out by believing. He thought things all out first, the ceremony they had had and the ceremony the Cheyennes and Arapahoes were having, and then he went to talk it over with Eagle Plume.

196

Searching to Know

Eagle Plume made room for him inside the tipi, and they sat and smoked there. It was late summer, and evenings were cool enough to make the fire feel good. When the pipe was out, Wooden Lance said,

"Have you seen this thing the Cheyennes have?"

"I have not seen it. I have heard of it."

"What have you heard?"

"That it will bring back the old days. The buffalo-hunting days and the buffalo-hunting people who are dead. All of the things we have loved will be brought back."

"Do you believe that?"

Eagle Plume sat still and thought for a few minutes.

"It's what I want to believe," he said. "When I was living in those days, there were many things I could see going on that were wrong. But the longer I keep living away from that time, the more good I see in it. It seems to me that I would give my eyes and my ears to be back in those times."

Wooden Lance bent towards the fire and tapped the heel of his hand on the ground, lightly, like a man getting ready to try a drum.

"You're older than I am," he said. "You remember those days better. I'm not thinking so much about bringing times back. But there's something else in this belief, there's bringing people back. That's what I'm thinking about, the bringing people back."

Eagle Plume knew then what he was talking about. Wooden Lance had just had one child, a little girl. When she had died a year ago, her father's light had gone out. That would be what Wooden Lance meant.

"It's hard to know," said Eagle Plume. "There are many different beliefs in this world. Some are good for some people, and some are good for others. Maybe this new belief is meant for you. Maybe it is good for you. Then you had better take it."

Wooden Lance shook his head. "I don't know about that," he said. "There was this buffalo coming out ceremony we had a while ago. It was about the same thing. If everybody believed, the buffalo would come back and the old days would come back. That's where these coming-back beliefs are different from others. Everybody has to believe, or they're no good. For just a few people to believe, just the ones who want to believe, won't work. Everybody, all the Indians, have to believe, or it's no good to anybody."

"That's so," said Eagle Plume. "That seems to be the way with these bringing-back beliefs."

"I can't make myself believe," said Wooden Lance. "There isn't any way for a man to do that; but I would believe if I saw that man, and he told me what was true."

"Where is that man?" asked Eagle Plume. "Is he in the Cheyenne country?"

"I think he is farther north," answered Wooden Lance. "I think he is in the Sioux country. That's where I'll have to go to try his belief. That's where I'll have to go to get my own belief."

Eagle Plume got up and went over to the northeast corner of the tipi. There was a little sack under his wife's bed there, and he dug in the earth and got it up. It was heavy with silver dollars. His wife always took care of it for him, but he could go and get it whenever he wanted it.

"Here is this thing," he said to Wooden Lance. "Here is this grass-lease money we don't use. You better take some of it to help you along. You better take all of it. You've a long way to go to get to the Sioux country, and this stuff is better than weapons for a man going on a journey these days."

"Thank you for helping," said Wooden Lance. He took the sack and put it away, tied inside his shirt.

It didn't take Wooden Lance long to get ready to leave. He had made his plan and knew what he would do, and now all he had to do was carry it out. The next morning he got his paint pony and started riding north. He had the money Eagle Plume had given him and some of his own, and other people had helped him out, too, so that he had enough for what he needed.

North to the edge of the Cheyenne country was one day on a good horse. North really into the Cheyenne country was two days. Wooden Lance found that the Cheyennes were ready to talk about their belief. They told him everything. It was what he had heard before, but it had worked on the Cheyennes until they were excited. They were so excited they could hardly hold in. They thought they would have to go to work and kill all the white people before the belief could do any good, and they were getting ready for the fighting. Wooden Lance had a hard time pinning them down so that he could find out where they got that belief.

When the Cheyennes told him, he went on, north and east, into the Arapaho country. The land had been getting flatter and flatter since he went out of sight of the Wichitas the day before, and here the prairie opened out and rolled flat like a piece of cloth spread out on a store counter. The Arapahoes were as stirred up as the Cheyennes, but he finally got one man pinned down long enough to tell him where they got the belief. It came from the Sioux country, the man said, and he jerked with his lips to the north.

Wooden Lance rode away from the Arapaho camp that was humming with drums and dancing and steady hunting for weapons. He would have liked to ride to the top of a hill or climb to the top of a mesa where he could be alone and think, but in all this flatness there was nothing to hide a man with his thoughts. He got out as far from the camp as he could and faced it so that he could see anyone who was coming, and sat and thought there.

In the old days traveling was easy for Indians. They had their horses, and there were no fences. Now there were not many horses, and there were fences and roads going across the country everywhere. Either one was enough to slow a man down, and the two together could almost stop him. The only things that went everywhere without worrying about fences and roads were the white men's railroads.

That was the way to go, then. If he went on horseback, it would take him a long time, and when he got back, it might be too late—too late for the Kiowas to join in if the belief were real and too late to get the other tribes out if it weren't. He would go by the railroad. He had money, much money. It ought to be enough to get him to the Sioux country. He went back to the Arapaho camp and found one of the young men who talked both sign language and English. That young man could be his interpreter. He could help Wooden Lance get on the railroad.

It took a while to get the young man to go with him. He was dancing, as the others were, and he didn't want to stop and risk missing the fighting when they ran the white people off. Wooden Lance got him to stand still and pay attention, and when he knew that Wooden Lance was going north where the belief came from and the man who brought it lived, he was willing to help. He got his horse, and together they rode north and east to the point where the railroad came to the edge of the Indian country and stopped.

Afterwards when people asked Wooden Lance how he felt about riding on the train that first time, he never could tell them. It was all so strange. It took all the courage he had to leave his horse with the Arapaho and get on the thing and sit down. He had seen it going, going through the country lots of times, but to feel it going and himself going with it was worse than he had ever thought anything could be. It was worse than dying could be, because dying would end sometime, but this thing went on and on, throwing you away from everything you loved and knew.

Men came and went past him; and men in blue suits and flat caps, a little like soldier caps, took away from him the paper they had given him so that he could ride on the train and punched holes in it and gave it back to him. Sometimes they tore pieces off of it and gave him back less than he had before. He wanted to talk to them and tell them it was his and that they had no right to be tearing it up, but he knew they wouldn't understand, so he gave up trying. He wouldn't even make the effort.

Other people ate and drank and even slept around him, but they were white people and at home with this wonderful thing of theirs and able to live with it. One of the white men in flat caps showed him where he could get water, and he drank; but he had no food and could not have eaten it if he had. He remembered a man he once saw shot in the middle of the back. That man was alive and his eyes moved and his tongue could even say little, simple words, but all the rest of him was dead. Wooden Lance felt as if he were the same way.

When the end of the traveling came, somebody took his shoulder and shook it until he ran away and off the train to get free of the grip. When he was outside, there was frost on the grass so that he knew it was morning and he knew he was a long way north. He sat still on the grass and the frost while the train went away and left him.

There was a little thin sun sneaking out of the sky and warming his body even if it didn't reach the thoughts in his heart. He gave up to it and stretched out and slept while the sun moved around him and warmed his head and his whole body and his knees and then at last his feet. When it stood at his feet and faced him, he waked and knew he was hungry.

There was a smell of smoke tickling through the air from somewhere. At first it seemed all around him; then he found that the wind was blowing from the north, and he followed it over a rise and into a fold of the ground, and there he found the camp that the smoke was coming from.

It was a Sioux camp, and the people there were good to him. They brought him food and waited while he ate it and while he smoked. Then he told them who he was and where he came from. The men sat and watched him while he told. When he had finished, they talked all together like crows chattering, the way Sioux always did, and then the oldest man, who spoke sign language best, turned back to him.

"The word came to us from the west," he said. "That's the way you'll have to go to find out—west and west to the Paiutes. They're the ones who know how."

Wooden Lance felt sick all over. He had thought that here was an end of traveling. Now he would have to get on that train again.

Searching to Know

"You can't go the same way you got here," the Sioux man told him. "The railroads don't go over in that country. You'll have to travel that way by horse. We'll sell you one." That was like the Sioux. They were always great ones for selling horses.

In the morning Wooden Lance took the horse and started out. It was a fairly good horse, not so good as the one he had left in the Arapaho camp, but all right. He was too tired when he started to care much, but by evening the feel of the horse between his legs and the open country around him had rested him, and he wished the horse were better. He didn't worry much about it, though. He just kept on going straight west. He had got dried meat from the Sioux camp to bring with him, so now he could eat while he was traveling.

It was the hardest horseback traveling that he could ever remember. It was coming winter in this northern country, and he was still dressed for summer in the south. Fuel was hard to get, and his food was giving out when he came up with a Shoshoni camp. The people gave him more food, and he bought a good, warm blanket that they said came to them from as far north as you could go before you fell into the water. It was a white blanket with red and green and yellow stripes across the ends and short black stripes in the middle. He bought the blanket for money, and he traded for a better horse, but he had to throw in money with his old horse. Then he kept on going. The Shoshoni said the Paiutes were still west, but not so far west as he had come from the east. They had a young man with them who spoke Paiute and sign language, and they sent him with Wooden Lance to interpret.

He had been too tired to know much about how the people in the Sioux camp felt about the new belief, but there was no doubt about the Shoshonis. They believed, hard. They were getting ready for the fighting that was part of the believing, and all the night they were dancing. At first the drums and the singing kept him awake, but then he let go, and they put him to sleep. That was the first time he began really to doubt, when he waked from that sleep. If there were something in it that made you believe, he couldn't have slept.

He and the Shoshoni boy went on west that next day. There were four more days of traveling, and then the Shoshoni boy signed for him to look. He looked ahead, and at first he thought there was no camp and the smoke was rising from fires on the ground. Then he saw that it was coming through holes, and that what looked like just bumps of earth were really piles heaped up on purpose. It was an Indian camp, but it didn't look like any camp Wooden Lance had ever seen before.

The Ten Grandmothers

They rode on into camp, and the meeting was the way it would be wherever Indians lived and were at peace. First, the dogs came out, and then the children, and then the women. After them came the men, and when everybody had come out through the same holes as the smoke, the visitors could get down from their horses.

The Paiutes were the ugliest people Wooden Lance had ever seen. They were shorter and blacker than Kiowas, or even Apaches, and they smelled just awful. That was from living in holes in the ground, where the wind couldn't get at them and blow them clean.

The Shoshoni boy told what they wanted. He told it slowly and went over it a good many times. The Paiutes chatted among themselves while he was talking, instead of listening to every word, the way a man who lived out in the open plains learned to. When the Shoshoni boy had finished, one word went around and around among them. "Wovoka," they said, over and over. "Wovoka. Wovoka. Wovoka."

Then they pointed towards a lodge in the center of the camp with a big red and white pole standing up in front of it.

The Shoshoni boy signed to Wooden Lance, "They say we should go over there. That's where the man named Wovoka lives."

The roof of the lodge was firm under their feet, not yielding and springy as Wooden Lance had thought it would be. In the center, where the smoke came out, there was a ladder poked out, and they went down the ladder across the fire, and stood on the hard earth floor. The place smelled worse than the people who lived in it. It smelled as bad as a white man's house. Over on the north side of the lodge a man lay sleeping, rolled up like a bundle of rabbit skins. When the Shoshoni boy waked him and he sat up, Wooden Lance saw that he really had been sleeping rolled up in a blanket of rabbit skins.

The man's face was tired and very sad. It looked old and alone, but his body was young. He came and sat with them beside the fire, and his women brought them food, boiled meat and a sort of soup made out of seeds. They brought it in baskets, and that was the first time Wooden Lance knew that there were people anywhere who ate out of baskets.

When they had eaten, they talked. Wooden Lance told who he was and where he came from. The man sat and listened. He had a little, young wife, who had not waited on them with the others, and she came and sat against the man, so that he could run his fingers through her hair. He seemed to keep her as a sort of pet.

"That is why you have come," he said when Wooden Lance had finished. "You came to test this belief that I am teaching. How will you test it? How can I prove to you what I know is true? I believe it, and I live by it. That is all I can tell you about it."

"You believe that by dancing the good days can come back?" said Wooden Lance.

"Listen," said the man. "This is what I know. When I am dancing, sometimes I lose this world. It drops away from me, and I am up in that Heaven the white people talk about. There are flowers and elk and buffalo. All of the people I have known and loved in my life before are up there. They come and talk to me. They are real to me. They tell me that they are happy and that I can be happy, too, up there with them."

"They are talking about the time after you die," said Wooden Lance.

"They are talking about that time," said the man, "but they are talking about this time, too. They are happy, but they would be happier if they were back on this earth. That is what they want, to come back and live again with the people they have loved."

"Do you think that they can come back that way?" asked Wooden Lance.

"Listen," said the man again, still running his fingers through his little, young wife's hair. "Why are they there? Why are they gone? What has taken them away from us? The white people. There are so many of them there's no room left for Indians on this earth. If we get rid of the white people, the Indians can come back. If we clean things out, there will be plenty of room for them. With the white people gone, nobody will feel crowded any more." He drew the little wife closer to him and began to play with her hand.

Wooden Lance watched and thought before he spoke. "Why are you the one to know these things?" he asked. "Why are you the one that's teaching this belief? That's what I want to know, too; why it comes to one man and not to some other."

The man looked down at his wife's hand that he was holding. "I was an orphan boy," he said. "White people took me. They brought me up. They taught me about Jesus. That was the only good thing they gave me, that teaching. Everything else was bad. When I grew up, I ran away from being whipped and scolded and came back to these people, where I belong. I brought that Jesus teaching with me. I knew that if God had one son, He could have more. Soon I knew that I was that other son. That's why I believe what I know. That's why what I'm teaching is what is true."

It was time for sleeping. Wooden Lance left those people in their hole and slept on top. It was cold, and it was going to snow; but that night he had to sleep where he could see stars if he waked up. The next morning he started back.

The Shoshoni boy didn't try to find out whether Wooden Lance believed. He was like a person who had seen God Himself, and he rode and rode, with his head up, singing those songs about good ghosts and their return under his breath all the way. Wooden Lance left him in the Shoshoni camp, got another horse there, and kept on eastward.

For himself he knew what he had to do and that he had to do it quickly. This man who said he was the son of God was just a man. He ate and slept and had women just as other men did. He wasn't living what he taught, so what he believed couldn't be true. Wooden Lance had to hurry, hurry, and tell the Kiowas what wasn't true.

It had been hard coming, and it was hard going back. He got some food in the Sioux camp; and when the Sioux questioned him, he tried to tell them what he had found out, but they wouldn't believe him. He wasn't telling them what they wanted to hear. They were all dancing all night and falling down in trances while they sang. They had made new white clothes, painted with suns and moons and stars, to welcome their loved ones back, and they were getting their guns ready for fighting. They said they would wear the new clothes in the fighting because the designs painted on them made them bulletproof.

Wooden Lance was less afraid of the train this time. He drank water, and he ate a little dried meat. He had only half of his paper left, and men were still tearing pieces off, but it seemed to be enough to take him home, even so. In a way he was glad of the train, because while he was moving, he was alone. He shut himself up inside himself and let the people come and go around him, and his heart was weeping because of what he had to tell the people.

It was mid-afternoon when he came to the Arapaho camp. The Arapahoes questioned him, and when he told them, they threatened him. But they saw that he believed what he said, and they respected his belief. They gave him the horse he had left there and let him go. As he went, the drums were singing the new ghost songs, and the people were coming out in their new, painted, white garments and lining up for the dancing.

The Cheyenne camp, which he reached the next day, was worse. Cheyennes were excitable anyway. They had been worked up when he left. Now they were so stirred up they were dancing out in the middle of the day in the autumn sun, and it frightened him to see them so careless of everything that they left the babies and the cooking and came to dance. It was bad when people were so busy thinking about the dead that they forgot about living.

Now he was only one day away from home. The horse was a good horse, his own good horse, and they went together easily, though they were carrying a double load, with the sorrow he was bringing. When he arrived at the Kiowa camp, he went first to Big Tree, and Big Tree brought the people together for him to talk to them. He told them everything that had happened to him—where he had gone and what he had seen and done and felt and believed.

"Now this is what I think," he finished. "Those people are getting all stirred up and excited. They are believing what they want to believe. They believe those special clothes will protect them from the soldiers bullets and that the minute they lick the soldiers the earth will open and the buffalo and the dead people will come back. That's not our belief. We've tried it. We know that when the soldiers fire, their bullets hit. Even if they aren't very good shots, if they're shooting at a whole lot of people, they're going to hit somebody. We know that a man can't bring the buffalo back because we've tried it. We had our own ceremony for that, and it failed. But those people are believing strong. We can't change them. We can't show them. We just have to let them show themselves. That way they will know what we know. They will know what's true."

Big Tree spoke. "That's all good," he said. "But there are some people who want their loved ones back. They say that when they are dancing, they go into trances. While they are that way, their loved ones come and talk to them. It comforts them. It makes them feel good. It seems bad to spoil what is making them feel better."

Wooden Lance could feel his tears coming into his eyes and rolling down his cheeks. "That's all right for those people," he said. "If they can get comfort that way, they ought to have it. They're lucky. I can't. There isn't any of that kind of comfort left for me. They ought to take what's good from a belief and use it; but the fighting part of this belief is bad and dangerous. That's the part they ought to leave alone." He sat down and bowed his head with the weight of his tears. All his heart was twisted into a hard knot inside him with envy for the people who could see their dead loved ones.

Winning Horse Race

The Summer of the Fourth of July Celebration (1894)

FOR A FEW YEARS AFTER THE KIOWAS CAME BACK FROM Texas, nobody thought much about anything. So many things had happened and so many things had changed that thinking did not seem to do much good. They just sat still and let things happen. It seemed as if people needed that time for resting and not caring, after all the working and feeling they had done.

Then they began to feel safer. The soldiers were at the Fort and the Indians had their own policemen to keep order. That was all right, because the policemen were all grown men who belonged to the dancing societies and would have been the ones to keep order anyway. Sometimes the soldiers appointed a man who didn't have the right to be a policeman, but one like that never seemed to last very long at the job, somehow.

When they felt safer about not having the soldiers come and stop them from doing things, they began to think about what to do. The country was full of people now; it was all settled. Everywhere you rode there was a house every few miles. That would have been enough to spoil the hunting if there had been anything left to hunt.

What they were going to live on besides rations was the first thing that bothered them. Rations were all right, but there didn't seem to be enough to go around. A family and their relations and friends could eat up the rations for a month in just a few days. Then they had to scatter out and go to stay with other people until it was time for the next ration issue. It made it hard for everybody, even if it kept you moving and didn't leave much time for just sitting around in one place.

The Caddoes, Wichitas, and Delawares at Anadarko were good farmers. They had been farming a long time, and people seemed to think that the Kiowas ought to be like them. But the Kiowas never had farmed, not as far back as anybody now living could remember. Their women did other things besides hoeing in the garden. And you certainly had to stay in one place if you were farming.

206

Winning Horse Race

A few of them tried it, but most of them didn't. Then some of the men, together with some of the Comanches, worked out a plan. There were ranchers in Texas who needed land to run their cattle. They needed it so badly they were willing to pay money to use land they didn't own. One man's land wouldn't do them any good, but they would pay money for all the land to the whole tribe, and then everybody would share in what they paid. The Comanches thought the plan was good, and they decided to lease their land. The Kiowas didn't like the idea so well. Some were willing, but others weren't, and when the ones who were willing out-voted the others and leased the land anyway, they sat around and sulked and wouldn't touch their share of the money for a long time.

The plan worked out all right, though. Nobody could farm range land with cattle running over it, because that spoiled it for the stock. Those who took the money had enough to buy food other than their rations, and they shared with the others, as they always had. The soldiers knew that something was being done with the land, and the land wasn't being cut up and hurt the way it would be by farming, and everybody felt better.

People began moving around more easily then. They didn't feel that they had to travel by night to visit their relatives; they could load up their horses and go in the daytime if they wanted to. They had time to think about their horses, too, and it was a good year for that. Spring was early and wet, and when the brood mares began dropping their colts, there was plenty of pasture and water, and everything went all right.

They came along to the middle of summer feeling easy and happy. This was the time when they should have been gathering for the Sun Dance, but now there was no Sun Dance left alive. The habit was strong, and when they heard the soldiers were going to have a celebration of their own called Fourth-of-July, they began to gather for that. They strung out in camps along Medicine Creek and watched. It was all like getting ready for a great big Sunday.

Eagle Plume did not have very far to travel to get there. He came from just north of Cutthroat Gap, and his wife came with him. It was slow traveling, because they had the Grandmother bundle to think about, and it had to be cared for just like a child, but finally they made it. They didn't try to cross Medicine Creek; they camped on the north side where the ground sloped upward and they could look along at the whole camp.

There were a lot of things going on. Some of the Comanches had come in for the Big Sunday, too, and were camped all together at the west end of the row of tipis. They had brought their best horses with them, and tied them out behind their tipis waiting. Some of the Kiowas had brought good horses, too, but they weren't showing them off too much, then. It was better not to try to tie horses up until just before you were ready to race them.

Corn Woman, Eagle Plume's wife, got the tipi set up and a meal cooked, and then she said to Eagle Plume, "You can look after yourself now," and she went off visiting among the camps. Eagle Plume rolled a cigarette and sat out in front of the tipi and smoked it, and felt good to be watching the people again.

Packing Rocks came along soon and sat down with him.

"Get down, friend," said Eagle Plume, and Packing Rocks told him, "Here I am, friend," and rolled a cigarette himself.

Packing Rocks was younger than Eagle Plume. He was a nephew of White Bear, and since White Bear and Sitting Bear had so much to do with each other, it made the younger men friendly. There was a Grandmother in Packing Rocks' family, too, and sometime he would have it, but not yet. Now he was still learning about caring for it.

There was much coming and going in the camp, people getting dressed up, men singing in their tipis, and drums going so softly you just felt them without hearing them. Children kept calling and dogs barking, and it was like old times, all but one noise. That came from the west end, where the Comanches were, and it was a funny sort of singing, different from Kiowa singing. It sounded more like Sioux songs.

"Where did they get those songs?" asked Eagle Plume.

Packing Rocks replied, "There's a Sioux fellow visiting Quanah. He brought those songs. They're dancing songs. They call them Forty-nine songs, because in the winter of forty-nine, when the white people began to go through their country they were all stirred up and restless and they sang those songs and danced all night."

Eagle Plume kept on listening to the songs. They were stirred-up and restless sounding, and he thought he didn't like them. When people were unhappy, they might cry about it, or mourn, but they didn't dance and sing at the tops of their voices. Something else was going with the singing that he didn't like.

"They're drinking, aren't they?" he said.

Packing Rocks replied, "They've been drinikng two days now. Seems like some of them would go crazy with drinking."

"Where they getting it?"

"Trader came in. Told the soldiers he had barrels of beads. It was barrels of whiskey. Quanah let him come into their camp, and he put up his tent and just stayed. All the young Kiowa men keep going in there, too. They say it makes them feel good."

Eagle Plume sat and watched. "That's Bird Woman going in there now. That's no place for a woman. What's she want to go in for?"

"I guess maybe she wants to get her brother out, Red Stone. He's been in there drinking ever since the trader got here."

The singing let up for a while now, and there were other sounds taking its place. Bird Woman was crying and pleading with her brother to come home, and Red Stone was yelling that he didn't want to come home and was going to stay where he was and race horses with one of the Comanches.

"You go home and get me a horse," he said to his sister. "Get me a good horse. Get me that bay mare you think so much of."

Bird Woman wasn't paying much attention to him. She kept begging with him to come home. She thought a lot of her brother and was proud of him, and it hurt her to see him like that. "You come on with me," she begged. "Get some sleep. Then you can ride a better race. The way you are now, you couldn't stay on a horse."

"I couldn't stay on my own horses, they're too spirited," said Red Stone, "but I could stay on that old bay mare of yours all right. She hasn't got enough spirit in her to walk, let alone run."

That was just talking. Everybody knew what that bay mare was like. She was fast as a streak and so wild nobody but Bird Woman could handle her. And as she had just foaled, she would be wilder than ever. When Bird Woman rode her in a race, it seemed as if the two of them were just floating, and they always won.

Red Stone couldn't shame his sister into giving him the horse. She knew that the mare could kill him or herself and would if she got a chance. Bird Woman kept on coaxing him to come home. It must have hurt her to do that, in front of everybody, the Comanches, too. She was a proud woman, and her people had always been well-to-do and proud. But as it hurt her worse to see her brother shaming himself, she kept right on begging him.

All of a sudden he gave in. "All right," he said. "I'll go home with you. I'll sleep some and eat some, and then we'll have the race. That mare of yours is the best. I'll race her against all the Comanche horses, one at a time. I'll even race her against that big black of Quanah's."

They went off together, and Bird Woman had to help him with walking, he stumbled so much. It was bad for sisters to touch their brothers, but she couldn't let him fall down on his face in the dirt. She helped him off to her tipi, and he went inside, and things settled down somewhat. The other men went back in the trader's tent and the Forty-nine singing started again.

"I don't like that," said Eagle Plume.

"I don't like it, too," said Packing Rocks.

It was quiet and cool where they were, and just sitting there should have made them feel good, but it didn't. There were too many bad feelings coming up out of the camp for them to feel any way but restless. It should have been all right, but it wasn't. Something was going to happen that was bad, and they became tired, sitting there waiting for it.

They could see Bird Woman's tipi and the mare tied behind it. The mare was too wild to put out on the picket-lines with the rest of the horses. Bird Woman had got Red Stone into the tipi and had gone off again to her husband's sister's camp. She wanted to leave everything quiet so that her brother would go to sleep.

That was where she was wrong. Red Stone had drunk too much to go to sleep. He waited a long time, so that she would see him and think he was sleeping and go away, and then he rolled under the tipi at the back, and got up.

When Eagle Plume and Packing Rocks saw him, he was standing up, and he was fairly steady on his feet. He went over to the mare, took hold of the halter, untied her, and got on her back before she knew it. Then he kicked her in the ribs and rode her off to Quanah's camp.

"I never saw that mare act that way before," said Packing Rocks. "Maybe her colt changed her."

"Maybe she knows he's drunk," said Eagle Plume, "and she's taking care of him."

Red Stone stopped in front of the trader's tent and shouted, and all the drinking men came piling out. When they saw him on the mare, they shouted, too, and Quanah's son went running to get his father's big black. Quanah raced the black a great deal, but he was too heavy to ride a race himself. All the men were running up and down and making bets and setting a course for the horses. By the time Quanah's son returned, they were all ready. The course was about a mile, along the flats on the south bank of the creek.

Packing Rocks wanted to go down and stop the race, but Eagle Plume wouldn't let him. "It's too late, now," he said. "The trouble has started. Trying to stop trouble now, you'd just make more. Later on we can help settle it."

It was a ragged kind of race to begin with. The riders were on bareback, and the horses were sleek with good grass and water, so that the men slid all over their backs. The men who were watching and betting were sliding around on the grass. It was all crazy. Somebody had an old gun, and when he fired it up in the air, the horses started.

Bird Woman heard the shot and came running from her sister-in-law's tipi. She was too far off to see what was happening, but she knew. She seemed to run almost as fast as her mare, and she was standing beside Quanah and watching when the racers reached the end of the course. Quanah's big black stopped, with his sides going in and out, so that they could see them from where they stood, but racing had made the mare crazy. She stood up on her hind legs and spun around, jerking the lines out of Red Stone's hand. She had won the race, but she wasn't going to stop. She stretched out even with the ground and started back.

It was too much for her. She shouldn't have been raced so soon after foaling, anyway, and there was certainly no sense in racing in the heat of the day. Just before the mare got back to Bird Woman, she dropped. Red Stone rolled clear, but she wouldn't have rolled on him. She died right there from a burst heart.

Bird Woman stood with her tears streaming. "My brother stole my horse!" she said. "He got drunk and stole my horse and killed her. Everybody knows about it. Everybody will talk about it. It was my own brother that shamed me this way."

But she didn't raise her voice or her hand. She went off alone, weeping, to her tipi. It was too bad for any of the women to try to comfort her then. Later on they would feel as if they had the right to go in and talk to her. Even her husband went off and stayed at his sister's tipi, to give her a chance to get over her grief.

Red Stone didn't seem to know what to do. The mare was dead, but she had won; and the men who had bet with him came and paid their bets and went away. Paying the bets had left most of them without anything to buy liquor with, and they didn't seem to want to drink any more. They went off to their own camps, and the trader shut up his tent for the rest of the day.

Packing Rocks stood up then. "I guess I'd better go," he said.

Eagle Plume shook his head. "You better stay here, I think," he answered, and Packing Rocks sat down again. "That isn't ending yet awhile," Eagle Plume said. "We're still going to have something we will have to do."

It grew later and later. End of the day was coming. People were beginning to let go again after all the excitement, and the women were thinking about cooking and the men were thinking about eating. Bird Woman's husband got up and left his sister's tipi and went over to his wife's. In the doorway he stopped dead. Then he turned and went as hard as he could go to his sister's tipi.

"You better come quick," he told her. "My wife just hanged herself from the tipi-poles."

His sister ran, and some of the other women heard and ran with her. They went into the tipi, and they must have cut the rope, because four of them came out carrying Bird Woman and laid her down on the ground. Nothing could be done now. Even from where they sat and in the late light, Eagle Plume and Packing Rocks could see that she was dead.

"That's a bad thing," said Packing Rocks.

"It's what happens when a brother doesn't show respect to his sister. He had no right to treat her like that," Eagle Plume answered.

Bird Woman's husband was mourning and weeping for her like a woman. He took his knife and cut slits in his face and neck and arms, and the blood ran down in streams. It was awful to see a man act that way. His own sister stepped up to him and told him, "That's not the way for a man to act. Enough brothers have shamed their sisters here, today."

Bird Woman's husband stopped mourning. "That's right," he said. "Her brother did this thing. He's the one who killed her. He's got to be killed, too. A man that would shame his sister that way has no right to live."

Whatever his sister felt, there were things that she knew. She knew that more killing wouldn't make anything right. She turned and ran to Red Stone's tipi as hard as she could. "Get to one of the Grandmothers," she yelled. "Get there quick. If you don't, my brother is going to kill you."

Eagle Plume was closest of all the Grandmother keepers. Red Stone ran up the slope and past Eagle Plume and Packing Rocks and into the tipi. He fell face down on Eagle Plume's bed under the Grandmother, with his arms stretched up to it, praying.

"Have pity, Grandmother. Guard me. Spare my life."

Eagle Plume looked at him as if he were dirt. "That's a lot of trouble for the Grandmother, saving a life like yours," he said, but he began getting ready. Packing Rocks helped him.

There was no time to build a sweat-lodge, and they could do that afterwards anyway. Bird Woman's husband ran up the slope and stopped in front of the tipi. He stood outside and called, and Eagle Plume picked up the old, black, stone pipe that went with the Grandmother and went outside to him.

It was only when Eagle Plume was curing or when he carried the pipe that you knew for sure he had power. Those times he looked bigger than ordinary men, instead of smaller, and he stood very straight. Now he looked as tall as a tree, standing there with the pipe in his hands.

"Why have you come here?" he asked Bird Woman's husband.

"My wife is dead," said the man. "I came for the one who killed her."

"What will you do when you find him?"

"Then I'm going to kill him."

"Will that bring your wife back?"

"No. But it will make me feel better."

"How will it do that?"

"If anybody ever killed your wife, you would know."

There wasn't much answer to that. Nobody ever had killed Eagle Plume's wife, and nobody was likely to. He just stood and thought and waited, with the black stone pipe held straight out in front of him. Behind him he could hear Red Stone's breathing being jerked across the tipi.

"I guess you'd better smoke this pipe," said Eagle Plume.

"That's what I'm not going to do," said Bird Woman's husband, "not until I kill that man, anyway."

"That man is going to be punished. He doesn't need you to do anything to him."

"All my life," said Bird Woman's husband, "I've been hearing about that pipe. In the old days, it was strong. It could make things right when they went wrong. If you smoked that pipe, it was a sign of forgiveness. But things are changing. This thing that happened; it came out of things that are changing. That's what I'm afraid of. The Grandmothers used to be able to punish the ones who did wrong, but with so many things changing, how do I know that hasn't changed, too?"

"Lots of things are changing," said Eagle Plume. He took a step towards Bird Woman's husband, with the pipe held out across the palms of his two flat hands. "Some changes are bad, and some are good. This thing came out of a bad change. But what is bad and what is good does not change. It is bad to kill anybody. The person who does that will be punished. Nobody wants him around. Nobody will have him. Even his own parents won't let him live with them. They would rather starve than eat food he got for them. His wife won't have him. Nobody will speak to him. Nobody will help him. All he can do is go off somewhere and live with another tribe."

"That won't bring my wife back," said Bird Woman's husband.

"Listen," said Eagle Plume. "This is the first time I ever heard of things being this way." He took another step towards the man, still holding out the pipe. "All my life it has been the other way. A woman's husband hurts her, and her brothers want to kill him. That's the way it always happened before. That's bad. This is the other way around, and that makes it worse. For a brother not to show respect to his sister is the worst insult there is. For a brother to kill his sister is the worst thing that could happen."

"I know all that," said Bird Woman's husband. "What do you want to tell it to me again for?"

Eagle Plume took the third step towards him. "I want you to understand," he said. "This is something that is bigger than you are, bigger than that man in there. This is something that darkens the whole tribe. Now it is over. You can't help it, and that man can't help it now. It's up to you not to make it worse. If it's any worse, it will be so bad the whole tribe goes underground."

"What do you want me to do?" the man asked.

"What did they do in the old days to a man who killed his wife?"

"They took everything he had, his clothes and his weapons and his horses and his equipment, and they turned him out of the tribe. Nobody could give him anything. He had to go naked and starving and thirsty. He never could come back. He had to go clear away. Maybe he found another tribe, and they let him in with them."

"That is the way it was," said Eagle Plume. "That is the way it is going to be this time. What this man has done is worse than killing his wife. He shamed his sister where everybody could see. But what will happen to him is worse. He has to go on living and knowing what he has done. That is the worst thing that could happen."

"That's what you want me to do?" asked Bird Woman's husband. "You want me to take everything he has and let him go?"

"You can take everything he has," said Eagle Plume, "but you can't keep it. That way he would be just paying you for your wife, as if she ran away with him on a war party. What you take you have to give away. There are lots of old, poor people around who need things."

Bird Woman's husband watched the ground for a while. His mind was balancing back and forth, but finally it settled down steady. Eagle Plume saw what had happened. He took the fourth step forward and laid the pipe across the backs of the man's hands. Bird Woman's husband turned his hands over, and the pipe rested on the palms. Then it was all over. If he held the pipe inside his hands, it was all settled for good.

Packing Rocks built a sweat-lodge on the east side of the tipi and heated the rocks. Eagle Plume and Bird Woman's husband took the Grandmother and went inside and sweated four times. When they came out, they were limp, and it was all they could do to walk. Bird Woman's husband couldn't have killed Red Stone even if he hadn't promised not to.

But Red Stone was gone. There was nobody left in his tipi, but all his things were there. His wife had left her things, too, and had gone to her parents. All the things they owned were in the tipi, waiting for Bird Woman's husband to give them away to the poor.

That was up to Eagle Plume. That was part of the job of being a keeper for one of the Grandmothers. When all the Comanches had gone off the next day to celebrate the Big Sunday with the soldiers, he called the Kiowas together and had the give-away. None of them wanted to go to the celebration. They were too sad after what had happened. Most times a give-away was a celebration itself, but this time it was a disgrace. People took the things that were given them in silence, and went quietly back to their tipis.

Allotments

*The Summer the Men Surveyed
for the Allotments (1900)*

PROBLEMS WERE NOT ANY EASIER TO SOLVE AS YOU GREW OLDER, Spear Woman thought. When you were young and life seemed hard, you could think ahead to the days when you would be old. Then things would be as easy for you to settle as they were for the older people all around you. Now, in her old age, she found that there were many things that she must still puzzle about.

Hunting Horse was one of them. For a long time they had gone along with a tipi for her and a tipi for Bow Woman, and he had divided his time between them. The babies had come and had been loved, and she and Bow Woman never felt quite certain in their minds which of them had borne one particular child. Then there were no more babies, and the children began to get married and move away, and they all three had moved back into one tipi and lived together the way they had the first years they were married.

That was a good life, too, even in a canvas tipi. They camped on the north side of Saddle Mountain, down the slope from Horse Stealing Gap, where there was a spring that stayed fresh all summer. There was good pasture for the horses, and back from the creek wild plums and cherries grew, and farther back where the flats were dryer, there were plenty of little, sharp-tasting sand plums. What deer were left were in the folds of the hills, and Hunting Horse had good luck in getting them.

But now there were more changes. All her life Spear Woman had watched changes, thinking that each one would be the last and that next there would be an end of changing so that you could sit still and let life happen to you. But no matter how still you sat, life happened in the form of changes, and you could never stop them. If they went on outside of you this way, they must be going on inside, too, and the worst part of it was that if you were changing inside, you couldn't know it.

The last two changes were about the biggest Spear Woman could remember, though. The first one was an outside change. The government said that the land for which they had all been getting grass money by leasing to ranchers for cattle was going to be divided. Then, instead of everybody's getting a share of the money when it was paid, each would get what he made from his own land. The people could build houses on the land, live in them, and farm the land if they wanted to. The government farmer had come twice to tell them about it.

The second change was an inside one. The missionaries had come years ago and built their church and a school at Rainy Mountain. Some people went to the church to see what it was like. The Rainy Mountain missionaries were two women, who were good and kind and tried hard to learn Kiowa so that they could talk to the people. People appreciated that and made them welcome, and soon there were many Christian Indians around.

That was all right. It was all right when more missionaries came and had a school at Fort Sill and went to the camps and held services. Then two of them, a man and his wife, settled at Saddle Mountain.

Spear Woman went to the preaching one Sunday because she wanted to know. All religions were good and helped people. Power could come one way or another, and the more power you had, the better and stronger to do good you were. What these people said was the same kind of good things she could always remember the old people saying to the younger ones: "Do good. Help one another. Be kind. Be generous. Live together in peace."

It was all so easy and true that it was like listening to her uncle talk when she was a little young woman. It made her cry a little, re-membering her mother and her uncle, who were dead, but it made her feel good inside, too. She went home and told Bow Woman and Hunting Horse, "That preaching up at the mission, it's true. It's what we always know."

The next preaching day the three went together. The mission church had not been built yet, and as the weather was good, they sat out-of-doors under a brush arbor. Spear Woman and Bow Woman sat with their shawls drawn together under their chins and listened. Hunting Horse threw his head back, with his chin in the air and his eyes closed, and listened, too. You knew he wasn't asleep because nobody who was asleep could sit that way.

When they came away, Hunting Horse said, "I guess we'll go back next Sunday. Talk like that makes you feel good." Afterwards they went regularly.

Some of the talk they did not understand. The missionaries spoke about "conversion" and "taking the Jesus road," and those were hard things to put into Kiowa so that everybody could understand them. But the little, simple things that they had known all their lives they understood, and as always they tried to do them.

One Sunday the man missionary came up after the service and talked to them. He had a young man with him, as interpreter.

"You come a lot," the missionary said.

Hunting Horse answered, "We like to come. Talk like this makes us feel good."

"That's right," said the missionary. "It ought to make you feel good. Do you feel good when you go away, too?"

"All week we feel good," Hunting Horse told him. "It's like listening to the old people talk in the old times. That used to make us feel good, too, when they said these things."

That seemed to puzzle the missionary when it was interpreted. He didn't say anything for a few minutes, but just stood with his head bent down, thinking.

"Do you believe—"he asked Hunting Horse then—"do you believe the things we say?"

"Sure," said Hunting Horse. "We always know these things. We always believe them. That's all a man's got to do to be good; live the truth and speak kindly and not get swelled up and proud with himself."

"Are you ready to follow the Jesus road?" asked the missionary.

"Seems to me like we're following it now," said Hunting Horse.

Then it came out. The missionary shook his head. He showed them what was wrong. "You can't follow the Jesus road," he told him, "as long as you have two wives. That's not right. Jesus said a man could have just one wife."

"What if she dies?" asked Hunting Horse. "What's he going to do then? Who's going to look after his children?"

"Just one wife at a time," said the missionary.

They went home, then, to think things over. It was the end of summer, with the grass too dry to make good pasture, and there wasn't really enough water in the creek for the horses. They should have moved away, up on the Washita near Rainy Mountain, but Hunting Horse didn't want to go. He wanted to stay where he was and think things out. Spear Woman told him there were missionaries at Rainy Mountain, too, and he could go and talk to them and still have the stock on better pasture, but he didn't want to go.

"I got to stay here," he said. "I got to find out why it's wrong to have two wives."

The next day but one the government farmer rode up. He came in the middle of the day, when the little dust whirlwinds were chasing each other along the creek bank on the edge of the cottonwoods, and he seemed to bring the dust and the heat into camp with him.

"Get down," said Hunting Horse.

The farmer got down and sat beside Hunting Horse under the arbor. He was a dark man, part Mexican, but the only way his Mexican blood showed was in his skin. As his father had been a captive, he spoke Kiowa and had good manners. He had been away to school and had learned there about farming and had prepared to work for the government.

"You have a good place here," he said, when he had eaten the frybread and coffee Bow Woman brought him.

"It's all right," said Hunting Horse.

"You want to go on staying here?" asked the farmer.

"Right now we'll stay," said Hunting Horse. "The women are getting restless. They want to move up to Rainy Mountain. Right now I'm not ready to go. After while maybe we'll move."

"You like it here, though," said the farmer.

"It's all right," said Hunting Horse.

"You want to take up allotments here?"

"What's allotments?"

"Government divides up the land—so much to everybody. Then that's your land. You stay on it; raise cattle, horses; make garden, farm. Everything comes off that piece of land, it's yours."

"Government divides up the land. Where does the government get the land to divide?"

"All this land around here. That's what they're dividing."

"Why do they want to do that? It's not their land. It's our land."

"That's right. They make it so everybody has a share, just the same as everybody else."

Hunting Horse was getting excited. "That's not right. This is our land. We don't have to cut it up and put fences around the pieces for everybody to have what he needs. We've been living here a long time. We all share what we have. We don't get into fights over it. White men always fighting over their land. Soon we'd be like that, too—fight, fight, all the time, over who gets what."

The farmer sat quietly. His head bent down, and his hand was beating a little drum on the earth, like an Indian's. All these things he had heard before, and he knew that in many ways they were true. But he had a job, and it got done better if he didn't argue.

"Indian ways were good ways for the old days," he said. "Now new days are coming, white man's days. Indian ways won't work. Everything's changing. Indians will have to change, too. Lots of old things were good things. Too bad to give them up. But the buffalo have gone. Deer are going. Indians want to keep on eating, don't they? Best way to get food is to raise it, like a white man."

"I guess that's right," said Hunting Horse. They had all gone hungry many times in the last few years.

"That's the way it is," said the farmer. "You think it over. You get three shares, one for each of you. Each of your children gets a full share. You take them all right here in this valley, and you won't have to move. You'll have all this land. Then you can stay right here. Government will build you a house." He laughed a little with relief at the end of the talking. "Build you each a house if you want it." He rode off still laughing.

Now they had more to think about: the Jesus way and the problem of the two wives; the land, and how many houses they wanted. Things to think about were just piling up on them. They all thought. Sometimes Spear Woman and Bow Woman sat side by side thinking, until Hunting Horse became hungry and called to them for food. He had never had to do that before, not since the first year he and Spear Woman had been married, but he didn't scold them for it. He just waited until they brought some food, then they ate it and went on thinking.

One day Spear Woman remembered about the food. She started cooking, and for a while her mind rested and her hands worked. She took the cooked meat and fry-bread to Hunting Horse and Bow Woman and put it down in front of them. Hunting Horse looked at the food and at her, and began to cry.

"I don't know what to do," he said. There were big tears on his cheeks. "It seems as if this is going to kill me. I want to take the Jesus road. That's the only way to do. It's what we know all our lives is right. But it isn't right to hurt somebody, even to take that road. We all live together happily. We have all our lives. We love each other. We have our children, and we love them. Everything was so nice, the way it was, and then everything has to change. I don't know what to do. I just can't make up my mind. Seems like I'm being pulled in two, two ways at once."

Bow Woman was crying, too. Whatever way they tried to work it out seemed wrong and hard. Then Spear Woman saw. She saw what she could do to make it easy for Hunting Horse and Bow Woman.

"I've been thinking, too," she said. "We all have had lots of thinking to do. This is what I thought. If you'll both stop howling, maybe I can make you hear when I tell you." She made her voice loud and cross so that they would listen. It went better with what she was going to say if she sounded cross, anyway.

"We're all old people," she went on. "We've got children and grandchildren. The only good a wife is to an old man is to feed him and nurse him when he's sick. He's no good to her at all. He just sits around. Sometimes he remembers to do things, but mostly he doesn't. He lies on the bed with his muddy feet and gets everything all dirty. He's just a bother to her."

She had never heard her voice sound like this before. Hunting Horse was sitting up on the bed with his mouth open and his eyes staring out of his face at her. Bow Woman had covered her mouth with her hand, and her eyes were big and black over it.

"I've had all of it I can stand," said Spear Woman. "I was married to you first, and I've had to stand it longer than my sister has. I don't like it, and I'm tired of it. It was bad enough when you just tracked around and got things dirty and forgot to do your share of the work. But lately you just sit, sit, don't do anything, don't seem to know anything. Then you get hungry and holler at me for food. I just can't stand any more of it, that's all."

She stood up over them. Her shoulders had bent as she got older, but she was straight as a young girl for this moment. "You won't make up your mind about allotments. You won't make up your mind about anything. Now I'll tell you. I'll make up your mind for you. That is your allotment up the slope. Next to it is my sister's. Down here at the bottom, where the creek is, that's mine. Then we don't have to put up a lot of fences. I can run my horses on your pasture, and you can let yours water at my creek. You and sister can have your house where you want it. I want mine here, where we're sitting. A little house, but big enough that I can have my grandchildren stay with me."

She looked at them again. They were both taking it in. They were understanding what she was saying, all right. In another moment they would understand what she wasn't saying, and then the worrying would start all over again. She turned her back on them and walked off, leaving husband and wife alone.

Healing Power

(1910)

POWER HAD COME TO EAGLE PLUME FROM MANY SOURCES. There was the mountain-boomer power of his vision. There was the Sun Dance power his brother had given him. The power of the Grandmother had come from his father, and Quanah had given him peyote power. All these forms and forces were in him, mixing and mingling, and they set him a little way alone, by himself, not where other people could not touch him, but where he might choose those who should.

People came to him, as they had to his father and as they came to Quanah, to be healed. Many of them he helped and sent away, and when they came again, it was to bring those whom they loved and wanted to see helped. Not always could he help them. Some of them could not bring all the things the power had to receive for helping. You had to bring the things, four sevens, seven times; nothing with blue or yellow on it, and nothing with green; before the power could begin to work through the Grandmother and the mountain boomer. It was not that Eagle Plume was greedy. He never kept the things. They belonged to the women in his family. But the power must receive the things that were owing to it before it could work.

Some people came many times for themselves, and some of them seemed not to have very much the matter with them, or to be much helped when they went away. Still they came and brought their gifts, and Eagle Plume knew that the power wanted them to be helped, if he could help them.

He sat now and watched Middle of the Heart Woman coming up from the draw to the east of the tipi. The bow of her saddle had a bundle tied to it; that meant that she was coming again to be helped with the pain in the middle of her back. Her husband was rich enough to pay money every time it hurt her. Eagle Plume didn't know about the power, but he did know that he was getting tired himself of Middle of the Heart Woman and the pain in her back that wouldn't go away.

"Get down, friend."

"There you are, friend."

Middle of the Heart Woman dropped the lines over her pony's head, and sat down with Eagle Plume in front of the tipi. He rolled and smoked a cigarette, and they watched the trees moving in the draw below them until she spoke.

"You are a good doctor, friend."

"I show the power where it can help."

"You have helped my back more than any other doctor."

"The power comes through four ways, when I show it."

"My back is hurting me again." She shut her eyes to show how bad the pain was, and when she opened them again, he had made up his mind what to do.

"The power has spoken to me about your back. It has told me what to do."

"Then will I be well?"

"This is what the power says: This is the fourth time you have come to me. Three times I have tried, and it has been better for awhile and then worse again. This time is the last time. The power says that if this time the pain does not go away, you will have to go to the white doctors to get better."

"Go to the white doctors!"

"Go to the white doctors' big sick-house at Fort Sill."

"That is a bad place. People have died there."

"Not everybody has died. And some have died who would have died anywhere. Just going there did not kill them."

"But they let it stand when people died there! They didn't tear it down."

"They have different power. It can clean the place. It is so strong you smell it all around the building."

Middle of the Heart Woman sat and thought for a long time. Then she said, "The power said you could work on me this time."

"That's what it said."

"All right." She got up and went to the horse. She untied the bundles on the saddle, and carried them off a little way and put them on the ground.

Corn Woman, Eagle Plume's first wife, came out of the tipi and began to help pile the things up. The two women got blankets and covered the sweat-lodge, and built up the fire, to the east of the tipi.

Swift Runner, Middle of the Heart Woman's man, came riding up the draw just as they were getting things ready. He helped the women with the fire and heating the rocks. When everything was ready, Eagle Plume got up and went into the tipi. He took off all his clothes, even the long white underwear the officers at Fort Sill had given him, and put on an old breechclout. Then he unbraided his hair and shook it down around his shoulders.

Swift Runner and Middle of the Heart Woman were standing outside the door of the tipi. Eagle Plume lighted his pipe with a coal from the fire, and they raised the tipi flap and came in. They had only blankets on, and their hair was loose over their shoulders like his. They had painted their faces black all over with the coals from the sweat-lodge fire.

Middle of the Heart Woman had a bag in her hand. She went around the south side of the tipi, and stood facing Eagle Plume, there with the Grandmother over his head on the west side. "Here is the first gift for your power," she said.

Seven pennies, seven nickles, seven dimes, seven quarters. That was good. The power could use that. He took the coins and laid them neatly in front of him. The colors were all right, too. Swift Runner and Middle of the Heart Woman went out of the tipi and came back with more coins. They did it seven times, and there was so much money in front of him that Eagle Plume wondered if the power felt very rich. He certainly did, and so would Corn Woman when he gave the money to her.

When the last coins were in place, he handed the pipe to Middle of the Heart Woman, sitting on the ground in front of him. She pointed it four ways, and blew four puffs of smoke, then promptly choked and gagged, the way women always did on the old, black, sacred pipe that went with the Grandmother. It was so old it was strong even for a man to smoke.

Eagle Plume prayed a long time for Middle of the Heart Woman. He didn't want her to feel that the power wasn't doing what was right and was best for her, so he prayed especially long and hard. Then Corn Woman came in and took the Grandmother from its place over his bed, tied it on her shoulders, and led them to the sweat-lodge.

They went four times around the inside of the tipi; then four times around the outside of the lodge, every time from left to right, before they went inside. Just he and Middle of the Heart Woman stayed in at first, after Corn Woman had hung up the Grandmother on the west side. The others stayed outside and rolled the hot rocks in to them.

It was hot in that sweat-lodge. It grew hotter and hotter. Corn Woman must be feeling the same way he was, that they didn't want Middle of the Heart Woman to feel that the power wouldn't try to help her, anyway. Four sweats, four smokes, and then they rolled the rocks out, and Swift Runner and Corn Woman came in.

Middle of the Heart Woman lay face down on the bed at the west side of the lodge, with her blanket pulled down below the middle of her back. Eagle Plume took his old, old, flint arrowhead, the one the mountain boomer had shown him on the ground at his feet the time it came to bring him power, and cut four times up and down the middle of Middle of the Heart Woman's back. Then he cut four times across the up and down cuts. He cut hard. Enough to bring the blood. He wanted to do just right. Then he talked to Middle of the Heart Woman. The blood was running good, even before he began to suck.

"You know your back hurts you. That is some bad power inside that wants to get out. You know when I treat you, you are better for awhile. That is because the good power gets out part of what the bad power puts there to hurt you. The bad power is strong. It puts lots of things there to hurt you. They're little stones, like what we find sometimes in deer and buffalo, in their gall bladders. You have a gall bladder inside you, like a deer or a buffalo. That's where the bad power puts stones, when it wants to hurt you. The good power is going to try to get all of those stones out. Maybe it won't be able to. Maybe some of them are in so deep the good power can't get them loose. Then it will take a different sort of power, to get them out. If they are in that deep, it will take white man's power to get them out. Maybe it is some kind of white man's power that is putting them in."

Middle of the Heart Woman sighed, and then she said, "All right. If the good power that you have can't get them out, then I'll try the white man's power."

That was good. Eagle Plume went ahead and sucked. He sucked four times, and the fourth time, he spit a little pebble out into his hand, and showed it to Corn Woman and Swift Runner. They nodded, and Swift Runner took the pebble and held it in his hand tight, while Eagle Plume sucked out three more. Then he told Middle of the Heart Woman, "You can sit up now."

She sat up, slowly, because she was pretty stiff from the cutting and sucking, and Swift Runner showed her the little pebbles. "That's what it is," she said. "It was one of those each of the other three times."

"That's right," said Eagle Plume. "That makes seven stones now. When it is more than four, it is seven, and if it is more than seven, it may be four sevens. If getting seven out doesn't help, then the others are in too deep. I can't get them."

The Ten Grandmothers

Swift Runner threw the pebbles into the fire, and when Eagle Plume had prayed again—he made it a short prayer this time because he was getting hungry—they all went out of the lodge and over to the tipi. Corn Woman led them the same way she had when they went in, and she hung the Grandmother up again where it belonged, and then they all dressed, and the two women started to cook the dinner.

Swift Runner never did talk much, but after a while he said, "Well, I guess she's better."

Eagle Plume answered him, "Maybe now. Maybe not after while. If she doesn't stay better, the power says you better take her to Fort Sill."

When he had said the grace and buried a scrap of meat, they all ate. Then Swift Runner brought the horses, and he and Middle of the Heart Woman rode off. Corn Woman cleaned things up and got them ready for the night, and then she came and sat beside Eagle Plume. After a while she said, "I guess maybe Middle of the Heart Woman won't get much better. Looks to me as if she likes doctoring. When she's ready, she'll try the new kind," and they went to bed.

It took Middle of the Heart Woman four months to get ready to try the new kind of doctoring. She came and talked to Eagle Plume once, and tried to get him to use his power again, but he told her he was afraid to do what the power had told him not to. Then she went to Packing Rocks, but he told her the same thing. She tried Wolf Lying Down, and then she even went to Big Tree, but they all told her the same thing, and finally she went to Fort Sill.

On the way, she stopped to see Eagle Plume. "You're making me go," she told him. "If I die down there, where all those other people died, it will be your fault."

Eagle Plume didn't worry. He prayed for her and sent her off feeling better. Corn Woman looked at him for a long time. Then she said, "I think you're making her go because you want to find out what they do down there."

"Maybe so," Eagle Plume answered. "Maybe I can learn something. If the white doctors have good power, I want to know how they use it."

Corn Woman didn't say anything else. He knew what she was thinking, so she didn't have to.

Middle of the Heart Woman was gone a long time. Then one day Eagle Plume heard that she was at home and told Corn Woman, "I think I'll go to see her."

He rode over, and Swift Runner saw him coming and came out to meet him.

"Get down, friend."

"There you are, friend."

They went into the tipi and sat down.

"Where is your wife, friend?"

"She's out gathering firewood."

"Then she is better."

"The white doctors made her well."

"Then their power is good."

"It's sure strong. They made her sleep a whole day, and parts of three others. I couldn't go in, but I know they cut her, because the scar is there."

"That's right. You got to cut to get out the bad power."

"They cut in front."

Eagle Plume sat and thought that over. That might be one reason why he hadn't made her better. He might have cut in the wrong place. But she said her back hurt, and that was where you cut, where the pain was.

"They took out the stones. You told her they were there. There were a lot of them—a big, double handful. They gave her some to bring home."

"That many! I thought there were too many for me to get out."

Middle of the Heart Woman came in then. She stood and smiled at Eagle Plume.

"There you are, friend. You are a wise doctor. You told me right."

"My friend says they cut the stones out."

"A lot of them. But they cut different from you. They cut in front."

"The stones must have gone clear through from your back. Pretty soon the pain would have been in front."

"That's right. They knew the stones were going through me."

"What did the stones look like?"

"Different from the ones you got out. Maybe they changed when they got in front."

She got up and reached under the bed for a rawhide case. When she had opened it, she took out a buckskin bag, and out of that she took a little bundle all tied up in buckskin. She laid it on the bed beside him.

"Here they are." She untied the buckskin and turned back the corners, and there they were; a handful of little, rounded, irregular pebbles, sort of greenish and smooth looking. He looked at them, and then he poked them with his finger. They rolled differently from ordinary pebbles. They were funny-looking.

"They gave me some of them," Middle of the Heart Woman told him. "I brought them home, so I could give some to you."

She picked them out, four sevens, and laid them in front of him on the bed. "Those are yours."

Eagle Plume picked them up, one at a time. She still had a lot left, but these were plenty for him.

"Thank you, friend. I am glad you thought of me."

He tied them up in a piece of buckskin Swift Runner gave him, and tied them around his neck with a buckskin string. He made sure they were down inside his long underwear, so that he couldn't lose them on the way home.

"Stay and eat with us, friend."

But he wanted to get home. He wanted to sit down in his own tipi and look at those things and think about them. So he got up and said, "I go now," and went out and got on his horse. They said politely, "All right, you can go," and stood and watched him out of sight.

Corn Woman was waiting for him when he got home.

"Did you see Middle of the Heart Woman?"

"Yes. She's all well."

"Did they tell you what it was?"

"It was stones, like I told her. They had worked around through her to the front, and the white doctors had to cut her there. Then they took out the stones. They made her sleep four days and four nights while they were doing it."

"That's strong power."

"They gave her the stones to bring home with her."

"Did you see them?"

"She gave me some."

They went into the tipi, and he spread the stones out, and they looked at them for a long time, until Corn Woman spoke.

"Sure are funny-looking stones."

"Sure are. They don't look like stones."

"No, they don't look like stones. Look more like pounded meat, all dried up."

"Too round and hard for that. You got a flat rock and a hammer?"

One of the best things about Corn Woman was that she didn't ask questions. She just went and got what he asked for. She brought him a flat rock and a hammer, and sat down to watch him.

He took one of the stones, put it on the flat rock, and pounded it up with the hammer. It was stranger looking than ever—sort of string, inside, not fine sand or gravel, like other rocks when you pounded them.

Corn Woman looked at him, poking it with his fingers, and then she got a pan of water. That time she knew what he wanted even before he said so. He took the pounded-up stone, and stirred it into the pan of water. It was strange. The water got discolored, as if it had blood in it, and the stone got stringier than ever, more like pounded meat.

"I guess that's it," he said. Corn Woman nodded.

"That's got to be it," she agreed.

"The reason she didn't get well, I got out the wrong kind of stones."

"Where did you get the ones you took out?"

"From the gravel bar, down in Arrowhead River."

"That's the wrong kind, then."

"Next time I won't take out stones. Next time I'll know what to take out. Got to be dried-up, pounded meat."

He sat outside the tipi while Corn Woman got their dinner ready. He thought about the stones a lot. Next time he would have to cut in front, and he'd have to take out dried-up, pounded meat, instead of stones. He wondered if the white doctors had got them all out of Middle of the Heart Woman, so that she wouldn't come back to him at all. Well, maybe somebody else would start having those pains in the middle of the back. Then he could try it out on him.

PART IV : *Modern Times*

The Interpreter

(1912)

THE FRONT PORCH OF THE HOUSE WAS SO HIGH OFF THE ground that there was room for two whole rooms under it. In front of the porch, the ground fell away easily, down to the flat where the ground leveled off before running up to the mountains. The head of the front steps was a good place to sit, because from there you could see all the different colors there were on the slope and in the prairie-dog town in the middle of the flat and across where the mountains turned blue.

Spear Woman often sat there with her granddaughter. In the old days, four years ago, she held the child on her back, but now they sat side by side and looked out to the spaces in front of them.

Leah was a big child and a smart child, Spear Woman thought. She was pretty, too, dressed in her blue calico dress, with her hair in straight little pigtails down her back. The place where her hair was parted should have been painted red and yellow, and her ears should have been pierced years ago, but Leah's mother had been away to school, and some of the old things she just didn't like. She wore moccasins herself, though, and she let Leah wear them. One thing Spear Woman did every month was make them each a pair of moccasins.

Frances and Stanley came out of the house and stood behind the two on the steps.

"Are you ready?" Stanley asked, and Leah said, "Yes, father," in her polite little voice. They went down the steps to where the team was hitched and climbed over the wheel into the wagon. Spear Woman and Leah sat together in the body of the wagon, and Stanley and Frances sat up straight on the seat above them.

The horses went down the road towards the prairie-dog town, and their feet made splashes in the dust to go with the splashy sound of their shoes hitting the ground. Spear Woman thought about the Trickster story of the prairie-dog dance, and began to hum their dance song under her breath, the sound more in her mind than in her mouth. But Leah heard her, and began to sing out loud:

233

The Ten Grandmothers

Prairie dogs, Prairie dogs, wag your tails,
NOW is the time to dance the best!
NOW is the time to dance the best!
Huh! Huh! Huh!

She made little slashes in the air with the side of her hand, to show
that she was Trickster cutting the prairie dogs' heads off. Then she
looked up and spoke to her father. "Please stop, father. Please let me
get out. I want to dance the prairie-dog dance with the prairie dogs."

Father laughed, but he stopped the wagon, and Leah got down.
They all sang the prairie-dog song, and she danced there in the middle
of the village with her pigtails flopping up and down across her shoulders. The prairie dogs were startled and ran down in their holes, but
she kept on until she had danced and sung four times.

"That's enough, now," said Frances. "You'll be all tired out and
hoarse when we get there if you keep on dancing in the dust."

Leah climbed back in the wagon, and now she sat down hard
beside her grandmother.

"Mother, do I have to talk when we get there?"

"Yes," said Frances.

That was all. It seemed hard to Spear Woman. Frances had been
away to school and had learned her English there, and Stanley had
learned his at school, too, and they both spoke all right. Ever since
Leah had been big enough to teach, Frances had been making her
learn English, and when they went to the store now, Leah had to
interpret for all of them.

Spear Woman gathered the child against her. She couldn't say
anything, because mothers had the right to bring up their children
their own way, but she knew Leah was hurting inside, and there
was a pain there in herself, too.

"It's hard, making the little thing talk to strangers," Stanley said.

"She's got to learn," Frances answered. "She's got to learn English,
and she's got to learn to talk to strangers. That's what's wrong with
Indian girls. That's what makes them backward. They're too shy—
scared to look at people, scared to talk to people. They don't have to
be that way. White girls learn. Indian girls can, too."

"It's that old storekeeper," said Spear Woman. "That's what's
hurting her feelings and making her shy. He looks and looks at her
all the time she's talking to him. No wonder she has a bad time."

"White people do that," said Frances. "It isn't rude to them. They
don't mean to hurt feelings."

"He calls me by name, too," said Leah. "I don't like that."

234

"All white people do. You got to get used to it."

There was no good in arguing with Frances. If she made up her mind, her spear was staked, like a warrior in the old days fastening himself in place in a battle. If she said Leah had to interpret, Leah had to interpret, no matter what her father and grandmother thought.

The town sprawled along the river bank like sinew laid out in the sun to dry. It was ugly and brown like sinew, but there was usefulness behind it, and that was like sinew, too. It was strong, strong enough to be smothering out the old life and the old ways by just sprawling there in the sun. Spear Woman hated it for what it was doing, not for what it was.

Wagons were hitched in front of the store, with people they knew sitting in them or leaning against the wheels and talking back and forth. Men spoke to Stanley and women to Frances, and Bow Woman got down from Hunting Horse's wagon and came and put her arms around Spear Woman. They hadn't seen each other for a week, and that can seem a long time.

Frances spoke to the people who spoke to her, but she had business to do, and she would get it out of the way first, before she talked and visited. That was Frances's way. She had learned it while she was away at school. At first she used to hurt people's feeling with it, but then they learned not to mind. Now nobody felt hurt.

"Come, daughter," said Frances to Leah.

Spear Woman watched the child stand up. There was hurt in every bone in Leah's body, but she minded her mother right. She climbed down from the wagon and went into the store with her. Spear Woman followed them.

There was a new storekeeper, not the old, red-faced man who looked as if his own mean temper were choking him, but a man with a thin, brown face and eyes that closed up to slits when he smiled.

"Hello, ma'am," he said to Frances. Then he saw Leah, "Hello, sis," he said, "You're mighty little to be running around loose."

Leah just looked at him. Her finger was going towards her mouth, like a little baby's, but Frances saw it in time and pulled it away. She had a list in her hand, under the shawl, and now she gave it to Leah.

The new storekeeper stood and waited, without asking questions. Maybe he knew that they knew what they wanted. The old one used to act as if you couldn't know and shove things at you until you didn't know what you were taking. You paid more money than you expected to and got home with a lot of things you didn't want. Spear Woman still remembered the time she got home with fifty pounds of beans and forgot the flour.

Leah looked at the list and began to read. She was always afraid she'd forget, so she read very quickly, in a high, tight little voice.

"Fifty pounds of flour, twenty pounds of sugar, ten pounds of beans . . . ."

"Whoa up, sister," said the new storekeeper. "You go too fast. If you'll read a little more slowly, I can get things for you."

Leah caught her breath, deep down inside her, and went back to the top of the list. She pointed her finger at each item as she read it, to make sure. Frances stood behind her, the shawl over her head, her two moccasins pointing straight together, side by side, and didn't move or make a sound. It was all up to Leah, as long as they were in the store.

Leah went down the list, one thing at a time, and the storekeeper got what she wanted, one thing at a time. He didn't look at her, and he didn't talk at all. He just got the things she called for. It was all making Leah feel better, and her voice grew louder and bigger. Stanley came and stood in the door, with some of the men behind him. They must have been telling him about the new storekeeper.

The man kept on getting things until they were all the way to the bottom of the list. He piled everything up on the counter and began to add the prices on a paper sack. Frances reminded Leah, "You got to add the prices, too."

"Please, mister," Leah asked politely, "you tell me the prices? I add my list."

The storekeeper looked clear over her head for a moment. "All right, sis," he said, "if you're big enough to interpret for your mother, I guess you're big enough to add, too."

Frances went deeper into her shawl as he began to call out the prices. Leah wrote them down on her list. The round, stubby figures looked odd next to her mother's tall, slender writing, but she went on putting them down.

"What do you get?" asked the storekeeper, and Leah answered, "Seven dollars and twenty-two cents."

The storekeeper nodded. "That's what I get, too," he said; and Frances drew a deep breath. She always made Leah add figures, but the old storekeeper always said they were added wrong, and that Leah had come out short. Then he added them over, and made a dollar more. When they got home and Frances could check them, she usually found Leah had been right in the first place.

Stanley came from the door and began picking up the sacks to carry them to the wagon. Frances folded her shawl just right and turned towards the door. Leah had done right, and everybody felt proud of her. Later, in the wagon, going home, they would tell her so. Spear Woman wanted to make a war-whoop, she was so proud. Leah was such a little girl that she got out and danced in the prairie-dog town, but here in the store she had walked up to a man she had never seen before in her life, told him what she wanted, and added up the figures just right. She was certainly a smart and good child.

Spear Woman looked around. There was a big jar of candy standing on the counter, round, clear balls, red and yellow and green striped with white. "Come here, granddaughter," she said. "I want you to interpret for me."

Leah looked about ready to cry. This had never happened before. All the other grown-ups made her interpret, but her grandmother never had. Spear Woman bought things by standing in the middle of the floor and pointing to them with her chin. Then she paid for each one as the man gave it to her, to make sure she had it right.

Leah was good about it, though. She said to the storekeeper, "Mister, my grandmother wants something," and the storekeeper came over and said, "All right. What is it, sis?"

Spear Woman jerked her chin at the jar of candy on the counter. "Tell him I want some of that. I want ten cents' worth." She wondered how many ten cents' worth would be, and if it would be enough to show Leah how proud she was of her. The man began to take candy out of the jar and put it in a sack. It made a big lot.

Leah watched his hands, but not his face. Spear Woman let her eyes rise, just for a moment, above his chin, and they met the man's blue ones. His lashes flipped towards Leah and down towards the jar, and Spear Woman nodded. He took out an extra handful of candy and added it to the already full sack.

Back to the Blanket

(1928)

LEAH SAT ON THE TRAIN AND WONDERED. WHEN YOU WERE going back to something that you didn't remember, except that it was there, you had much to wonder about. Her parents had sent her to school in the East when she was nine, and all that she could remember before that was blurred, with a few sharp points sticking out of it, like tablelands coming up out of the Plains.

There was no knowing what she was going back to. There would be space all around her, that she knew. Even in these past years, set in the warmly curled Pennsylvania valleys, she has missed that feeling of flat width. But what would be inside the space was what made her uneasy—maybe nothing and maybe something.

Her step-mother and her father and older sister were clear enough, but they had come East to see her twice. Her father was a smile— what she thought of as a good smile—and a square, chunky, brown block. Her step-mother was short and thin and quick, like a bird. Even coming East she wore her blanket, and her hair was in two smooth, flat braids. Never shoes, always moccasins for both of them.

It was her sister for whom Leah felt sorry. She had had too many babies, too soon. On the trips east she had tried to dress up and do Leah credit. She wore white woman's store-bought dresses and shoes that hurt. But she never could give up her braids, and she knew herself that the dresses were ugly. She was always looking for an excuse to say she was chilly so that she could wrap up in her shawl. All her English seemed to leave her and go back to the mission school where she had learned it. Father and Mother did all right, because when their English gave out, they could smile at people and get along that way; but it was bad for Jane because she thought she ought to talk to people and the words weren't there to be said.

This was the ending of the second day on the train. The people at the school were generous about these things. When the students went home, they were sent first class, in the sleeping cars. It amounted to something, coming home in style like that. When you got off the train, people knew you amounted to something.

238

Back to the Blanket

She had slept all right the first night, but this second one was harder. Sleep kept running away from her, and she tired herself out trying to catch it. When morning came, she couldn't be sure whether she had slept or not, and it made her slow and uncertain in her dressing not to know.

Girdle, brassiere, bloomers, slip, blouse, skirt, jacket. Her hair braided, and the braids twisted around her head. A pin at the throat of her blouse, and then her hat and gloves. She looked at herself and pulled her veil down. The outfit really was stylish. Now that you couldn't see the color of her skin, she could pass anywhere for a white girl.

The school people had given her money for her meals, and when she had had breakfast, she went back to her seat and looked out of the window. It was half-past eight, and the train would be in at ten. Already they were running through space that opened beside and beyond the train and where nothing ever seemed to end or begin. She was a little afraid of the space, and glad of the train window that held it back, but at the same time she was eager and glad to see it, excited by it, wanting to plunge into it.

When the train stopped, she walked squarely and solidly, like her father, down the aisle and carefully got off. The platform was flat ugliness blotting the clean space about it. Beyond it the earth spread red as the Pennsylvania barns. She had forgotten that anything in the world could be so red. Down under the air ran a current of coolness that wasn't a wind, but that made everything feel like moving.

The wagon stood beside the station, and was as ugly. It was painted a green that was the only green in the world that would fight with the red of the earth. The paint ponies, with their homemade harness, drooped their heads and pulled up a foot apiece and looked two-thirds asleep. There was a general feeling that the wagon and the ponies were waiting. When something happened, they would go along, but not because they wanted to.

The three of them, mother, father, and sister, sat on the high seat of the wagon, crowded close together. Behind them there were two chairs fitted into the wagon box. They were old chairs and broken down, and you knew that even when they were new, they weren't good. Packed into the wagon box around the chairs were what looked to Leah like all the groceries in the world.

Father threw the lines over the ponies' backs to touch the ground. He got down from the wagon-seat one muscle at a time and fitted himself to the ground as if to be sure that his feet hit the right places. Then he came across to her and stood and looked straight at her. It gave her a funny feeling, as if nobody had ever looked straight at her before. As far as she could remember, her father never had.

"Is this Leah?" he asked in Kiowa.

She got her name and nodded, looking at the ground as if there were nowhere else to put her eyes. Then she heard her name again, and her step-mother's arms went around her.

"Na-na-na-na! Na-na-na-na! How big she is! And dressed like a white girl. But this is Leah. Couldn't be anybody else."

They stood there a moment, all three of them, smiling and talking in Kiowa. All of a sudden, Leah found words coming back to her. She had thought they were all gone, but she could understand what her step-mother and her father said, and she even began to make little easy words with her tongue and throat herself. It was funny to do it, because in the East, when they came to visit her at school, she had had no words and no understanding of them.

Then she remembered her sister and went towards her with her hand out. Jane had pulled her shawl clear over her head, with just her little hand, as little as people said their grandfather's had been, showing. When Leah spoke to her in English, she let go of the shawl and held out the little hand to shake. She didn't say a word.

Leah turned then, back to her parents. They were bringing her luggage. It startled her to see her little step-mother carrying one end of the trunk like a man. She went over and tried to push her away and take it, but her mother shook her head and went on with the trunk. Father was carrying his end of the trunk and the suitcase, and between them they put the things into the back of the wagon. The train was gone. She was here to stay.

Leah fitted herself into one of the chairs in the back of the wagon, and her step-mother took the other. They had to crawl over a hundred-pound sack of flour, a fifty-pound sack of corn meal, and a big bag of sugar to get there. The sacks of food were just tumbled into the bed of the wagon. Beyond them were sacks of feed for the horses and a can of coal-oil and a quarter of beef that wasn't even in a sack.

Father said something in Kiowa. Jane moved on the seat as if she were turning to face her sister, and explained.

"Old Man say you got excuse things in the wagon. He don't get to town only once a month, got to get lots groceries then."

"That's all right," said Leah. "I don't mind."

She minded that quarter of beef terribly. It hurt her to see the meat lying out like that with the flies all over it. Everything that she had been taught about germs and keeping things clean and keeping coal-oil away from groceries was piling into her head and bothering her.

She wanted to turn around and look at the meat, but she knew if she did, it would make her sick.

She looked ahead and around, and then she remembered. The earth curved just right, not flat, but running away to the foot of the mountains as if it were alive. Underneath, it was red, always red; but on top it was green, the right greens to go with the red. The mountains were the edge of the world. Not big, high mountains like the Alleghenies, but little, warm, round, grey-white mountains that could be big and cold and grey-black some times. There was a creek to the right of them, running south, and out ahead she could see the big bend of the Washita River and the corner that the creek made emptying into it. The ponies were coming to life and stepping as if they liked the feeling of earth instead of cinders under their feet. There was warmth in the day and there was warmth among them in the wagon. Only Jane sat on the edge of it and let herself be cold with shyness.

It was a long trip home. Going along in the wagon, it took all day. There was time for thinking and time for talking. Sometimes Jane spoke, pulling Leah's mind back from its secret place with a jerk, but most of the time mother or father just talked easily.

"The missionaries will be looking for you," her father said, and she answered, "I want to see them."

"They're sure proud of you, what you done. First Kiowa girl going away to college like that. They want you to work at the mission. Make translations. Put Bible stories and church songs into Kiowa."

"That's good," said Leah.

"They think it's pretty important, what you do now. Got to set an example to everybody. Got to show everybody what to do. You're pretty important, all right."

Her step-mother spoke, "That's right, pretty important. Grandmother says she's going to make war-whoop for you, like for a young man coming back from the raids in the old days." She laughed. "Then you have to give her a horse."

Father laughed too. "Where's she going to get a horse? Took all her horses to keep her in school. Had to sell all her horses to buy those good clothes she's got on."

That was a new thought. Leah had never wondered much about where her clothes came from. She leaned forward and spoke directly to Jane in English.

"Is that true? Did they have to sell all my horses?"

"We all had to sell some horses," Jane said. "You don't get good clothes, lots books, all like that, without money. Sometimes missionaries writing us. You got to have things. You needing them. Then we sell horses, send the money to the school."

Leah had never had any money herself, except her dollar weekly allowance. The missionaries said they gave the students an allowance to teach them responsibility and the use of money. She had never thought about how she was kept in school. The missionaries had said they were sending her to a mission school, and she had supposed it was like the mission church, kept up by the white people to help the Indians. It didn't seem fair to tell people you were doing things to help them and then make them pay for it.

"I'm sorry you had to sell horses," she said to Jane, and Jane said quietly, "That's all right. We sold them to the soldiers. They weren't very good horses, just work horses. Couldn't run."

Leah wondered about selling off the work horses and keeping the ones that could run, when you lived on a farm and needed work horses for plowing. That wasn't what she had been taught at school, but that was why she had gone to school, so that she could come back and educate her people. She'd have to start doing it, but this didn't seem a good place to begin.

Jane let her shawl go back over her shoulders so that it lay in soft folds, like her step-mother's. She seemed easier now. She began to talk a little more.

"What they teaching you at that school? Just books?"

"Lots of things," Leah answered.

"What things?" Jane persisted.

"How to work in the house, scrubbing and sweeping and dusting. How to take care of things, mending and washing and ironing. Making clothes last a long time."

"That's good," said Jane. "Those clothes you got on won't last long out here. Dust just cuts through that soft cloth. Won't have any hem left on your skirt in four days."

That was about right, too. The dust had got through her clothes to her skin already, and the various layers of clothing were all rubbing against each other and against her, and against every separate grain of dust. It felt like things crawling over each other and over her. It was bad, and she wanted to scratch.

"I got wash dresses in my trunk," she said.

"You got shawl, too?" Jane wanted to know. "You going to need shawl. Hat's blowing off, getting lost out here."

It was a mean, mischievous wind. There had been none all morning, and now it came out of the noon that was drawing the mountains close. It twisted up handfuls of dust from the red earth and twined them around the wagon like vines going around a tree trunk. When it was gone, Leah's hat was gone with it.

"Na-na-na-na!" mother cried, and father stopped the wagon and got ready to move himself down to earth to go after it.

"That's all right," Leah said, "Let it go. Don't go after it. It's a heavy hat anyhow. Makes my head ache."

Father chuckled deep down and got back on the wagon seat. "Maybe she's some Indian anyhow," he said to Jane.

"She looks like an Indian," mother said. The braids would never stay up against her head without her hat to hold them, and already they were slipping down and hanging to her waist. They felt better that way, lighter and not so thick.

"I guess we better eat," father said, and stopped the wagon.

They had gone over one of those sudden folds in the earth and had come upon a creek that you didn't expect, going through a grove of cottonwoods and willows that surprised you, too. It was all green and cool and quiet, held in the clear space as if nothing could touch it.

They all got down from the wagon, and father unhitched and turned the ponies loose. Mother and Jane went off up the creek, and when they came back, their shawls were over their shoulders, full of little limbs and branches and dead stuff.

"Pecan wood," mother said. "That's what makes a good cooking fire. Flavors the meat like salt."

Leah watched while Jane built the fire. She was neat and quick about it, with small, tidy gestures that seemed to waste neither wood nor movement. Leah turned to see what her mother was doing. She had pulled the piece of meat across the floor of the wagon, and was whittling off some of the ribs.

The fire was like perfume, but Leah knew that however sweet the smoke smelled, she could never eat any of that meat. She took off her jacket and folded it carefully on the chair, and said to Jane, "Is there anything I can do?" as if she were speaking politely to one of the lady teachers at the school.

"You can get water," Jane told her, and jerked her chin towards a bucket that hung under the wagon.

"Where's the well?" Leah asked.

"Down there," Jane jerked her chin towards the creek.

"You drink creek water?"

"Sure. That's all the water there is around here."

"But it isn't safe. It might be infected."

Jane forgot about the fire for a moment. "What's that?"

"It might have germs in it."

"What's germs?"

"Little animals that you can't see that make you sick."

"Hum." Jane went back to her fire. "If you can't see them, what makes you know they're there?"

"You can see them through the microscope."

"What's micorscope?"

"It's a thing to make little things look bigger."

"Like missionary's glasses?"

"Sort of."

"Missionaries need glasses to see things they want to see," said Jane. "It's the things they say they don't want to see they spot without no glasses. I guess they want to see those old germs all right if they look at them with glasses. You got one of them things with you?"

"A germ?"

"One of them 'scope things."

"No. They cost too much. Just a few people have them."

"I guess you could have one if you wanted it. We can always sell more horses."

That hurt. Leah took the bucket, and, germs or no germs, went down to the creek for water. It was hard, coming back to this life. The missionaries made it sound easy. You went away for most of your life and forgot your own language, but you learned lots of other things to take the place of it. Then you went back and taught all the new things to the people at home, and they did better and lived better, like you. There was just one danger that you had to look out for. That was going back to the blanket. If you ever went back to the blanket, you were lost. Then there was no hope for you any more. You would be just Indian all your life.

It was really hot when she came back through the sun to the shade with the bucket. At first she thought it was the fire that made things hot, but all of its heat was going into cooking the meat. It was just time moving around to noon that made the heat. Nobody else seemed to be hot. Jane was watching the meat, and mother had got a paper bag of things from the wagon and was spreading out store bread and some oranges and stick candy.

The meat and the smoke together smelled good. It was cooler in the shade, and Leah found that she was hungry. She still didn't want to eat that meat, but when Jane gave her a piece laid on a slice of store bread, she didn't want to hurt her sister's feelings and she bit into it.

"Look out for germs," Jane warned her.

"I guess maybe cooking will kill them. Scalding water will."

She hadn't said "I guess maybe" since the first year she was at school. You could say it two ways. One way was when you made up your mind to do a thing and nothing could change you. The other way was, as now, when it meant you were making a joke. The English teacher said "I guess maybe" was redundancy and you didn't need all those words. Jane must have thought you did need them, because it made them both feel easier.

They ate, and then they rested against the grass. Leah wondered if she slept and thought she did because she hadn't last night, and knew she didn't because she knew everything that was around her. She had never thought about the shapes of grass blades or that they had different colors on their two sides before. She had always thought of shadows as grey or black but they were blue when father got up off the grass and began to hitch up the ponies.

It was cooler than at noon, but she didn't put the jacket on. She still felt hotter than her mother or sister looked. She asked Jane, "What you got on underneath?"

Jane just turned and looked at her feet. "Nothing," she said.

You couldn't have told it. She looked perfectly well covered up in the straight, cotton dress with full sleeves. Of course the overskirt kept her legs from showing through. It was just as modest as anybody else's clothes, even if it weren't stylish. It looked all right in this country.

The house had been built by the missionaries to be a model Indian home. It was square and solid, with its fields around it. There was a high porch on the front, looking south and south to the mountains that dusk was pushing away from them again. Under the porch was storage space for canned goods. It had some in it, but there was a lot of harness there, too, because it was closer to where they unhitched the wagon than the barn was.

They ate again, and then slept on their beds. The bed was hard, just a thin mattress over boards, but it was sleep that Leah had forgotten that took hold of her and held her. It let her go with the first movements of morning. She wondered which moved first, her mother or the mockingbird in the tree outside the kitchen.

It would be hot again today. It would be hot every day until the rains came, and then it would be cool suddenly and quickly. Jane had been sleeping in the arbor, and she came in now for a clean dress.

"You got another dress?" Leah asked her.

"Sure," said Jane. "I got four dresses." She opened the dresser drawer. Showing off, like women in the old days who had lots of buckskin clothes. All Indian.

"You lend me one?" Leah asked.

"What you want with it?" Jane sounded suspicious.

"I'm hot," Leah replied. "These clothes are hot. I want to put on something cool. Then I'll make over some house dresses to be like yours. That way's cooler, and you don't need a slip."

Jane handed her the dress and overskirt. "Sure is funny," she said. "You go away, learn to be white woman. First thing when you come back, you put on Indian clothes."

"Indian clothes are better here. You got to wear clothes you can work in."

"That's right," Jane said. "I got to work today, too. Got to dry that beef."

She went about it after breakfast, slicing the meat away from the ribs in sheets as thin as tissue-paper, then gashing each sheet against the grain of the meat. She threw them up over a bar in the sun as she finished, and the sun and the flies fought over them.

Leah wanted to help her, but when she said so, Jane said, "This is Indian way. Gets lots germs on the meat. That's what makes it taste good," and Leah went off to unpack her trunk.

That took all day, and when she had finished, she had just re-packed it, with her books and heavy clothes at the bottom and her cotton dresses at the top where she could get at them. Even in the thin cotton of Jane's dress she was hot and sweaty, with her braids tied together at the back of her neck making her even hotter. She went out on the porch and unbraided her hair and got ready to brush it before supper. Father sat down on the steps.

"Wagon coming," he said presently.

Mother was sitting on the porch floor behind Leah's chair.

"Missionaries' wagon," she said.

Leah could see a spot in movement, that was all. It could have been a horse or a cow until she squinted her eyes up. Then she could see a small spot ahead of a big one—a horse pulling a wagon.

The spots turned across the fields head on, and lost their two shapes and became one big one. A blue roan was pulling a black wagon. The black looked worse against the fields even than father's green wagon. The roan plopped his feet up and down in the dust until he came to the steps and stopped there.

"Hello, there," said the man missionary. "Good evening."

"Get down, friend," said father, and the missionary laughed and repeated the Kiowa words and got down. He went around to the side of the wagon and helped his wife to the ground. Leah remembered her mother, climbing down all by herself yesterday and felt ashamed of her father for not helping his wife. Jane came and stood in the door behind them.

"Where is Leah?" asked the lady missionary. "My, I can hardly wait to see her. Such a little thing when she went away, and a grown-up young lady now. We're so proud of her. I said to father this morning, 'We'll just harness up in the cool of the evening and drive right over and get Leah,' that's what I said; and he said, 'Mother, you're just right,' he said. Where is she?"

She was coming up the steps with little nervous hoppings all the time she was talking and now she was standing right in front of Leah, looking at that sheet of black hair pouring down and hiding her face.

"That's her," said Jane, pulling her chin around to point.

Leah shook back her hair and stood up.

"Good evening, Mrs. Gaines," she said.

"Why, Leah! Why my dear child! Why, what has happened! Look at her, father. Look at this poor creature. Something terrible must have happened. Where are your clothes, my dear? Did you lose your trunk? What happened to your hair?"

"I was unpacking my trunk, and I got hot. I took down my hair to brush it."

"Oh, that's all right then. I thought something had happened. I thought maybe—Where did you get that dress?"

"That's her dress," said Jane suddenly from the door. "I made it for her."

"You made her a squaw dress? Jane, that was wrong. You had no right. You know she's educated. She wouldn't want to wear those clothes."

"She's Indian," Jane's voice was stubborn. "She's just educated Indian."

This was harder than anything Leah had dreamed. She thought she would come home, go to the mission, work to uplift her people. It would all be easy. Then she would marry some good young man, not an Indian, a missionary, and go away and do good all her life. And here was her own sister calling her Indian.

"That's just it," said Mrs. Gaines. "She's educated. She's got intelligence. She knows better than to dress like that and run around like everybody."

The English teacher at school had said intelligence was capacity for learning, and that having learned was knowledge. Jane had capacity for learning all the things Leah had learned. She just hadn't learned, and so she lacked knowledge. But the missionary woman didn't seem to know the difference between the two. She couldn't be very intelligent herself.

"Get your bag, Leah," said Mr. Gaines. It surprised you to hear him because most of the time his wife drowned him out. "We want to get home at six o'clock in time for supper."

Why, supper was when you were hungry. That was the time to eat. They had all been working and were hot, and they wouldn't eat until they had cooled off. It was silly to say you must be hungry at six o'clock or ten o'clock or any other one time. It had always seemed silly, even at the school. Leah shook her head.

"I guess I won't go," she said. "I guess I'll stay here awhile. I haven't seen my folks for a long time."

"But we have your room all ready for you and the things laid out for you to go to work." That was Mrs. Gaines all right, making plans and making everybody stick to them. Too many plans kept you from living. You were all the time trying to catch up with the things you'd planned to do.

"Maybe Leah wants a little visit with her folks first," said Mr. Gaines more quietly. He wasn't so tied down to living in a certain line. "It's been a long time since she saw them. Maybe she wants to get acquainted again."

"Of course it's a long time since she saw them! That's the whole plan of Indian education. How can these children learn to be good, upright men and women and set a good example if they aren't given an opportunity? If they have to see the old things going on around them all the time and live the old way, how are they going to make the others change for anything better?"

Well, father and mother had changed all right and had done it without going away, although father had gone to the school at Fort Sill. They had a house instead of a tipi, and they rode in a wagon instead of on horseback. They could buy flour and bread and sugar and cloth in stores instead of going out and killing something to eat and tanning its hide for clothes—those were all things the white people meant when they talked about being progressive—and they had learned staying at home.

"I guess I better stay here awhile," she said. "You want me to translate some things, but I couldn't right now. My Kiowa's not good enough. I better stay home and learn it again."

"It'll come back to you," said Mrs. Gaines determinedly. "When you've been here a month, you'll find you remember it. You don't have to stay at home to learn it. Why, you'll pick it up from father, here. He preaches in Indian once a month."

Back to the Blanket

Leah's father just didn't smile, but it was only because he was too polite. Leah remembered one thing they had said about Mr. Gaines, years ago when she was just a little girl. "He thinks he's talking Kiowa, but all he's doing is shaking the arbor poles." They had even named him after that. That was one of his names Mr. Gaines didn't know about. He always told visiting missionaries about the name he did know, because he was proud of it. It meant "Loud Talking Man."

"Thank you for asking me," Leah told them. "I bet I could learn a lot from Mr. Gaines. But this is where I belong. I think I had better stay here and learn."

"If you stay here, you ought to teach. That's what you're equipped for. There's nothing these people can teach you, they have everything to learn from you."

Leah didn't like that, calling her family "these people," with all of them standing there understanding every word. "I guess maybe I stay here," she said. Jane came out of the door and stood beside her. They were suddenly alike. You knew they had to be sisters.

"I can't do good to people if all they think about when they see me is how different I am," Leah said. "You have to be enough like people so that they will stop thinking about how you look and just remember that your mind feels right to them. I have to stay here until we all feel that."

"That's the way it is," said Mrs. Gaines. She didn't sound angry so much as tired and hurt. She went back to the wagon and stood waiting for her husband to help her up to the seat. She looked little and old and sharp, like an old flint arrow in a museum.

"You take these children away and put them in a good environment. You do everything in the world for them that you can. Just when you think you've changed them and made something out of them, they fool you. They'll go back to the blanket every time, even the best of them."

Mr. Gaines helped her into the wagon and turned the blue roan. At the corner of the fence, he turned to call, "Try to come to church Sunday," and they went away, with the two spots of the wagon and horse getting smaller until they turned into one spot.

Leah sat down again. Her knees folded under her and she missed the chair and sat on the floor. The sun was sloping across from the west end of the porch, and she sat in a puddle of it with her hair still down around her shoulders.

So she had gone back to the blanket. She had quarreled with her sister, and they had hurt each other's feelings. She had tried to get near her step-mother and her father, and there was always something between them that prevented her. She was different from them and they all knew it, and none of them felt right about it. Mrs. Gaines said she had gone back to the blanket because she wouldn't come and live at the mission.

What good would it do to live at the mission? There was no warmness from her to Mr. and Mrs. Gaines. There was respect, that was all. Here there was warmness towards the people around her and towards her, anyway. Yes, and there were the beginnings of respect. They hadn't tried to hold her back or force her to go. They had left it up to her to make her own decision. That was what people did when they had respect for each other. Then they could sit still together and think things out, too, as now. There was privacy in that way. You didn't have to go into another room to be alone. People knew without telling when your mind needed leaving alone and were careful not to touch it with theirs.

She got up, then, and braided her hair. Jane stood up, too. "Come on," said Leah. "I guess maybe we better bring that meat in for the night. Dew might make it spoil."

"That's right," said Jane. They went towards the drying bar.

"That old Mrs. Gaines," said Jane. "She's got a lot to learn. All these years she's living in Indian country, and she still looks right at us when she's talking to us."

Leah began taking down the meat and piling it on a piece of canvas. Jane went on talking. "But we got things to learn, too. All that talk about germs. Makes things sound like they're dirty, animals crawling all over them. Maybe they are. Maybe we better learn things like that. Indians sure like to have things clean."

Breaking Camp

(1930)

THE BAD THING ABOUT GETTING TO BE VERY OLD, TO Eagle Plume, was the feeling of having lived away from everybody he knew. Your parents died, and then your wives and your brothers and sisters died. That was all right. You expected that. But after a while your own children died, and then you were left going on living. Living was a thing that didn't get any easier with practice, either.

Maybe one reason he had been left living so long was so he could go on taking care of the Grandmother God. It was hard to find one of the young men who would want to do that. It was hard, having that Grandmother to take care of. It had to live in its own tipi, and nothing must ever strike against the tipi-cover. Just getting a tipi-cover was hard, and with no woman to put it up, it looked bad. Instead of being stretched tight and smooth over the poles, it was loose and bagged in like the seat of an old man's pants.

It was good, in a way, that his sight was going. With his eyes dimming, he couldn't see that kind of fault so sharply, and if he just glanced at the tipi without stopping to look, it was the way a Grandmother God's tipi ought to be, tight and smooth and white.

There was another thing that was worrying him. He didn't get hungry now the way he used to when he was a young man, but there never seemed to be enough to eat. Farming was too hard for him, and his tenants were always behind with their rent, so that he never had money to buy food. Even if he did, he couldn't go off the place and leave the Grandmother all alone. He had to wait until somebody else was going into town and have them get food for him.

But all those things weren't so bad as the feeling of aloneness. Sometimes it took one form and sometimes another. His dead brother who had given him his power would be standing before him, reminding him of the time when they were young men and the power was given. Eagle Plume never asked his brother to take the power back. You couldn't return power once it was given to you. There was always a reason for your having it. But sometimes he did tell his brother what hard kind of power it was to have.

Other times it was his dead sister, the one who had gone to mission school and studied in the East, and had married Hunting Horse's son, Stanley Hunt. She was little and round, the way he remembered her when she was just a young girl growing up. Sometimes he cried when he saw her, and once he said to her what he wouldn't say to any of the other gone people when he saw them. "I wish you were back here with me," he said. "I wish I had somebody like you to take care of me."

Later he knew that it was just dreaming when he saw the people of the past so clearly, but at the time it was always true. They were realer to him than his tenants or the other people he saw most often.

When he saw the green-painted wagon like his own old wagon coming through the gate, he didn't know whether it was a bygone wagon or a live one. It didn't make much difference. He sat and watched it come. Three people on the seat and a lead horse behind. There was no way to know who the people were, but their shapes were those of a man and a woman and a boy.

The woman was short and round, and she let herself to the ground over the wheel slowly and easily, and came over to him the same way. She came and stood straight in front of him where he could see her, and for a moment he thought it was his sister again. Then she spoke.

"There you are, mother's brother."

Then he knew her. It was his sister's daughter. He hadn't seen her for a long time. He got to his feet and put his arms around her to embrace her.

"There you are, niece."

She turned and gestured to the man on the wagon seat. He came over and shook hands, and the boy followed. Eagle Plume knew his niece's husband, Packing Rocks' son, but the boy was strange to him.

"This is my husband's nephew. His name is Fred."

They all sat down, and the younger man rolled cigarettes. When the old man's was lighted and the two of them were smoking, Eagle Plume said, "It's good of you to come here, niece."

She pulled the fringe of her black silk shawl to and fro through her fingers as she answered. "I saw my mother, uncle."

Eagle Plume nodded. "I see her sometimes. She comes and talks to me."

The husband said under his breath, "It's all just dreaming."

The woman shook her head. "No, I don't think so. I saw my mother plainly, just the way she always looked. She was standing in front of her brother and holding out her hands to him. There were tears in her eyes and on her cheeks. She was mourning over him. She wanted me to take care of him."

She stopped and bent her head over the shawl fringe.

"I have seen her that way, too," said Eagle Plume.

"That's why we're here," she went on. "That's what brings us. My mother wants you to be happy. She wants you to live with us and be taken care of. Over at our place things are nice. Lots of people there to help. Everything goes easy."

Eagle Plume was quiet for a few minutes, thinking. The younger man gave him another cigarette and he smoked it through before he spoke.

"That's good and kind of you," he said. "That's the right sort of thing to do. I'm grateful to you for thinking of me. But if you take me to live with you, you don't take just one. You take two, and we got to live a certain way. We even got to travel a certain way."

His niece looked at her husband, and they both nodded.

"That's all right," the man said. "We thought about that. That's why we brought the boy. He's just young, so it's all right. He can help out. He can ride the horse with that other one you have to take care of. It can't go in the wagon and you can't ride, but with the boy to carry it, it's all right."

Eagle Plume took a big breath. Things were working out. Some young people knew the way they ought to act. They cared enough to find out, if they didn't already know. He should have believed his sister's daughter would know the way things ought to be done, but it hadn't seemed possible. Young women got so careless nowadays.

"That's all right," he said. "Tomorrow we can start. We better start early. Where do you live now, niece?"

"Just north and east of the hot springs, along the creek," she said, and he knew the place. It was the same place where Packing Rocks always used to have his camp in the old days. That meant most likely they were living on Packing Rocks' place, and that explained a lot. Packing Rocks had one of the Grandmothers, and anybody that lived around him would know the right way for things to be done. He was that kind of a man. He cared about doing things right.

"It's a long way over there," Eagle Plume said to the boy. "It's going to be a hard trip. Did they tell you the things you have to do?"

The boy was very quiet. He was a little scared because he was taking part in something sacred, but he answered politely, "I got to ride the horse and carry that sacred thing on the saddle horn. I got to start right after daylight and keep going until we get there. All day

I have to go fasting. I can't eat until the tipi's set up and that thing's inside it."

"Do you think you can do it?" Eagle Plume asked. He really wanted to know. If the boy had any doubts, it would be better to wait and try to find somebody else.

"I can do it," the boy said. "I think that sacred thing will help me do it."

Packing Rocks must have told him that, but it didn't matter how he had learned it, because it was true.

The woman got up now and brought food from the wagon. She built up the fire and cooked, and they all ate. There was meat and store bread and coffee with sugar. After they had eaten all they wanted of that food, she gave them sweet cake with jam on it. There was much food, and they were all hungry. Eagle Plume ate and ate, trying not to let the food spill on him. When he was alone, it didn't matter, but with the others looking on it was different.

When they had finished, his niece brought him warm water, and her husband helped him wash. It was too dusk and his eyes were too dim for him to see the tears that ran steadily down her face, and somehow she kept them from showing in her voice. Everything they did must be done not because they were sorry for him. It must be because it was duty. They had the privilege of helping this old man along.

Sleeping was easy and dreamless for Eagle Plume. When the woman laid her hand on his shoulder to wake him, the world was already shaping itself out of the darkness. While he and the younger man ate, she and the boy packed up his clothes and took down the tipi.

"You come now," she said, when he had finished eating. "Come and get the sacred things all together."

There was the bundle on the west pole, and the pipe on the north side of the fire-hole. His buffalo-skin robe lay on the bed beneath the bundle, and he wrapped it around him and stood up. He spoke to his niece.

"The woman has to carry those things out of the tipi," he told her. "You got to take them out to the boy."

She put the bundle on her back the proper way, with the pipe tied across the top of it. Then she went around the north side of the circle of tipi-poles, and out through the place where the door had been. The boy was already mounted, and she carried the bundle across to the horse. On her way there, she made three stops. The fourth time, she was standing beside the saddle horn. The two men were already in the wagon.

When the bundle was tied to the saddle horn, she lifted herself to the wagon-seat, and they started. They went slowly, and as they passed through the gate, the shapes of things, that had been growing clearer, were all at once hard and sharp, and the sun was a hard red plate against the east sky.

The road went up and down, up and down, along the Washita valley. Sometimes it drew near the river and other times turned away from it. When the river was near, there were trees and shade, but away from the water there was the sun and the shapes it cast and the dusty red earth. That was all; there was no shade away from the river.

They kept on going slowly. The Grandmothers had been living for men for longer than any man knew, and they never had hurried. They took care of people and put things right that were wrong with their lives, but they never hurried about it. They always did everything in their own time and in their own way.

Nobody talked much. That wouldn't have seemed right. They were all small and weak beside the bundle that was tied to the saddle horn, and if it didn't want to talk, there was no reason why they should. Besides, they were doing something sacred, and when you did sacred things, you had to be careful not to go wrong. Just one wrong act could make it bad for everybody.

The road and the plowing had changed the shape of the country. Where once it had run together and been an even, smooth, soft color, brown or green or red with the seasons, now there were edges to the colors, and they lay in sharp-cut patterns. There were ditches beside the road that had never been there before, and with the change in the color and the shape of things, the feel of the world had changed. Still it felt good, riding along this way with people who belonged to you and took care of you and knew the way things ought to be done.

In the middle of the morning they came out beside the Washita, and Eagle Plume held up his hand for them to stop in the shade. He stood up in the wagon and faced back to the east and prayed, softly at first, just muttering under his breath, and then as he felt them praying with him in their hearts, aloud. The boy sat quietly, leaning forward in the saddle, knowing that three stops were necessary before they came home.

"Give the boy water," said Eagle Plume when he had finished praying. His niece looked startled.

"That's not the way they did it in the old days," she said.

"In the old days we didn't do it this way at all," Eagle Plume answered. "We didn't have any wagons, and a man gave up sacred things before he was too weak to care for them. There was always someone ready to take them from him, in the old days."

They gave the boy water and he drank it and they went on. At noontime, when they stopped, it was the same way. Prayer and a drink for the boy, and the others sat and waited. None of them spoke of eating, and none of them wanted to eat. There was something with them, inside of them, that made fasting easier than feeding. Still they went on and turned south.

By mid-afternoon things looked more the way they used to, to Eagle Plume. They were getting away from the part of the country the white people had taken over, and you knew they were going through Indian country. The fires smelled different, and there was a brush arbor near every house. It was like coming towards a camp in the old days. It was like coming home. The third stop was on the south side of a hill, where the wind could come and run its fingers over his face, as if it, too, were losing its sight and wanted to know who the person was that it touched.

Then the way was all downhill and over smooth, round, curving ground, without sharp angles or harsh colors, but just the dusty red-grey of late summer to make all the colors run together softly as did the shapes of the earth. They came along a little ridge, and the valley with the creek through it shaped itself in front of them. There was a house on each side of the creek at the north end of the valley, and at the south end on the west side was another house with a big brush arbor. To the west of it was a cleared space. The woman touched the old man's arm.

"That's where we're going to put your tipi," she said. "That is the best place for it. The brushes are all cut to put up a windbreak for it, too."

They circled around so as to come up to the tipi-place from the south, and they went around the cleared circle four times and stopped on the east side of it. Then the woman got down from the wagon, and began to put the tipi up. She worked quickly, and she knew how. It didn't take her very long to get things ready.

When she had finished, the tipi looked the way a tipi should. The canvas was tight and smooth over the poles, and you knew it would stay that way no matter which way the wind blew. You could look straight at the tipi and know it was all right. It was the right kind of home for a sacred thing and the man who had the right to take care of it.

Eagle Plume got down from the seat of the wagon and gathered the buffalo robe around him. His niece's husband would have helped him, but he felt better not being helped. He went over to the tipi and around it three times, and the fourth time he went inside and sat down on the west.

They had to lift the boy down from the saddle and rub his legs before he could walk. When he was able to go, the woman tied the bundle on her back and led the way around and into the tipi. She went around the south side and kneeled down in front of Eagle Plume.

"Here is this sacred thing, uncle," she said. "Now it is home again in its own place where it belongs to be."

Eagle Plume unfastened the bundle from her back, and hung it up in its own place on the west above his bed. Then anything trying to get it would touch him first. He untied the little, old, black stone pipe from the top of the bundle, and filled it with mixed sumach and tobacco, and lighted it.

"Grandmother," he said, when he had blown the four puffs, "Grandmother, you are very old. I am very old, too, but not as old as you are. We are such old people we can't always take care of ourselves the way we used to, but we can still take care of each other. I cared for you as long as I was able, and now you have found these young people to take care of both of us. This is where we are staying. We have set our spear here. All my life I will stay here, and you will stay with me. And when my ribs fall in and I die of old age, you will keep on staying here. This is where you want to go on staying, or you wouldn't have come here. That's all."

He put his hands on the young people's heads and shoulders and blessed them, and they went away out of the tipi so that he could sit and talk to his god.

Strength of Power

(1936)

LATE SUN MADE LONG BROWN SHADOWS OVER THE BROWN GRASS. The end of summer covered everything with a fine, dusty coating that was like a film between your eyes and the shapes of things. Nothing quite had edges any more, not like the blue haze of early summer when everything showed sharp-cut and distinct against the softening color.

William wondered whether the ending of a season was like the ending of a life. Things were there; they were the same and you felt the same about them, but the edges were a little bit hazed over and the keenness of the feeling seemed to be lost. His father rode the short distance between the two houses, dropped the lines over his horse's neck and was looking at him while he was still wondering.

"Get down, father."

"Here I am, son."

Packing Rocks put his feet on the ground and moved his bulky body to a place beside his son. They sat without speaking, and without speaking Jane brought them coffee. There was plenty of sugar in it, but no milk. The cows had all been eating ragweed and the milk was good only for pigs.

"How is Fred?"

"Jane says he's just the same."

"He just sits?"

"That's all, father."

Packing Rocks set the coffee cup behind him, for Jane to reach, and watched the shadows run together on the ground in front of him.

"It's hard for a man, having a sick son."

"Harder if the son is sick in the head."

"When he was little," Packing Rocks said, and it was the first time William had ever heard him go back to the childhood of his children, "when he was little, he was different from the rest of you. Quieter. He would sit still and study for a long time at a stretch. Seemed like he was thinking things out."

William nodded. "I remember that. He was younger than the rest of us, and we teased him. Maybe that hurt his feelings."

Packing Rocks shook his head slowly. "I don't think it was that. Most boys get teased by their brothers. It won't hurt their feelings for long. I think he just wanted to be thinking things out, even then."

"Maybe so. He did lots of thinking things out afterwards."

"That's right. He was good at it. College professors all said he was good. They paid respect to him for his mind."

"They all said he had a good mind, one of the best."

"Seems like a long time ago," Packing Rocks said. "Seems like as long ago as when he was a little boy."

"Not but a year."

"I know that. Lots can happen in a year."

"Well, anyway," said William, and there was hate in his mouth and inside him, too, "that boy who was driving the car got killed in the wreck."

"Yes," Packing Rocks sounded as if he had been thinking about it for a long time. "He got killed, all right. That's all over for him. He doesn't have to go on living without knowing. Whatever happened to him, he knows it or he doesn't know it. It's not like just catching at things you ought to have known once."

"He was lucky."

"Yes, he was lucky, all right. It's my boy who got punished, and he never hurt anybody. He was good."

All his life Fred had been good. He was kind and gentle, and he never did hurt anybody. Even now, with his mind, that had been the best part of him, gone, he wasn't bad. He was sweet, and he minded Jane better than any of the children. It seemed to worry him if he got dirty. That was about all he knew, to keep himself clean.

Jane stood in the door behind them. She couldn't speak to her father-in-law any more than in the old days, but her words went through her husband to the older man.

"Indian Service doctor was here today."

Packing Rocks, too, spoke to William to reach Jane.

"Did he see Fred?"

"He saw him."

"What did he say?"

"He said he might be able to help him."

"Can he make him well?"

"He doesn't know that. He can try."

"How do they do that?"

"They put him to sleep first, so he won't feel anything."

The Ten Grandmothers

"That's good. Better if the sick person sleeps." Packing Rocks spoke as one who knew, for he doctored in his own way.

"Then they take a little sharp knife, cut through his scalp and his skull."

"They scalp him?"

"They can make the hair grow back so the scar won't show."

"Then what?"

"They cut through the skull, take out a little piece of bone. Then they can reach his brain."

"He's still living while they're doing this?"

"He's still living, only he's sleeping."

"What do they do when they get to the brain?"

"Then they take out the bad thing that's pushing on it. Old, dried-up lump of blood, they think. When the pushing on the brain stops, then he's all well."

"That's what's making him sick? Old, dried-up piece of blood pushing on his brain?"

"That's what the white doctor says."

The shadows were all one big shadow, now, and that was bluish, brownish night. It rolled up from the draw and covered them and shut out everything but their voices from each other. They were all still, and even the voices were covered up in the dark.

"What does the white doctor do to know what's wrong?"

"I don't know," Jane answered. "He looks and looks. Sometimes with a little light in Fred's eyes."

"That's funny. He ought to look inside himself to know."

"He says he can tell better at the hospital. Got more things to work with there. Wants to take Fred to the hospital and study about it there."

"Would he do the cutting there?"

"That's where he wants to do it, but not right away. Wants to study about it some more first."

"Then some morning when he gets tired studying, just gets up and goes to cutting."

"He won't do that." William knew enough about the hospital to feel sure. "He won't do any cutting unless you say he can. He's got to have your word to go first."

"That's all right," Packing Rocks rose. "If it seems like the right thing, I give my word. But I got to study first, too." He rode away and left them silent in summer darkness.

Packing Rocks sat in his tipi and studied. He built a little fire, in spite of the heat, and sat over it with his rawhide rattle and sang his own medicine songs quietly to himself. Eagle Plume heard him and felt his way into the tipi and sat and helped with the singing. Even if Eagle Plume's eyes were gone, his voice was still strong, and he knew the old songs. All the talking they did was through the singing, because they could understand the sound better than other people understood words.

The white doctor came again at the end of the week. Packing Rocks rode over to William's to see him. No one was at home but Jane and that made it hard because he couldn't speak to her. But he came in and looked at a beam in the ceiling and spoke to it.

"Please tell that woman who is married to my son that I want her to interpret for me."

Jane looked at the same beam and talked back to it.

"Please tell my husband's father I'll do it."

"Ask the white doctor some things for me."

"All right."

The doctor came out of Fred's bedroom and spoke to Jane.

"What does he say?" asked Packing Rocks.

"He says that Fred isn't any better. He won't get any better. Maybe he won't get any worse for a long time, then it'll all be over quickly. He'll just fall over dead."

"Can that white doctor make him better?"

"He says he thinks he can."

"Is he sure?"

"He isn't sure. Sometimes it works, sometimes it doesn't."

"Where did he get his power?"

That was a hard thing to translate. Somehow Jane made the doctor understand it, but it took her a long time.

"He says he studied a long time. He went to colleges. Then he worked in a hospital. Older doctors, who knew how, taught him there."

Packing Rocks nodded. "That's all right. That's one way to get power. Study with older men. They can give it to a young man."

The doctor stood quietly with his bag in his hand.

"I have power, too. I have power to heal. I have made lots of people well. Tell him that." All was spoken to the beam, as was Jane's answer.

"He says that in the old days, men could heal many times. They healed by belief. Their belief and the sick person's belief."

"That is true. That I have seen."

"But now doctors have different power. Now they heal by belief, but they have to act to help the belief."

"We act to help belief, too. We sing. Sometimes there are motions we have to make. We suck out the thing that's making the person sick."

"He says he cuts out the bad thing, instead of sucking."

"That's all right. Maybe his power showed him different."

"He says the main thing is to make the sick person well."

"That's right. That's what you've got to do."

"He says he wants permission to take Fred to the hospital and cut the bad thing out."

"If Fred goes, will this man do the cutting?"

"He's the one who will do it."

"And what if he doesn't do it right? What if his power doesn't work?"

"Two things can happen. Fred may stay just the same way, if it doesn't work. Or maybe if it doesn't work, he'll die."

"If he dies, what will happen to the doctor?"

There was a long silence after Jane translated that question. The doctor thought about it heavily. Jane didn't help him with an answer; she couldn't. Men knew the answers to these questions, and they must make those answers to each other. Only very old women could have healing power, and it was different for every person who had it, anyway. At last the doctor spoke.

"He says nothing will happen to him. He will feel bad inside, and he will be sorry, but nothing will happen to him."

"His power won't hurt him."

"He says his power is good. It doesn't want to hurt anybody."

"My power is good, too," said Packing Rocks. "My power doesn't want to hurt anybody. But if I fail with a patient, my power can hurt me. Maybe it will kill me; maybe it will kill somebody I love. That shows I haven't used it right. I have to run that risk every time I heal somebody, that maybe the power will be used wrong and will hurt me."

"The doctor says his power is different. Sometimes it's strong and heals. Sometimes it isn't strong enough, and the person dies or just doesn't get well enough. Then he feels bad, but that's the only way it hurts him."

Packing Rocks thought for a long time. It was hard, but the decision was up to him. He had to make it himself, alone. Then he knew what he must do.

"Tell the white doctor," he said to the beam, "that I've made up my mind. My own power can't heal my son. It's not for that kind of sickness, in the head. But when I heal I'm sure of my power. Nobody has ever been hurt by it yet because I used it wrong. If that doctor can't put his own life and his family's life on his power, then it isn't strong enough to use. My son has to stay here. He's not any worse off than if he went to the hospital. He's alive. He's with people who want him to stay alive. He's taken care of. He'd better stay here. If the doctor's power gets stronger, so he can trust it, then Fred can go to the hospital."

Jane told the doctor, and for the second time in that long talk, he spoke to her.

"He's made up his mind?"

"That's what he says."

"Can you make him change it?"

"I can't even speak to him. How can I make him change his mind? He knows what he's got to do. This is right for him, what he's doing."

The doctor picked up his bag to go. "I guess he knows. I wish I had his power to know."

Packing Rocks turned to the door of Fred's room. "I guess I'll go in and sit with him a while. Might make him feel better to have somebody sing to him."

They Do Come Back

(1937)

"SOMEONE IS COMING ACROSS THE FIELD," WILLIAM SAID.

Jane crossed to the window and looked through the slanting lines of the rain.

"That old Mrs. Loughton again."

"She's all right," William offered. "She's been pretty good to us, these last weeks."

"She's all right," Jane was doubtful, "but she asks questions."

"She's got to—she's a white woman. Got no other way of finding out."

"I guess." Jane went to open the door, and stood aside to let the white woman pass into the kitchen.

"Good evening," Mrs. Loughton seated herself in the chair William vacated for her. "What you folks doing?"

"Oh, nothing." Jane began to poke the fire. April was late for a fire, but the house was damp and lonesome—she took her mind away from that.

"Where's Thomas?"

William answered after a moment. "He's staying out in the arbor. He doesn't like the house."

Mrs. Loughton shook her head in mournful agreement. "Too lonesome for him, I bet, poor fellow, with Mary gone. Hard on a man to lose his wife."

Jane put up her hand to stop the name, but it was too late. Mrs. Loughton didn't mean to be insulting, she just didn't know any better. But you mustn't say people's names until after they'd been dead at least a year. Not like the old days, though, when you mustn't ever say them.

Mrs. Loughton went on talking, "—and you've got a lot of things moved out of the house. Did you take them out to the arbor for Thomas?"

William got up. He wouldn't stay now. "No," he said from the doorway. "We just moved them out."

He was right. It was no good explaining, telling why you gave away furniture and bedding and things to the people who helped you when a relative was sick and died. Mrs. Loughton had helped, too, good. Just like an Indian that way. Jane had felt that they should have given her some blankets, maybe that quilt that she and Mary had pieced, but those were things that had never been used, and when everything else had been given, Thomas had needed bedding, out there in the arbor.

"The rain's nice." Jane was looking for something to say. It wasn't nice; she hated it right now; it made her want to cry and cry. If the sun would shine, she could get out of the house, down by the creek and sit and rest. Here in the house she moved restlessly; she was alone. She and Mary had always done everything together.

"Good for the corn," Mrs. Loughton agreed brightly. She stood up. "Well, I got to go. Just thought I'd run over and see how you were getting along. I got to worrying. Didn't sleep much, last night. There's an owl down in the brush by the creek that kept hooting and hooting. I guess she's going to build, but she sure kept me awake."

An owl down by the creek. An owl that kept hooting and hooting. Jane sat down suddenly, her feet folding beneath her against the floor. An owl that kept hooting and hooting. They did come back, then. Even in the rain that slanted through the trees, they came back. Mrs. Loughton was moving towards the door, and she forced herself up.

"You come back—" there was smoke coming from the arbor, thick clouds of it. She just stood and looked at it.

"What's that?" The white woman was staring too.

"Thomas was out there. He said he'd lie there and smoke—"

"He must have gone to sleep with a cigarette in his hand—"

They were running then, towards the arbor. The smoke got thicker and thicker, billowing out to meet them.

"Thomas! William!" Jane could feel her own voice coming out of her throat, feel it, but not hear it. It was funny, she thought, running to the pump, to feel your voice without hearing it. William was running, now. Somehow he had come from the corral and was running with buckets of water to throw on the roof, and Mrs. Loughton was helping him. All the time Jane kept pumping.

Then there was steam and not smoke, and William was doing the pumping. Thomas was there, with one arm and one side of his face looking terrible.

"Put grease on it," Mrs. Loughton kept saying, "put grease on it. Then the burns won't set in."

They led him into the house and put grease on the burns, the good fresh pork grease with no salt in it that Jane had been saving for the next peyote meeting. You mustn't eat salt with peyote, she kept thinking, but all the time she was smearing the grease on Thomas's face and putting clean cloths on it. It didn't matter anyway; they couldn't hold a meeting now; all the good blankets were gone, and there would be nothing for the people to sit on. All the good blankets were gone.

"What happened, Thomas?" Mrs. Loughton was asking questions again. "What happened? How did it all happen? All them good blankets burned up!"

"I don't know," Thomas shook his head. "I lay down on the blankets on the bench to smoke. I guess I went to sleep. Anyway, the next thing I knew there was smoke all around."

"You lay down on them blankets to sleep. And then they caught fire from the cigarette."

"I didn't want to go to sleep. It just sneaked up on me."

Mrs. Loughton shook her head mournfully. "All them good blankets, and that quilt you and Mary pieced. It's too bad." Again she moved to the door. "Well, I'll be going now. Try to get through the woods before dark gets that owl started hooting."

Jane did not try to stop her. She just stood and watched her go, and said politely, "Come again sometime," without knowing that she said it.

Thomas sat on the floor near the stove, his face and arm bandaged. He was looking at her out of one eye; maybe he never would have but one eye to look with again.

"What was that she was saying about an owl?"

"There was an owl down in the brush by the creek last night. It kept hooting and hooting so she couldn't sleep."

"What did she think?"

"She thought maybe it was going to build a nest down there."

"You tell her you thought so?"

"No."

"No. It won't build no nest."

"It won't build no nest. She just came back for them blankets."

"Sure. She come back for them blankets."

"I told you you ought to give them away, ought to give them to Mrs. Loughton."

"That's what the owl come to tell her. It wanted her to know about them blankets."

"That's what I thought."

"Well, anyway, she wouldn't understand. She's a white woman."

"That's what I thought. She wouldn't understand."

"Did you tell her?"

"No, I didn't tell her. And anyway, the blankets are gone."

"Are they all gone? And the quilt, too?"

"I guess I'd better go see."

Dusk was thickening as she walked towards the arbor, but there was still light enough to see a little. Even under the arbor the light came through the hole in the roof enough that she could see the charred pieces of blanket still smoking on the bench.

"Whooooo! Whoooooo!"

Jane stood in the arbor door and listened. She did not shiver, there was nothing left of her to shiver. The sound had gone clear through her and cleaned her all out, so that she stood there empty like the arbor with just a hole in her.

"Whooooo! Whooooooo!"

It was like a command, like a voice speaking to her and giving her orders. She walked across to the bench. There were three blankets, a new Pendleton, a good Navajo, and a new store blanket. In the dark she could still tell what was left of them apart. There was very little left. Three blankets and the quilt.

"Whooo Whooo!"

It was like giving an order to a soldier, like giving an order to the women at a buffalo hunt in the old days. "Get ready," it said. "Get everything cleaned up," it said. "There's got to be room for the new robes and the new life. All these old things got to be thrown away," it said.

Jane picked up the quilt and walked out of the arbor, away from the house and down towards the creek. Wet as it was, she didn't want to go into the brush; it might burn, too. But she stopped on the edge, as near as she dared, and built a little fire. It took a while to find enough dry wood, and all the time the voice was talking to her, just a little, down deep in its throat.

When she got the fire built, she held the corner of the quilt in it. If she laid the whole quilt on the fire the blaze would just go out, so she put it in a little at a time, until the quilt was all gone, and the black rain dripping from the trees was all she could hear. Then she turned to face the woods.

"You can go, now," she said, "I did just like you told me. Everything you had is all gone. I'll take care of Thomas and see that he gets some blankets. But yours are all gone. You can go now."

Then she turned back to the house in the totally silent dark.

Plains Painter

(1938)

PHILLIP'S FEET MOVED HIM AROUND THE PILE OF SAND AND gravel and up the post office steps, whether he wanted to go or not. At the doorway he stopped their forward movement, and turned to look back at the workmen who were preparing to lay the walk in front of the building. Well, it wouldn't be long now. His hand opened the door, and he followed it into the lobby.

Spaces for twelve murals, and three only on the wall. The nine gaps accused him. Universities were fine things, but they changed you. They gave you the feeling that things must be done when someone said they were to be done. That was white man's way. He knew it, but he could not always feel it. And what was completed when you were told to have it done was never as good as what was done when you felt it ought to be done.

Scaffolding, paint-pots, brushes. The sketch was blocked on the fourth wall-space, waiting for him. That was the trouble. There was always something waiting, and then it got in the way of the things that weren't waiting, but wanted to be done.

He clambered up the scaffold. There was peace here, of a kind, up under the ceiling.

"Good morning." Phillip looked down. The postmaster, installed in his new office though the building was not officially open, passed below.

"Good morning." That was one of the clerks from the Agency office upstairs.

"Good morning." "Good morning." "Good morning." They all said it, whether it was a good morning or not. And it wasn't. It was a bad morning in many ways. Wearily he answered them, and wearily he began the first blocking in with color.

"There you are, grandson." At least the old man made no pretenses about its being a good morning. He knew it wasn't. He knew what the drought had done to the wheat and what it was doing to the cotton.

Plains Painter

Phillip answered with equal politeness. "You have come, grandfather. Get down." You still said "get down," the greeting of the days when a man arrived on horseback or not at all. Probably he would always say it. Universities didn't take everything out of you, even though they tried.

"You're painting."

"Yes."

"It's good that you're painting the new Agency. It shows respect, for you to paint the pictures instead of a white artist."

"Time they let an Indian paint pictures in Indian Agency."

"Indians have always painted." There was no reproof, simply a reminder of the days when shields and tipis were decorated as walls were now. "Indians don't stop painting."

"I guess they don't." Phillip frowned at the colors. He had had to buy his own, and he couldn't remember the names of all of those the art department supplied to its students. Some of these didn't seem to be turning out quite right; the red was pink, and there was something wrong with the blue.

"What are you painting, grandson?"

"It's a camp, as in the old days. Men and boys and horses, and women scraping hides and drying meat."

"That's good. You never saw those camps, but you ought to know. Us old folks, we've told you a lot."

Too much, sometimes. The old people were always telling you about the camps. It made good stuff for pictures, but you got tired of it occasionally, hearing the same old stories over and over.

"Whose camp is it, grandson?"

"I don't know. Just a camp." What difference could it make whose camp it was? It had to be finished tomorrow, and whether it were Big Bow's or Sitting Bear's didn't matter. All camps were alike.

"I guess I'll stay and watch you." The old man dropped to his heels, back to the wall, face up-turned to the painting. Phillip was suddenly glad he hadn't put on his smock. It might keep the paint off his clothes, but it did look funny.

"There you are, friend." Another old man had joined his grandfather. They would sit for hours, smoking and spitting and occasionally speaking, and he would hear every word. It wasn't that they raised their voices—you just heard them. It seemed like a mile, sometimes, when they spoke across a camp.

"What is your grandson doing?"

"Get down, friend. My grandson is painting a camp picture."

"Like the old camps."

269

"Like the old camps." The old man sounded proud. At least he was glad it was a camp, and not a modern-day dancer. That was something.

"Whose camp is it?"

"It is just a camp." The words were stripped of meaning, and the tone held neither pride nor shame.

"It should be Big Bow's camp. That was yours."

"That was mine, in the old days."

"It was a good camp."

"Big Bow was a good man."

There they went again. Now they would tell the stories of how Big Bow escaped from the soldiers, and how he came back to his camp and led the people away into Texas, where the whites couldn't find them for three years. There it went.

"Big Bow was coming along on his fine bay mare—"

"There you are, friends." An old woman this time, some sort of distant relation of his grandfather's. Phillip peered over the scaffold for a second, and saw her looking upward at him.

"Get down, sister." The two old men looked towards her, and she sat a little removed from them, her feet folded sideways beneath her.

"What is your grandson doing, brother?"

"He is painting a picture of a camp, sister."

"Are there any women in it?" Well, that was a change. She didn't care whose camp it was.

"There will be women in it when the men are painted."

"What will the women be doing?"

"Some will be scraping hides, and some will be drying meat."

"That was good meat, in the old days. In Big Bow's camp, before we went to Texas, we had good buffalo meat."

"Buffalo meat tastes good." Both old men nodded solemnly. Would they really like it if they had it now? It couldn't be as tender as beef, or even pork. Well, they didn't like pork and wouldn't eat it, because they thought it tasted like bear, so how could they know what it was like?

"I will stay here for a while, brother. Perhaps I can tell your grandson some things about the old days."

"I have told him, sister."

"You have told him the man's part."

"That's what a man should know."

"That's what a man should know until he paints women's work. Even in the old days, men didn't paint women to look like women;

just square with a head and some arms sticking out. How do men know how to paint women's work if they can't paint women?" She chuckled and was silent, chin on palm. She seemed to look at the floor, but Phillip knew that she saw every movement that he made.

Time moved among them and added to the group. Phillip peered down. It was almost noontime, and he would have to take everybody to lunch, his grandfather was so sure that he would. You couldn't let the old man be hurt, even if at the university you could just walk off and go eat alone if you wanted to. The noon whistle at the cotton gin exploded around him, and he laid down the paints.

"Will your friends eat with me, grandfather?" Wordlessly they rose, folded about them the sheets that replaced blankets for summer, and followed him across the street to the cafe. This was the Indian main street and the Indian cafe; the whites had their main street and their cafe on the other side of the building.

Eight old people sat about the table. There was no need to order. The waitress knew as well as he did what they would eat—soup and beef and store bread. "You want something else?" The woman's recognition of the difference between an old-time Indian and an artist was flattering, but he shook his head. It would be bad manners to eat what your guests did not.

"That is not Big Bow's camp you are painting," one of the old men spoke. "Big Bow had a striped tipi, but it was yellow and black. It stood in the middle of the camp, and sometimes he sat with his society outside it and sang."

"That might be the green and orange tipi that Sun Boy took from the Arapaho." His grandfather was careful not to offend his guests, while still aiding his grandson.

"Sun Boy's tipi had stripes going around, not up and down," the old man argued. "I never saw a tipi with stripes going up and down before. Always around."

"Maybe he had a dream to paint the tipi that way," his grandfather offered, and Phillip grasped the suggestion.

"I saw it that way," he said. They would drop it now. If you saw a tipi a certain way, no one could argue about it. It might have stripes going up and down instead of around, to give a vertical movement to the composition, and you wouldn't have to explain either vertical movement or composition or the fact that you put them in because the art professor said they should be there.

"When do you start on the women?" the old woman wanted to know. "Maybe I can help you paint women's things."

"I'll start a woman right after lunch." What was the harm? She wanted to see the women painted. It was all right. He didn't have to paint the men first.

Back on the scaffold, he considered the sketches of women's figures. That one with the hide on the stretcher, scraping it, would be all right. The voices came from below and hung around his head as he began.

"Big Bow would never let a woman scrape a hide right in the middle of the camp."

"It won't show if he puts it in a corner, the way Big Bow would."

"That's right."

Well, they didn't mind that part too much then. But he would have to hurry, if he were to get half this picture done today and the rest tomorrow. If it didn't get finished, it was too bad; he'd never finish the others in time for the dedication.

"Brother, your grandson is painting wrong." What was the matter now?

"What do you mean, sister?"

"That woman is a bad woman. A good woman would not wear a skirt that short."

"The skirt is short."

"Even today, when the girls dress for dances, they don't wear their buckskin dresses that short."

"My grandson should have thought about those things."

"He has been away a long time. Perhaps at the university he saw skirts like that. White women don't care if they show their legs."

Why pick on the skirt? It had to be that way, or the whole picture was out of balance.

"I am going home, brother. I can tell your grandson nothing about women's ways. That woman does not know how to scrape a hide, and he'll never teach her. A bad woman like that wouldn't be scraping a hide; she'd be running off on a war party with some man."

"My grandson won the government competition. He was picked as the best. He's an Indian, and they want an Indian to paint this building."

"Maybe a white man would be better. White men could make mistakes but it wouldn't be like lying."

Her going took away the old men, all but his grandfather.

Phillip returned the paints to the turpentine can and came down from the scaffold.

"Grandfather, I am going to stop work now."

"It is three o'clock. White painters work until five."

"I'm not white. I'm Indian. They hired an Indian to paint this building, and he's going to paint it Indian way."

His grandfather grunted softly. "That's good if you do it. How you going to start?"

"I'm going to paint at night. In the old days"—forgotten scraps of knowledge he had heard all his life were coming back, pouring over his mind—"in the old days, a man painted at night, alone. That's the way I'm going to paint. Janitor will let me in, and I'll paint by myself."

His grandfather nodded. "That's good. When a man shows his work before he finishes it, it's everybody's work, everybody's that he shows it to. You sit up there, paint all day long, everybody can come in and see. Then they have the right to tell you what they think. You paint at night, alone, then it's your work. Nobody got the right to bother. You do it your way."

There was something in that, thought Phillip as he cleaned the brushes. Maybe that was why really big artists had studios and didn't let other people in when they were painting. It wasn't to hurt other people's feelings; it was just to keep their work to themselves until it was ready for other minds to touch.

"Through for the day, Phillip?" the postmaster leaned out of his window. "How are you going to get them things done in time for the dedication if you quit at three?" he smiled with his face, but behind it there was no warmth.

"I'll get them done." Phillip somehow knew that he would. "But I want to paint at night for a while. The light's different then. I want to see how the colors work."

"Them old people bothering you?" The postmaster was shrewd from many years behind the window of a post office where more Indians than whites came for their mail. "Just can't keep their tongues off what anybody does."

"It isn't that." How should this grinning white man know what it was? "It's just that things look different at night. I kind of want to see how that tipi would look with the stripes going around instead of up and down."

Playing Indians

(1941)

LEAH WONDERED HOW IT HAD HAPPENED THAT THE SCHOOL principal had decided to favor the Caddoes. Even now, grown up and out of school as she was, she didn't have much use for Caddoes, and didn't think she ever would. With Caddoes and Kiowas both in the same school, it seemed strange to be passing the Kiowas up.

She didn't have to ask anybody about it, though, because when she went to the office to get her mail, the newspaper was lying on the desk. It was the feature section of the Sunday paper that she saw, with smeary photographs and clear, hard, black type looking up at her. "Prehistoric Site Identified," it said. "Spiro Assigned to Caddoan Culture."

Then she could understand. It was part of the Indian Office system of making Indians proud of being Indians. Caddoan must mean Caddo, and that was why they were planning to take the Caddo children to see the things from that place.

The sun was pouring heat out of the sky, but Leah shivered all the same. Those things were buried hundreds of years ago, and all the people who had made them were dead. It seemed wrong to dig them up, even for white people. For Indians to go and look at them was worse. Those dead people were Indians. Once they were buried, they did not want to be dug up and handled. They surely didn't want other people pawing over them. They would try to get even. It would be unlucky for anybody who touched those things, or even looked at them.

The boys' adviser drove the yellow school bus to the foot of the steps and nodded solemnly at her. He was an Alaska Indian, and he never seemed to have fun the way Plains Indians did. "You coming, too, Miss Hunt?"

Leah shook her head. She had been a little bit peeved all day yesterday because one of the other unit matrons was going, but now she did not care. She did not want to go around where dead people's bones and belongings were. "I don't want to see those old things."

Playing Indians

The boys' adviser looked at her and nodded grimly. "They're dead and can't hurt you, but that's all you can say about them. No fun looking at them."

He felt the same way she did, Leah was sure, and she began to feel that maybe he was more of an Indian than she had thought.

"My folks wouldn't like it," she said. "My father is educated, and he speaks English; but there are some things he wouldn't do. He won't stay outdoors when the hoot-owls are flying, and he wouldn't go near a dead person, unless it would be to help lay him out."

The boys' adviser shook his head slightly for "yes," a way he had when he forgot sometimes. "I think they're making a mistake," he said. "Principal says it's the ancestors of these Caddo children made this place. Maybe so. Maybe not. Anyway, they're dead. What's the use of making the children look at them?"

"Indian Office say it's to make them proud of being Indians."

The boys' adviser sat up straight at that. "Indians don't have to be made proud of being Indians," he said. "Indians are too proud of that as it is. That's what's the trouble with them. They're all the time running around telling the world how proud they are of being Indians, when what they need is to quit being Indians and settle down and just be people."

That was the other side of it. Leah had heard that before from old-timers in the Service, both Indians and whites. Make Indians forget they were Indians. Make them live and think and believe like everybody else. Since they had to live in the other fellow's world, let them get ready to fit right into it so that nobody could tell the difference.

That was wrong, too. Indians would always be Indians. Like herself, standing and shivering in the sun-heat because some of the children were going off to look at dead people. She didn't know why she shivered, but she couldn't help doing it. It went back and way back in her mind, to the stories grandmother used to tell, about how dead people that weren't happy turned into owls and came back to see to things they hadn't finished when they were alive, and about how your nails would drop off and your hair would fall out if you got too close to dead people when you didn't need to. All those things. You knew they weren't true, but you didn't forget them.

The children fell out of the dark building into the brightness, through the brighter sun. They were yelling and yipping like little coyotes, but not as wildly as Kiowa children would have yelled and yipped. They tumbled into the bus and settled down quickly, and you knew they were Caddoes, because Caddoes got quiet easily.

There was one little Kiowa girl who always stayed close to Leah when they were in the girls' building. She was a pretty little round-faced child, and Leah found herself favoring the girl in little ways; brushing her hair easy instead of hard, and sometimes giving her pieces of candy. Her name was Gladys. She came and stood beside Leah now, and looked as demure and quiet as those Caddo children going off in the bus.

"Where they going?" she asked.

"To the State University, to see things in the museum there."

"Why are the Caddoes going?"

"Principal thinks those things in the museum belonged to the Caddoes."

Little Gladys wandered off then, and Leah got busy. She had plenty to do all day, without worrying about dead people and owls and why one tribe went off on a trip and the other was left at home, and what was going to happen. Something would, because you could always tell when the Kiowas were getting restless and jealous. They got off in corners and talked in Kiowa, and more than once she came across two or three together, and they were always saying the same word. It meant "bad, evil," but it meant "bad" in an unnatural sort of way, not just ordinary wickedness.

Late evening was shaping under the trees when the yellow bus stopped in the deep shadow in front of the school building. The Caddoes got out, all quiet and polite, almost like white children, standing there in a group at the foot of the steps. The Kiowas waited until the bus drove off, and flowed up and around the Caddoes like water. Something was going to happen. Leah slipped out of her quarters, into the shadow where she could hear them.

"Where you been?" That was the biggest and oldest of the Kiowa boys.

The oldest Caddo answered him, "Been to State University museum."

"What you go for?"

"Went to see things there."

"What sort of things?" That was little Gladys. Leah gasped in surprise. The child never had spoken up like that before.

"Oh, pots, and carved shells, and pearls, and copper things."

"Where did they come from?"

"People dig them out of the ground. They say they used to belong to the Caddoes."

"What Caddoes?"

"Dead Caddoes. We saw them."

There was a little hissing around the group of Kiowas. It was that word "bad" or "evil" again. You could hear them draw in their breaths to say it.

"You saw them."

"Sure. We even got to touch their bones."

It was like the spring rise in the Washita. The living water rose and slipped around things and carried them away with it, and in the same way one group of children rose and flooded around the other, and carried them away; away from the school buildings and the dormitories, away from the barns and the fields, and over the hill and down into the gully where the cedar trees grew.

Leah, following, wondered, and knew they were going to the right place. Who pulled the cedar branches for the fire she didn't know, nor how the Caddoes were all kept in one place while the fire was built up and lighted. But they were. It was a small fire, with rolling grey smoke streaked with yellow, and still the Kiowas were not speaking and the Caddoes were tied hand and foot with silence. When the fire was going strong, the big boy spoke again.

"You got to get clean," he said. "You all got to get clean before you can sleep in the building with us."

The flood rolled the Caddoes into the smoke, and the smoke from the cedar washed them clean of the touch of the dead. The smoke poured and flowed around the whole group, soaping and saturating them. Leah turned and went away. Nobody was going to get hurt. It would all be all right. When it was over, you could sleep easily in the building with the Caddoes.

She met the boys' adviser as she came past the garage. The bus was put away, and together they started up the hill towards the school for supper. As they reached the girls' building and paused, there were yells and shouts behind them. Children, Caddoes and Kiowas mixed, were tumbling uphill towards them, rolling and shrieking and yapping like gay puppies. Over them all hung a strong smell of smoke.

"Where you boys been?" yelled the boys' adviser, "What you been doing with fire?" But they rolled and frolicked past without answering. Leah saw little Gladys and drew her towards them with her eyes.

"What have you children been doing?"

There was a little Caddo girl standing beside Gladys, and she was the one who answered. She looked straight at Leah and spoke.

"We been playing Caddoan village," she said, and the two little girls went on, following the supper bell into the dining hall.

"There," said the boys' adviser, "What did I tell you? Indians think too much about being Indians. Right away they even have to start playing they're dead ones."

The War Party

(1942)

THE BIG POSTERS WERE OUT ALL OVER TOWN, ANNOUNCING THAT the Indian Fair would begin tomorrow. Phillip walked down Main Street and felt proud of his work; he really liked the picture of the dancing man that he had designed for these posters. His grandfather and old Eagle Plume had looked at it a long time, and agreed that it was lifelike.

You could always tell when a fair was going to begin, because the day before it started felt different from ordinary days. People began to come in well ahead of time, and they camped all over the two-acre field southwest of the Fair Grounds. The old people said it wasn't like an old-time camp, but there was something about it that must have felt right to them, for the very first things to go up on the campgrounds were the tipis that the old folks saved for occasions like this. It was a good thing they did put up tipis, or present-day artists would never know how to paint them.

He turned into the post office. The little room at the end of the corridor had been turned over to the Draft Board. He walked under his own paintings and knew without looking at them where each one was. Buffalo hunt, travel, camping scene—they could stand. They would be there when he was gone and when he got back, if he got back.

The interview didn't take long. He'd had his physical and was all ready to go. You couldn't really say he had dependents. He sometimes helped his grandparents, with whom he lived, but that was just what anybody would do. When he was gone, they'd get along all right. The others would help them then.

The sergeant said, "You have until tomorrow to finish things up. Be here at nine o'clock, here at this building. We'll give you boys a break, a ride in a jeep in the parade, and down to the station."

Phillip went down the steps more slowly than he ever had. Even when you knew it was coming and you had to do it, it was hard. He forgot his car and walked, walked eastward to the Fair Grounds and his grandfather's camp.

278

The War Party

Hunting Horse sat in the tipi doorway, with old Eagle Plume beside him. It was not that they were such good friends, but being the two oldest men left living threw them on each other. Eagle Plume was almost blind and was getting deaf, but grandfather had his sight and could hear well. He helped Eagle Plume along a lot of the time when the old man began to give out.

"Get down, grandson."

He sat and rolled a cigarette for Eagle Plume and one for himself. His grandfather wouldn't smoke. It was wrong for a Christian, he said. Lots of old-time white ideas were mixed in with his old-time Indian ideas. It was odd to get things mixed up that way.

"Have you news, grandson?"

"I'm leaving tomorrow."

Hunting Horse turned to Eagle Plume. The older man always said he could hear Hunting Horse and Spear Woman because they spoke such good, clear Kiowa. The younger people just mumbled and forgot half the words. Now Hunting Horse spoke without raising his voice.

"My grandson says he is going away to fight tomorrow."

"Is there a war going on? Who are they fighting? The Germans, like the last time?"

"The Germans again. And some other people, too, called the Japs."

"Those Germans," said Eagle Plume, "make me think of the Navajos. No matter how many times you go out and lick the Navajos, after while they grow more young men and come at you to be licked again. That's the way those Germans are. Are the Navajos fighting on the German side?"

"No, the Navajos are fighting on our side."

"Seems like a funny kind of business, Kiowas and Navajos fighting on the same side. Don't let your grandson have much to do with the Navajos, friend. They might change their minds."

Phillip laughed at that, remembering Navajo boys at school who had been his good friends. Indians were getting to know and like each other because they were Indians. Indians had to hold together for that reason. That was what peyote religion taught, and it was right.

Eagle Plume was talking again. "It's a long time since any of us saw the young men ride out and fight. Will they make a ceremony for them?"

Hunting Horse glanced towards his grandson, and Phillip nodded. It would make the old men feel better about it. "Tomorrow. It's a kind of a ceremony. When they have the Indian Fair parade, we'll be in it. We'll be riding in a special kind of car, all of us that are going away to do the fighting."

"That's good," said Hunting Horse. "That's the way it ought to be. Showing honor and respect for the brave young men. That's the way we always did."

Eagle Plume put out his cigarette and sat there thinking.

"Will you lend me a horse tomorrow, friend?"

What did the old man want with a horse, Phillip wondered. He was too shaky to stay on if he had it, and had sold all his own long ago.

"Will you need it, friend?" Hunting Horse's politeness led up to all the things his grandson was thinking right out.

"I'm going to need it. I need it to ride in the parade and bless those young men. They're going away to fight, and they ought to be blessed before they start out. I'm the only one left that has the right."

"You are brave, too, to take that ride."

"I know what you're thinking," said Eagle Plume easily. "You think I'm old and shaky and probably I'll fall off. Well, I won't. I still have power, no matter how old I am. I can ride that horse if I'm doing it to bless the young men."

"Thank you for blessing, friend," said Hunting Horse. "I will give you that horse that you will ride."

"Tell your grandson to come here. He must give me another cigarette first."

Phillip rolled the cigarette and passed it across, and the old man took it and blew smoke to the directions, the way he would with a pipe: east, south, west, north, up, down. The smoke went over Phillip.

"Kneel down, young man." That was a term Phillip had heard only when they were telling stories of the old days. It was an honorable term, and it really meant "young man who is going bravely out to fight the enemy." He kneeled in front of the old man, sitting flat on the ground below him. Eagle Plume put his arms out and up, to embrace him.

"This is the power that I have. This is the power that my brother got in the Sun Dance and gave me. It is good power and strong power. I've had it a long time, and I'll have it a while longer. This is the power to live until your ribs fall in and you die of old age. This is the power to go through war and sickness and all those bad things, and come out safe. This is the power I am giving this young man."

He took Phillip's hands in his, and blew four times into the palms of each one. Four times on each of his feet. Four times over his heart. Then he made him get up and turn around and kneel down again, and blew four times in the middle of his back.

"Now you have this power. It is good, strong power, and it will keep you alive through the fighting and bring you back to us safely. This is my gift to you, to keep the power going on. When you are as old as I am, you can hand it on to somebody else."

It had always sounded funny when they talked about handing on power, but maybe there was something to it. He didn't feel any different, but he knew he had been through a ceremony. He went into the tipi and lay down on his back and looked up at the ears to think, his knees up and one knee over the other, his foot swinging in time to his thinking. That was the best way to lie when you had to think. All the men he knew did it.

Outside he could hear the voices of the two old men going on. They were making plans for the next day. Strange. They were the ones who were making the plans, and he was the one who would be doing the fighting, but he made no plan. Now all the plans were made for you. Not like the old days, when each man made his own plan and worked it into one general plan for all to follow. You didn't take orders much, in the old kind of fighting. Now fighting was all taking orders.

He went from thinking into sleeping without knowing it. When he waked, the voices were gone, and there was the throbbing of a drum along the earth from somewhere. He sat up and listened. That was a peyote drum. Nobody ever held a peyote meeting in this camp, though. It was too easily interrupted by white people who just wanted to know what was going on. He went to the door of the tipi and looked out. The drum came from Packing Rocks' camp. Packing Rocks' deep voice went with it, singing a blessing song. When he stopped, the drum began again, not so strongly, and Eagle Plume's old voice sang a song for strength and help. Phillip went back and lay down. Those old men certainly believed in singing to give them power.

When he roused again, it was morning, and Bow Woman, his grandmother, was bending over him. "You better get up," she said. "I got food all ready for you to eat."

He went outside and sat with his grandfather while she brought the food to them. Meat and broth and fry-bread and coffee—what the old people liked best in all the world. There were other things that he'd rather have, but this was what they thought was the best food in the world. He ate it.

Hunting Horse was dressed in a blue silk shirt. There were bright yellow yarns around his braids and a pair of beaded moccasins on his feet. He had put a spot of red paint on each cheek-bone, and his long, beaded pipe-bag lay on the ground beside him. When they had finished eating, he stood up.

"You better get dressed, grandson."

"I got my clothes on."

"Those aren't your good clothes."

"I'm leaving my good clothes. I won't need them. They'll give me a uniform to wear."

"That's not what counts. When you ride in a parade, you got to dress up. You got to look your very best. All the people are there to do you honor. You got to show them that you appreciate it."

It was a foolish way of looking at things, but the old man never would give up, if he had his mind set on something like that. You might as well give in to him, because that was what you'd end by doing. Phillip got his suitcase out from under his cot and took out his best bright blue suit and a clean white shirt. He had better put on a tie, too. The old man would expect it. He tied the few things he would take with him in a small bundle that he could carry.

His grandfather would probably like to paint his face, he thought, and wondered how he could get out of it. But when he came out, Hunting Horse said nothing about that. He handed Phillip the lines of the horse he was holding, and said, "You'd better take this over to Eagle Plume."

It was a good horse; it was the best horse he had, a bayo coyote. He took the bridle and led the horse across the camp to Eagle Plume. When he saw the old man, all Phillip could think of was that he was just right to go with the fine horse. All those years, Eagle Plume must have been keeping his Gourd Dancers Society costume. He stood now, coated with yellow paint and with the long breechclout covered with crow feathers trailing behind him. There was a bundle of crow feathers tied in his hair, and all his hair but his scalplock was unbraided. The pink shell he always wore was still tied to the scalplock, but something else was tied to it so that it showed black in the middle of the pink. It looked like an old-time, black, stone arrowhead.

Eagle Plume took the horse. He thanked Hunting Horse and his grandson. One of Packing Rocks' grandsons mounted to ride the horse into town, and the old man came across the camp and got into the wagon with the rest of them.

Riding into town in the wagon was something Phillip had always done. The dust was deep along the road, powdering out over the camps that lined it and turning tipis and tents and brush arbors all the same red-brown. People and their clothing had the same color as their shelters. It should have flattened things out, but it didn't, because what was going on inside people was sharpened by excitement.

They came to the place where people were lining up to be in the parade. Packing Rocks' grandson was there already, with the horse. Eagle Plume got out of the wagon and sat on the grass by the side of the road, waiting.

Color and movement sang without voice around them the rest of the way in. The feathers, the paint, the beadwork; all the gay, good things that meant the fair and gay, good feelings were around them thick. Somehow they even made the jeep look gay, but the sergeant looked worried.

"There," he said, when he saw Phillip, "that's the last one. Let's go."

They rode back through the singing color and movement that was the most important part of the world right now. Girls' hair that shone; and girls' white buckskin dresses that gleamed like smoke against the blue sky. Silver ornaments and shell ornaments. Smell of sage and herbs for perfume. All the things that women knew how to use to make themselves beautiful. All at once Phillip knew that it was all these things that he was leaving, too.

When they got into line behind the Comanches, where they would be leading the Kiowas, Eagle Plume got up and went to his new horse. Phillip started to get out of the jeep; then he saw that Packing Rocks' grandson was helping the old man mount. He supposed the boy would go along and lead the horse, because it was pretty spirited, but Eagle Plume took the lines in his own old, small hands, that were still strong enough to hold them. There was a minute when they were all standing still, and then the band struck up and the parade started.

It was a loud band, and it was right in front of the Comanches, so that the sound kept coming back over them in spurts. But it wasn't that sound so much as another one that Phillip heard. He heard Eagle Plume singing the Journey Song.

> *Going away on a journey,*
> *That's the only thing.*
> *That's the best way there is*
> *For a young man to make himself rich and famous.*

Some of the boys in the jeep knew that song, and riding along through the crowds and the morning, they all began to sing it too. When they had sung it four times, Eagle Plume began to talk to the people.

"This is where you're supposed to look," he told them. "This is what you are to see. These are the young men to give honor to. These are the young men who are going away to fight for you. They will go far away and fight with a strong enemy. Maybe some of them will get killed. Maybe some of them will be hurt. They are brave; they are doing you honor, fighting for you."

Not all the people along the sidewalks knew what was happening. They thought at first it was a parade joke, like the Mud-Heads that were there every year throwing mud at the people. But the old man was in earnest. What he was saying was almost a prayer. Even the white people could feel that he meant it. Voices that had been raised and clamorous began to drop and become easy, and against them Eagle Plume's voice rose more clearly.

"This is the song that my father sang when he was killed. All the men that were with him then in having the right to sing it are gone now. Nobody is left who has the real right to sing this song. But my father would want them to know. He would want these young men to hear his song so that they could fight bravely. This is a song that will make a man strong in fighting if he thinks about it.

> *I live, but I will not live forever.*
> *Mysterious moon, you only remain,*
> *Powerful sun, you alone remain,*
> *Wonderful earth, you remain forever.*

They were even with the courthouse, now, and Phillip could see his grandfather's wagon and his grandfather standing up in it. His grandmother was doubled and twisted on the seat of the wagon as if something were hitting her and hurting her, but she straightened up when she heard Eagle Plume sing. Her eyes went down along the line of the parade and hit the jeep and found Phillip's. For the first time in his life he was looking full into his grandmother's face, and it was beautiful. When she was a young woman, she must have been lovely. She raised her chin and threw back her head and a sound cut through Eagle Plume's song and finished it off. She was making the war-whoop for both of them.

They went all through the town and came back to the edge of camp. Packing Rocks' grandson came and took the lines and helped Eagle Plume dismount. The old man got down and came across the road to the jeep. "That is the best I can do for you," he said. "All an old man can do for young ones is give them his blessing. I hope it's strong enough to carry you through, and you all come back all right." He shook hands with each of them and stepped back to the side of the road.

"O K, boys," said the sergeant, "Start 'em rolling."

Buffalo Grass

(1944)

FOR LEAH THE SOUTH PORCH OF THE BIG HOUSE WAS THE BEST part of home. Here you could sit and watch sunrise or sunset; watch the shapes of the earth change and move as the sun moved. Then you knew, when you sat out there, that the earth was alive itself.

Spear Woman sat beside her granddaughter and thought that the earth had gone dead. Lights played and moved, and cloud shadows came and went, but the earth itself had somehow died. It was all one color now; not like the old days when its shades really changed and flickered like flames under the wind. She stirred and sighed and spoke.

"When the buffalo moved across it, there were other colors and other lights."

The thought was near enough Leah's own to startle her. "There are lots of colors there now."

Her father spoke behind them. "Not like there used to be. In the days that even I remember, there was one color when the wind was from the north and another when it was from the south, one from the east and another from the west. Now the grass is all one color on every side, and it doesn't change with the wind."

"Sometimes the colors change. Down near Lawton there is a prairie where the grass takes different colors."

"In Buffalo Park. The government made it to be like the old days."

"Is it, father?"

"Pretty much. Grandmother would know better than I do. The buffalo were gone already when I was a young man."

"Is it, grandmother? Is that buffalo park like the old days?"

Spear Woman shook her head. "How do I know? I have never seen it. A buffalo park—Are there buffalo there?"

Leah's father nodded. "Lots of buffalo. They were there last autumn when I went with the army officers, looking for old battlefields. We saw the buffalo. They came close."

Spear Woman was sitting straight up now, like a young woman. "Lots of buffalo and they came close. I wish I could see them. I want to see them."

The Ten Grandmothers

Leah stared. Grandmother often said "I wish," but never "I want."

"Do you really want to see them, grandmother?"

"I need to see them. That time they hung the red blanket, I was the one that kept the buffalo from coming back. I was too scared. I thought them back into the hole in the ground. But maybe some are out now. I want to see them. I want to tell them how sorry I am, to keep them shut up down there. I am an old woman, and soon it will be too late. I want to see the buffalo."

Father nodded. "I guess you better. Daughter, can you take your grandmother?"

Leah spoke English. "Casings are pretty bad, and it will take just about all our gasoline."

"You make it. Just one-day trip. Leave here early in the morning, be back that night. You don't got to hurry."

Leah thought. "All right. I never saw a whole lot of buffalo myself. Just two one time, in a circus." She changed into Kiowa. "When do you want to go, grandmother?"

Spear Woman thought. "You can't hurry with these things. Buffalo don't hurry. Got to plan buffalo hunt ahead. I guess we go four sleeps from now."

"All right." Her son rose slowly. "I fix the car. Leah will make a lunch. Then you can go."

It didn't sound like much to do, just to fix the car and a lunch, but Spear Woman kept them at it for the whole four days. Everything had to be just right. "You owe respect to buffalo. They kept us alive," she said when Leah protested that the upholstery didn't need scrubbing. Even her son went so far as to suggest tying a rawhide saddle on the hood, so that she could ride the car like a horse. "In the old days, you wouldn't make fun of the buffalo, wouldn't make fun of your mother. You'd know you needed them both."

But by the next morning she had got over her hurt feelings. Even after the four days of getting ready, she still had things to see to at the last minute. She brought her best Pendleton blanket from the trunk and spread it over the seat. She put on her very best clothes and painted her face. Leah, already thinking of fifty miles of dust each way, of the crowds of white people that hung around government parks, of all the things that could happen to a car with two women in it, wished that the paint had been left off. But grandmother would have to show respect for the buffalo.

The sun was low in the morning, and the shadows of the little hills were on the grass, changing its color in Leah's eyes. Grandmother looked at it and said, "All brown," and got into the car. She arranged her dress carefully and set her moccasins firm on the floor of the car, as if they were in stirrups. Then she said, "All ready," and Leah let out the clutch, and they started.

She took the back road, down through Cutthroat Gap and around Saddle Mountain. It was longer than the highway, but it was pretty. Grandmother showed her places as they went along.

"That big bend there, by the river, Buffalo River. That's where they held the Sun Dance the year I was born. That little butte over there. That's where the three boys froze to death, the time they ran away from the first government school. See where that hole is, where the ground kind of dips down? That's where the old trading post stood. It burned down, the Year They Ran Away to Texas."

On and on. Every little dip, every bend and curve—the spring where they stopped to drink and water the radiator, even the beds of water cress below it—had their histories and their names. It was all alive, this country; people walked across it that Leah could not see, but Spear Woman could. She did not call their names, for they were dead, but she told to whom they were related, and how that made them kin to her and to Leah. Some places were happy; there had been Sun Dances and ceremonies. Other places were unhappy; people had died there, and been mourned. Leah could feel the mourning, even now. On, with the sun rising higher and the shadows drawing up under the objects that cast them. On and on.

Two lines of high, tight fence spread across the prairie from a gate, and Spear Woman sat stiff, suddenly. "What is that? That is grass like the old days. Real grass. All different colors."

It was, too. It was like changeable silk, the kind the Delawares used to trim their blankets. Yellow as the wind struck it; rose-color as it died away; then a sort of in-between color, with patterns that moved like the patterns in silk when you folded it.

"That's the buffalo park. Buffalo ought to be here. I don't see them."

Spear Woman looked quickly overhead. "Not now. Nearly noon. Sun's too high. Now's the time when the buffalo lie down by the creeks and rest. They're wise. They don't run about in the sun as we do."

Leah nodded. "I guess you're right. We'll go find some shade, too. Lie down ourselves."

All these past four days she had been in a hurry. Her plans had been pushing her. It had been the most important thing in the world to get here quickly, to find the buffalo and look at them, and to be gone. That the buffalo might not be there to be seen had not come into her thoughts. Now the hurry had rushed itself away; she was no more pushed for time than her grandmother or the buffalo themselves. She could find shade and lie down and sleep. It would take until late at night to get home. That was all right. They could sleep again when they were there.

Shade was not even in sight, and when they had driven through the gates, with the lines of fence on either hand, it was still not easy to find. Spear Woman didn't care. She sat and watched the grass turn over in the sun, flickering and bending and straightening like little campfire flames, and was happy. It was the old kind of grass, the old, rippling, running prairies, even if there were fences. She was glad her eyes were dim, because she didn't always see the fences, and could forget about them. It was all peaceful and alive again.

There was a creek, with a pebble bank, shelving down to clear, shallow water. Spear Woman took her Pendleton blanket from the seat of the car and spread it on the ground for them to lie on. Leah brought the lunch from the car, to find that her grandmother had gathered up little sticks and twigs and boughs, and built a fire. "Long ago I camped here. I had forgotten. Your grandfather and I were hunting for some horses that had run off. We stopped and ate here, and built a little clear fire like this."

They did not really need the fire, for coffee would stay warm a long time in the thermos jug, but it was nice to heat it in tin cups. They let the coffee get stone cold to cool the handles, and sipped it, and slipped into sleep as if eating and drinking and sleeping and being were all one thing.

Shadows were running away from the things that cast them, and there was blue light in the wonderful rose color of the prairie when Leah waked. Spear Woman was sitting still beside her, just watching the wind walk across the grass. Leah stretched, and her grandmother nodded at her. "You had a sleep. That's good. Now we will go and see the buffalo."

It had taken a long time to put things in the car this morning, but it seemed to take only a minute now. Their fire was out, everything packed away, and the blanket spread on the car seat almost without their moving. They started back along the fence.

There was a little draw ahead of them, across the blueing prairie, and there was something dark moving along it. Spear Woman saw it before Leah did. "There they are. You'd better stop. I'll call them this way."

She stood up in the car and lifted her voice out of her throat, not loud, but clear and high and true. It ran across the grass to stop the herd and turn them, and Leah understood why women always went on the hunts in the old days It was to draw the herds to them with their voices No man had a voice that could do that.

The buffalo had changed their course, and were moving jerkily along and up the draw. They were coming nearer, and Spear Woman called to them again. They actually began to hurry then.

Spear Woman stood in the car beside her granddaughter. Tears ran down her face, and her mouth tasted salt, but she was singing; she who had never made a song before found words in her heart and sang them aloud.

> *Once we were all free on the prairies together.*
> *Blue and rose and yellow prairies like this one.*
> *We ran and chased and hunted.*
> *You were good to us.*
> *You gave us food and clothes and houses.*
> *Now we are all old.*
> *We are tied.*
> *But our minds are not tied.*
> *We can remember the old days.*
> *We can say to each other,*
> *Those times were good.*

Something had happened to the buffalo. They were near to the fence, now, but they had stopped. The clear, high call they had obeyed; the song puzzled them. The herd broke apart, shuffling and snorting against the wire, and Spear Woman, dropped from her song, stared at them.

Then she saw. They were yearlings, little more than calves. And she had been singing to them about the old days. The tears were still on her cheeks, but she began to laugh. She laughed and laughed, and Leah stared at her, in wonder and fright.

"Of course you don't understand my singing," Spear Woman said. "Of course you don't know what it's about when I sing about the old days. You're just calves. You don't remember. You were born inside the fence, like my own grandchildren."

Then she sat down in the car and waited to be driven home.

The Kiowa Calendars
and Bibliography

YEAR	MOONEY	GEORGE POOLAW
1826		
1827		
1828		
1830		
1832		
1832–33	Money captured from American traders.	The year the Osages cut their throats.
1833	Massacre by Osages and capture of Taime.	
1833–34	Meteoric display.	The winter the stars fell. The Osages captured the Taime and several Kiowa women, one of whom brought the god back in March.
1834	Dragoon expedition.	Cat-tail sun dance (tonpa).
1834–35	Bull-tail killed by Mexicans.	
1835	Cat-tail sun dance.	Wolf Creek sun dance.
1835–36	Big Face or Wolf-Hair killed by Mexicans.	
1836	Wolf Creek sun dance.	Crooked Neck killed in a battle with government soldiers.
1836–37	K'íñähíate killed in Mexico.	
1837	Cheyenne massacred on Upper Red River.	Mourning sun dance.
1837–38	Head-dragging winter.	Winter of the bringing of the Pawnee's head.
1838	Kiowas and allies defeat the Cheyennes and Arapahoes.	Attack by Cheyennes on way to sun dance. No dance.
1838–39	Battle with Arapahoes.	Visit to Crow country. Attacked by Cheyennes on the way home, and six-day battle.
1839	Peninsula sun dance.	Big Bend sun dance.
1839–40	Smallpox winter.	Smallpox winter.
1840	Red-bluff sun dance.	Red Bluff sun dance.
1840–41	Hide-quiver war expedition.	Raid into Ute country for horses.

Calendars

GEORGE HUNT	MARY BUFFALO
Peace-pipe ceremony introduced to the Kiowa by an unidentified tribe who wore large earrings.	
Rawhide sun dance.	
Cedar River sun dance.	
Big Face (t'oedl) killed by a war party.	
Wolf River sun dance.	
The winter the Osages cut off their heads.	The year the Osages cut off their heads.
The winter the stars fell.	The winter the stars fell.
Cat-tail sun dance.	First corn sun dance.
Unexplained drawing.	Nothing happened.
Cheyennes massacred by Kiowas.	Sun Boy (baita'li) painted yellow at the sun dance.
Black Bear (setkŏ'giă) killed.	
	Guik'ade (Wolf Lying Down). No sun dance.
	Tsent'ainta organized.
Kiowas attacked by Cheyennes on Wolf Creek.	Tall weed sun dance.
Arapaho Taĭ'pego (gourd Dance Society) killed in a battle with Kiowas.	Smallpox winter.
	Tägudl (red herb) sun dance.
	Rag quiver made this winter by the Kiowas.
Peninsular sun dance.	Sitting Bear's brother killed. No sun dance.
Smallpox winter.	Alabak'i (Hair cut off on One Side) killed.
Smallpox sun dance at Red Bluff.	Double sun dance.
Quiver-captured winter.	Septoyoy'te (Heap of Bears) killed by Utes.

YEAR	MOONEY	GEORGE POOLAW
1841	Pawnees massacred on the South Canadian.	Kiowas killed Pawnees near Pike's Peak. No sun dance.
1841–42	Â'dalhabä'k'ia killed.	One Braid (alhaba'ki) was killed.
1842	Repeated sun dance.	Double sun dance.
1842–43	Crow-neck died.	The winter Crow Necklace died.
1843	Nest-building sun dance.	Bald Eagle nest sun dance.
1843–44	Woman stabbed; raid into Mexico.	A woman named Polaï'e (Rabbit) stabbed in a brawl.
1844	Dakota sun dance.	The Sioux sun dance.
1844–45	Expedition against Mexico; Ä'taha'ik'i killed.	Winter Little War Bonnet was killed in New Mexico.
1845	Stone-necklace sun dance.	No sun dance. Woman With a Rock Tied Around her Neck died.
1845–46	Bent's post on South Canadian established.	Thunder Boy killed in New Mexico.
1846	Kâ'itséñk'ia organized.	K'oïtsengo (Real Horses) organized.
1846–47	Mustache-shooting winter.	Sitting Bear shot in the teeth by a Pawnee.
1847	Fight with Santa Fé traders; Red Sleeve killed.	War Bonnet Man died of sickness. No sun dance.
1847–48	Camp on upper South Canadian.	The winter of the thunder storms.
1848	Kâ'itséñko initiated.	First koïtsengo sun dance.
1848–49	Antelope-driving winter.	Deer-tracking winter.
1849	Cholera sun dance.	Stomach-cramp (cholera) sun dance. Many deaths.
1849–50	Fight with the Pawnees; scalp dance.	Winter battle with Pawnees; one man held off the Kiowas all day.
1850	Chinaberry sun dance.	Chinaberry sun dance. Yellow Wolf born.
1850–51	Tañgíapa killed in Mexico.	Buck Deer (t'apä) killed in New Mexico.
1851	Dusty sun dance.	Dusty dry sun dance.
1851–52	Woman elopes and is frozen.	The winter the woman was frozen.

Calendars

Unexplained drawing.

The winter they killed the Pawnee.

Double sun dance.

Black Bear (setkŏ'gia) pierced by a lance.

Nest-building sun dance.

Something happened to a woman.

Kiowas captured a war bonnet from another tribe.

Antelope-driving winter.

Sett'ohate's tipi painted. Also unexplained drawings.

Thunder Man (pasotk'iata) killed.

Second smallpox sun dance.

Setaingia (Sitting Bear) shot in the mouth.

Red Sleeve (Mänkägudl) killed.

Dusty camp sun dance.

Inauguration of koĭtsengo.

Circle-timber winter camp.

Some event connected with koĭtsengo.

A Pawnee shot in the back and killed.

Chinaberry sun dance. Yellow Wolf (guikute) born this year.

Buck Deer (tagi'pa) killed. Iseeoh born.

Pawnees or Osages visited the sun dance.

The winter the woman froze her feet.

Crow nest built on sun dance pole.

Nothing happened.

(Atohoyk'a't'o) war bonnet sun dance.

Top Bird (gutotaide) stole the enemy's horses

War-picture tipi of dähäsăn given to Black Buffalo (päkon'giä) his sister's son. Sun dance.

Thunder God (paso[t]dak'i) was killed.

Smallpox sun dance.

Setain'gia shot in the teeth with an arrow.

No sun dance. Red Sleeves (mä-[n]kägudl) died.

Yellow Tipi (taguk'ok'i) died.

K'oĭtsengo took in new members.

White Horse (tsentain'de) killed on the Arkansas River.

Standing on Top of the Arrow (zebatai'de) killed. Sun dance.

A Pawnee killed after an all-day battle.

Chinaberry sun dance.

Deer Fur (t'apa) died.

Big Bow (zepk'ayepte) killed by Utes. Sun dance.

T'agi(ă)ma, a woman, froze her feet in a blizzard.

Surrounded Many Times (dohat'e) received his name.

Captured Pawnee boy escaped and returned to his people.

Rainy sun dance.

Black Bear (se[t]kŏgia) died in the sweat lodge.

YEAR	MOONEY	GEORGE POOLAW
1852	Allied tribes defeated by Pawnees.	Raid into New Mexico. No sun dance.
1852–53	Race horse stolen by Pawnee boy.	Winter the Pawnee boy escaped with the Kiowa's best horse.
1853	Showery sun dance; Taime sacrilege.	Rainy sun dance.
1853–54	Raid into Mexico.	The winter koïtsenk'i was killed in New Mexico.
1854	Medicine-lodge creek sun dance.	Attack by Skidi during sun dance.
1854–55	Gyai'koaóñte killed by the Ä'lähó.	The winter Big Head was killed in a night attack by Osages.
1855	Sitting summer; horses worn out.	Another tribe visited the sun dance to ask for horses.
1855–56	Big Head kills an Älähó—raid into Mexico.	The winter Big Head's brother killed an Osage in revenge.
1856	Prickly pear sun dance.	Prickly pear sun dance.
1856–57	Tipis seized by the Cheyennes.	The winter the horses froze to death.
1857	Forked-stick sprouting sun dance.	Growing of the Chinaberry sun dance.
1857–58	Horses stolen by the Pawnees.	The winter of the epidemic of colds.
1858	Timber-circle sun dance.	Sun dance in a semicircular grove of cottonwoods.
1858–59	Gúi-k'áte killed by Mexicans; expedition against the Ute.	Sleeping Wolf (guik'a'de) killed in New Mexico.
1859	Cedar-bluff sun dance.	Sun dance at the mesa in Greer Co.
1859–60	Gúi-k'áte abandoned to die.	The winter the drunk woman was lost.
1860	Attacked by troops with Indian allies.	Rising Bird (t'enepä'de) was killed by Wichitas.
1860–61	Crazy bluff winter.	Crazy dancing winter.
1861	Horse sacrificed at sun dance.	Paint horse tied sun dance.
1861–62	Smallpox.	Smallpox winter.
1862	Sun dance after the smallpox.	Smallpox sun dance.

Calendars

Attack by soldiers; a Kiowa killed.

Winter the boy horse was stolen by Pawnees.

The one-arm sun dance (?)

The winter Black Bear died in the sweat-lodge.
Attack during the sun dance.

The winter Big Shield (Kiĕp) died.

A man who belonged to a tribe with Long Hair shot.
Drawing of a man in a scalp-fringed hair.

Prickly pear sun dance.

Unexplained drawing.

Forked-stick-growing sun dance.

Horse-stealing winter. Big Foot (asobi'ă) died.
Circle-timber sun dance. Appearing Eagle (Tĕnebä'de) killed.
Something happened to Yellow Wolf.
They cut all available timber for the sun dance.
Attack by Pawnees; one Pawnee killed.
Eagle summer.

Crazy Bend winter. Much recklessness.
Paint pony tied sun dance.

Smallpox winter.

Smallpox sun dance.

White Bear (setaint'e) made a sacred arrow.
Kiowas defeated by Osages.

Long Hair (adlkiui) killed. No sun dance.
A young Ute man captured.

Prickly pear sun dance.

Autsenpa (Feathers Tied On His Head) killed.

Forked stick growing sun dance.

Pawnee boy stole horses and went back to his own tribe.

(Atabu'yi) Trees grew like the camp circle sun dance.
Guik'a'de killed.

Whiskey sun dance. Everybody "haywire."
Standing on the Gun (hazeptai) died.
On Top of the Bird (guutotaide) died. No sun dance.
Cheyenne woman opened a store and sold things to Kiowas.
Painted horse tied to the sun dance pole.
Big Head (adlto'edl) died.

Two Feathers (aeude) died. Sun dance.
The horses ate the ashes.

Black Bird (gutokogi[ă] died.
Sun dance on Arkansas River.
Big Head—brother of first Big Head—died.
Flat tin (German silver) sun dance.

YEAR	MOONEY	GEORGE POOLAW
1862–63	Expedition against Texas.	Tall cottonwood winter camp. Informant born.
1863	Sun dance on No-Arm's river.	One-arm sun dance.
1863–64	Death of Big Head and Kills with a Gun—Anko's calendar begins.	Big Head died.
1864	Ragweed sun dance.	High weed sun dance.
1864–65	Muddy travel winter—Kiowas repel Kit Carson.	Surprise attack by Utes; Kiowas were victorious.
1865	Peninsula sun dance.	Big Bend sun dance.
1865–66	Death of Dohásän and Tä'n-kónkya.	The winter Little Bluff (dohäsăn) died.
1866	German-silver sun dance.	The silver-plate sun dance.
1866–67	Attack on Texas emigrants.	Leaning on a Tree (apemä'dlte) killed in Texas.
1867	Horses stolen by the Navahos—Kâitseñko initiated.	K'oĭtsengo sun dance.
1867–68	Medicine Lodge treaty, expedition against Navajo.	Medicine Lodge treaty.
1868	Sun dance on Medicine Lodge Creek. Experition against the Utes—Taime captured.	Attack by Utes; Heap of Bears (setoy'oyte) killed.
1868–69	Tän-gúădal killed—Burial expedition.	Keeper of the Arrows (zebat'kok'i) killed in Texas.
1869	War bonnet sun dance—expedition against the Utes.	Sun dance at End of the Mountains; warriors returned from raid on Utes with the war bonnet.
1869–70	Bugle stampede.	The winter the bugle was blown.
1870	Plant-growing sun dance.	Corn-growing sun dance.
1870–71	Set-ängya brings home his son's bones. Negroes killed in Texas.	Negroes killed in Texas and their scalps brought back.

Calendars

Unexplained drawing.

Arkansas River sun dance. Wild Horse (ta[t]sete) killed by Caddoes near Richards' Spur just after leaving Fort Sill.
Gun-on-Top-of-Head (hãzeptai) killed.

Unexplained drawing.

Apparently a lance was captured.

Peninsula sun dance. Kiowa attacked on the Canadian by Kit Carson and the Utes.
Death of dohäsan, who had owned a wagon.

Sun dance. Unexplained drawing.

Unexplained drawing.

Medicine Lodge treaty. Timber Hill sun dance.

Unexplained drawing.

Heap of Bears (setoyoyt'e) killed. No sun dance.

Black Kettle (daadlko[n]giă) killed; Fort Sill established.

War bonnet captured from the Utes.

The winter they were scared of the bugle.

Corn-growing sun dance.

Big Foot (asobi'ă) the Taime keeper, died. Brick Johnson, a negro, killed in Texas and his scalp brought back.

killed.

Bird Tied to his Head (guitoapa) K'oïtsengo reorganized.

Door Pole's (satguut'e) son was killed.

Warrior Foot (ausote) died. Sun dance.

Owner of many arrows (zebatok'i) died.

Ute war bonnet captured sun dance.

Black Bear (setkongiă) died. Bugle-fright winter.

Top Bird (t'enetaide) whipped by other societies for breaking dance rules.

Crazy winter. Young man accidentally shot.

Big Pipe (sato'biet) killed by whites. Sun dance.

Osages visited the Kiowas.

T'enezept'e died. No sun dance.

Päkongi(ă) became permanent owner of Dohäsan's tipi.

Black Buffalo's horses killed at sun dance.

Otter Head Gear (p'po'ohon) died (1874–75).

Kiowa volunteers enlisted (1875).

YEAR	MOONEY	GEORGE POOLAW
1871	Arrest of Set-t'aiñte and other chiefs.	Sitting Bear, White Bear, and Big Tree captured.
1871–72	Peace with Pawnees; removal to Indian territory.	Winter visit from Pawnees, and formal peace.
1872	Bíako shot by whites in Kansas.	Bird Arrow (t'enïzepte) killed by Sun Boy (Baită'-li).
1872–73	Visit of the Pueblos; Dohásän's tipi burned.	Horses burned in Devil's Canyon.
1873	Sun dance on Sweetwater Creek; Guibadái's wife stolen.	Horse-killing sun dance.
1873–74	Set-t'aiñte released; Lone Wolf's son killed.	The sons of Lone Wolf and Red Buffalo killed at San Antonio. The winter the two sons were killed.
1874	Sett'ainte gives his medicine lance to Ä"to-t'aiñ.	White Bear gave a päbon to White Black Bird. Western migration of part of tribe under Plenty Stars.
1874–75	Fight at Anadarko—Gi-edal killed.	Return of emigrants; imprisonment at Fort Sill; suicide of White Bear.
1875	Sun dance at Love-making spring.	Heap of Stars, Taime keeper, died just after the sun dance.
1875–76	Sheep and goats issued.	The winter the sheep were issued.
1876	Sun dance on North Fork—Sun Boy's horses stolen.	The sun dance Sun Boy's horses were stolen by Texans.
1876–77	A'gábaí killed by her husband; enlistment of scouts.	Winter camp west of Mangum. Plenty of meat.
1877	Sun dance on Salt Fork. Ravages of measles.	The measles sun dance.
1877–78	Buffalo hunt-fever epidemic—houses built.	Buffalo hunt winter.
1878	Repeated sun dance.	Double sun dance vowed by Lone Wolf.
1878–79	Hunting party attacked by Texans. Ä'to-t'aiñ killed.	White Black Bird killed by Texans.
1879	Horse-eating sun dance.	Horse-eating sun dance.
1879–80	"Eye-triumph" winter.	The victory dance over the Navajo's eye.

Calendars

Setain'giă, setain'de, and aday'-et captured. No sun dance.

Lots of Tipi Poles (gunaa'de) ran away with a Kiowa girl at the sun dance (1876).

Pawnees visited the Kiowas.

Goats and sheep captured (1876–77).

Bird Arrow (t'enezep'te) killed by Sun Boy (baita'li) in a drunken quarrel.

Sun dance. Sun Boy's horses were stolen. (1877).

Unexplained drawing.

Village destroyed by fire (1877–78).

Black Buffalo's (pekongiă) horses killed.

Measles epidemic sun dance (1878).

Winter the woman was stabbed.

Feathers on Arrow (adute) died (1878–79).

White Bear (setain'de) made an arrow. Sun dance.

Double sun dance (1879).

Winter camp at Signal Mountain. Scouts enlisted.

White Black Bird (a[p]totain'-de) killed by Mexicans (1879–80).

Lovers Spring sun dance.

They brought the enemy's eye. (1880).

Goats and sheep issued.

Red Buffalo (kädlgudl) died (1880–81).
Big Bow (zepkayetk'i) died (1881).

More scouts enlisted.

Kiowa government school established (1881–82).

Measles epidemic sun dance.

Lots of sweat houses made at sun dance (1882).

First government houses built. Informant born.

Year they tied the red blanket to bring back the buffalo (1882–83).

Double sun dance. Eclipse of the sun during the dance.

Bear Cap (set'bohon) died. No sun dance (1883).

White Bird or Cow Bird (at'at'-aite) killed in Texas.

Standing on Top of the Mountain (k'optaide) killed (1883–84).

Horse-eating sun dance.

Hair-cut sun dance (1884).

Eye-trumpet winter.

Government issued cattle (1884–85).

YEAR	MOONEY	GEORGE POOLAW
1880	No sun dance. Päbóte dies.	No sun dance. Summer at Anadarko. Big Bow died.
1880–81	Zoñtam's (?) house built— Last visit of the Pueblos.	The winter Big Bow went home with the Pueblos.
1881	Hot or hemorrhage sun dance.	The dry summer sun dance.
1881–82	The do'a' contest. Dátekâñ's medicine tipi.	Cattle issued, two cows to each person.
1882	No sun dance because no buffalo; Dátekâñ the prophet.	Gagum died at the cutting of the center-pole.
1882–83	Bot-édalte dies—Talk of grass leases.	First grass leases.
1883	Nez Percés visit Kiowas— Taimete succeeds to the taime.	The summer that sampt'e was shot.
1883–84	House built by Gákiñǎte— visited by the Sioux.	The year agiatote died.
1884	No sun dance.	Big Bend sun dance.
1884–85	House-building. Woman stolen.	Komalte and polǎte arrested.
1885	Little Peninsula sun dance— first grass money.	No sun dance. The summer Big Bow shot a white man.
1885–86	T'ébodal's camp burned.	The winter it hailed grass and chips.
1886	No sun dance—Anko a policeman—grass payment.	The sun dance tonkia'ba was given a päbon by Yellow Wolf.
1886–87	Suicide of Peyi.	The winter paingai made medicine.
1887	Buffalo bought for sun dance. Grass payment.	
1887–88	Cattle received for grass leases.	The winter Sun Boy (baitǎli) died.
1888	Permission for sun dance refused.	Young Woman (yakoyte), a beautiful girl, died.
1888–89	Sun Boy dies. Anko splits rails.	Bay Horse (asontsema) died.
1889	No sun dance. Grass payment.	The year they put the sun dance pole up.
1889–90	Grass payment—The Îâm dance.	Riding on a Buffalo (pa-[a]nkia) brought the ghost dance from the Arapahos.

Calendars

Big Bow (zep'gayep) visited the Ute country.

Visit from the Pueblos.

Ten times seven sweat houses built for medicine.
The man set up his tipi for the buffalo-returning ceremony.
No sun dance. Visit from the Nez Percés.

Somebody died. Timber camp.

Nez Percé sun dance.

Cattle were issued.

Wichitas presented a peace pipe to the Kiowas.
Snapping Turtle (tonagat) stole K'onma.
Little peninsular sun dance.

The winter t'ebodl's tipis were set on fire.
Big Bow killed a horse thief in Wheeler Co.

Unexplained drawing.

Oak Creek sun dance.

Cattle issued.

A man died in a peyote tipi at Mt. Scott.
Somebody died.

No sun dance. Unexplained drawing.
Unexplained drawing.

Charged through the Line (edelopa), a woman, killed by lightning (1885).
Snapping Turtle (to'nagat) ranaway with Otter Tail's wife (1885–86).
Small peninsula sun dance (1886).

Agency established at Anadarko (1886–87).
U. S. marshal killed. Ghost dance started (1887).

Young Sand Bird (p'ei) accidentally killed himself (1877–88).
A corn sun dance (1888).

Second issue of cattle (1888–89).

Running Calf (tsapiadl) died (1889).
Looking at Something (sampteanmas shot (1889–90).
Comanche man adopted and named Running Calf (1890).
Sun Boy died (1890–91).

Sitting Buffalo, an Arapaho, visited the Kiowas (1891).

Boys frozen to death (1891–92).

Tonaga[t] accidentally shot a young man (1892).
Regular troop of Indians organized (1892–93).
Smallpox summer (1893).

Coming Ahead First (teemtoda) died (1893–94).
Big Boy born; Caddo killed by outlaws (1894).
Black Buffalo and d'ohasä'n died. Cornett's trading store was burned (1894–95).

YEAR	MOONEY	GEORGE POOLAW
1890	Last attempt at sun dance.	The year poläte was killed by Texans.
1890–91	Ghost dance inaugurated.	Indian troop formed. Informant enlisted.
1891	P'ódalä'ñte killed. Cheyennes visit Kiowas.	The summer of the run on the Cheyenne reservation.
1891–92	P'ódalä'ñte killed. Enlistment of Indian soldiers.	Lease payments at Anadarko.
1892	Measles epidemic—delegation to Washington.	The winter they first built houses.
1892–93		The year Big Bow visited the Pueblos.
1893		Behodlte won the Fourth of July beauty contest at Anadarko.
1893–94		The winter komalte and his friend exchanged gifts.
1894		The summer of the first issue at Rainy Mountain.
1894–95		The year they took the horses away from us.
1895		The summer of the big camp meeting.
1895–96		The winter the girl was burned to death.
1896		The year tepde'a died.
1896–97		The time they had the winter race.
1897		The summer they voted for the lawyer.
1897–98		The winter they made the trip to Washington.
1898		Camp meeting at Rainy Mountain Church.
1898–99		The winter d'omaide died.
1899		Smallpox summer.
1899–1900		
1900		The summer the men surveyed for the allotments.
1900–1901		

Calendars

Unfinished sun dance.

The winter the boys froze to death.
Informant's wife born.
Snapping Turtle accidentally
killed. Polante killed.
First Kiowa troop enlisted.

Measles epidemic; grass payment
received.
White Horse died.

Unexplained drawing.

Big Bow visited the Utes.

Fourth of July celebration; policemen played ring and pin game.
Cornet's trading store burned.

Fourth of July celebration at Anadarko.
A payment received and house
built.
Cattle issued.

Unexplained drawing.

Unexplained drawing.

Winter horse race.

Voting on tribal attorney.

Unexplained drawing.

A house burned.

Unexplained drawing.

Man killed by a wagon; accident
on the Fourth of July.
Smallpox epidemic; allotments
made.

Scalps on Sleeves (adltongiai)
died (1895).
Cornett's store rebuilt (1895–96).

Two Kiowa girls eloped with
Cheyennes (1896).
White Feathers (tsongiat'ai) shot
in the shoulder (1896–97).
First tracks laid through reserva-
tion (1897).
Bringing in Peace Pipes (sato[e]-
odl) died (1897–98).
Utes visited the Kiowas (1898).

First excursion train through res-
ervation (1898–99).
White Skunk (t'adlt'ai) died
(1899).
Api'aton whipped by White Fox
for meddling in his affairs (1899–
1900).
Ghost Dance ordered stopped
(1900).
Hair (adla) died of smallpox
(1900–1901).
Government schools overflowed.
Children sent home (1901).
Smoking (Tabai) died in peyote
meeting (1901–1902).
Black Beaver (Bakangia) and
Crow (mäsä) died (1902).
Nothing happened (1902–1903).

Nothing happened (1903).

Agent tried to abolish the Ghost
Dance (1903–1904).
White man first at Rainy Moun-
tain. Kiowa bitten by a mad dog
but recovered (1904).
Otter Cap and Frizzle Head died
(1904–1905).
Annuity payment (1905).

Red Buffalo's wife died (1905–
1906).

Bibliography

Brill, Charles J. *Conquest of the Southern Plains.* Oklahoma City, Golden Saga Publishers, *c.* 1938.

Catlin, George. *Letters and Notes on the Manners, Customs, and Condition of the North American Indians.* 2 vols. Edinburgh, John Grant, 1926.

Ewers, John Canfield. *Plains Indian Painting.* Stanford University, California, Stanford University Press, 1939.

Foreman, Grant (ed.). Marcy and McClellan's *Adventures on Red River.* Norman, University of Oklahoma Press, 1937.

Fulton, Maurice Garland (ed.). *Diary and Letters of Josiah Gregg, 1840–1847.* Norman, University of Oklahoma Press, 1941.

LaBarre, Weston. *The Peyote Cult.* New Haven, Yale University Press, 1938.

Mooney, James. "Calendar History of the Kiowa Indians," *Seventeenth Annual Report,* part 2, Bureau of American Ethnology. Washington, Government Printing Office, 1893.

Nye, W. S. *Carbine and Lance: the Story of Old Fort Sill.* Norman, University of Oklahoma Press, 1939, 1942.

Schultes, Richard Evans. "Peyote and the American Indian," *Nature Magazine,* Vol. XXX, No. 3 (September, 1937).

Tilghman, Zoe. *Quanah: the Eagle of the Comanches.* Oklahoma City, Harlow Publishing Company, 1938.

Vestal, Paul A., and Schultes, Richard Evans. *Economic Botany of the Kiowa Indians.* Cambridge, Mass., Harvard Botanical Museum, 1939.

Wissler, Clark. *The American Indian.* New York, McMurtrie, 1917.

———. *North American Indians of the Plains.* New York, American Museum of Natural History, 1937.

DATE DUE

3/29			